Women and Gender in the Early Modern World

Series Editors: Allyson Poska and Abby Zanger

In the past decade, the study of women and gender has offered some of the most vital and innovative challenges to scholarship in the early modern period. Ashgate's new series of interdisciplinary and comparative studies, 'Women and Gender in the Early Modern World', takes up this challenge, reaching beyond geographical limitations to explore the experiences of early modern women and the nature of gender in Europe, the Americas, Asia, and Africa.

Titles in the series include:

POETIC RESISTANCE

Poetic Resistance

English women writers and the early modern lyric

PAMELA S. HAMMONS
University of Central Florida

Ashgate

Published by
Ashgate Publishing Limited
Gower House
Croft Road
Aldershot
Hampshire GU11 3HR
England

Ashgate Publishing Company
131 Main Street
Burlington, VT 05401-5600, USA

Ashgate website: http//www.ashgate.com

British Library Cataloguing in Publication Data
Hammons, Pamela S.
  Poetic resistance : English women writers and the early modern lyric. -
  (Women and gender in the early modern world)
  1.English poetry - Early modern, 1500-1700 - History and
  criticism 2.English poetry - Women authors - History and
  criticism 3.Government, Resistance to, in literature
  I.Title
  821'.04.099287'09032

Library of Congress Control Number: 2001099634

ISBN 0 7546 0780 1

Printed and bound in Great Britain by MPG Books Ltd, Bodmin, Cornwall

Contents

Acknowledgements

The assistance, encouragement, and support of many mentors, friends, colleagues, and institutions across several years have made this book possible. Barbara Correll has seen the project through from its initial conception to its realization. I am very grateful for her kind guidance, keen criticism, and overflowing garden. I will always admire her for her professional integrity and her courage in defending her intellectual ideals. William Kennedy, Dorothy Mermin, and Rachel Weil have always been generous in sharing their expertise and advice, for which I am deeply thankful. Likewise, I am truly indebted to Andy Galloway; his enthusiasm for intellectual inquiry and his painstaking attention to Katherine Austen's commonplace book, "Book M," were indispensable to my completion of this book. He saw the value of "Book M" immediately and encouraged me to pursue my studies of it at a time when I was unsure whether or how to approach it. Margaret J.M. Ezell provided me with extensive, invaluable advice about how to improve this book when it was in its crucial last stages, as well as with important feedback when I presented a conference paper on Katherine Austen at the University of Tulsa's Annual Comparative Literature Symposium in 1997. I am similarly thankful to Nigel Smith for his helpful comments on my work at that same conference. Teresa Feroli has consistently been an insightful and gracious reader of my work. Likewise, Bernadette Andrea, Timothy Billings, and Heather White have helped to make my work better than it would otherwise be through their careful, attentive readings of it. Mark Blackwell, David Garcia, Nate Johnson, Rohan Maitzen, Philip Virgen, and Rich Weldgen were among the earliest readers of my work; their insights had an important influence in shaping it. I am thankful to Debra Castillo and Marilyn Mumford for their enthusiastic support and professional advice, as well as to my mentors in the University of Central Florida's Department of English: Judith Hemschemeyer, Stuart Omans, Pat Rushin, Jerry Schiffhorst, and Dawn Trouard.

I am grateful to Barbara Smith and Ursula Appelt for their inclusion of an earlier version of part of Chapter 4, under the title "Widow, Prophet, and Poet: Lyrical Self-Figurations in Katherine Austen's 'Book M' (1664)," in their anthology of scholarship on early modern women poets, *Write or Be*

Written: Early Modern Women Poets and Cultural Constraints (Ashgate Press, 2001), and for their constructive criticisms of that piece. I am especially grateful to Uschi for her precise feedback and her energetic, scholarly conversations. In addition, I would like to thank the editors and anonymous readers of the journals *ELH: English Literary History, SEL: Studies in English Literature*, and *Tulsa Studies in Women's Literature* for their helpful comments. A shorter, earlier version of Chapter 2, also entitled "Despised Creatures: The Illusion of Maternal Self-Effacement in Seventeenth-Century Child Loss Poetry," originally appeared in print in *ELH* 66 (1999): 25-49. I would like to thank the Johns Hopkins University Press and *ELH* for permission to use revisions of this material. Similarly, a section of Chapter 4 was first published as "Katherine Austen's Country House Innovations" in *SEL: Studies in English Literature* 40, 1 (Winter 2000): 123-137. I would like to thank the William Marsh Rice University, the Johns Hopkins University Press, and *SEL* for permission to publish the revised version of that essay in this book. Robert L. Patten, editor of *SEL*, gave me especially useful, supportive advice about how to make my work on women poets as accessible as possible to scholars outside my field. I am thankful to Allyson M. Poska and Abby Zanger, the editors of Ashgate's series, "Women and Gender in the Early Modern World," for including my work in such a dynamic series. Erika Gaffney, Celia Hoare, Ruth Peters, and Frances Britain of Ashgate have been consistently helpful and courteous in the preparation of this book. I am particularly grateful to Erika for her sensitivity to authorial anxiety.

Several institutions have provided material support without which I could not have written this book. I am grateful for the award of a Mellon Fellowship in the Humanities, which supported my graduate education at Cornell University and the timely completion of my dissertation on early modern women poets. Also while I was at Cornell, funding from a Margaret Werly Fellowship and a Women's Studies Beatrice Brown Award supported my graduate education and my initial foray into archival research respectively. Likewise, I am thankful for an in-house research grant from the University of Central Florida, which enabled me to have the time away from teaching necessary to complete this book. I am also indebted to the Department of English at the University of Central Florida for its material support of the book's final revisions. I could not have performed the research necessary to write this book without access to the fine collections at Cornell University's Olin Library, the British Library, and the Bodleian Library and without the assistance of their skilled librarians.

Finally, the ongoing emotional support of my friends and family gave me the strength to see this project through every stage of its creation. In many cases, I have been lucky to have had friends who provided scholarly advice as well as emotional support, as is true of many of those mentioned above. In addition, I am deeply thankful for the friendships of Phil and Carol Acree Cavalier, Lee Behlman, Rose Beiler, Maria Bullón-Fernández, Adenike Davidson, Ana Echevarría, Thamora Fishel, Elizabeth Frost, Derek Hackett, Siana Laforest, Jeanne Leiby, Eric Lindemer, Lisa Logan, David Nagle, Rachel Preiser, Heather Roberts, Jean-Daniel Saphores, Heather White, and Jordan Yin. Thanks, too, to all those friends at Cornell willing to play soccer, and those there and elsewhere who have granted me their kindness and stimulating conversation. I offer my deep, enduring gratitude to my parents--Lynn Duncan, Charles Hammons, Curtis Olsen, and Anna Suttle--for everything they have given me, which is far too much to describe. I am also grateful to Tim Hammons and Duncan Hammons, my brothers, who have supported me in their own unique ways; no one could ask for better brothers. I am thankful to Blanche ("Nannie") Baird, Clara Hammons, and E.E. Suttle for their pride and love: I will always remember them. Finally, I dedicate this book to Anna Grace Suttle, my mother, in thanks for her love, encouragement, example, and many questions, and to Gema Pérez-Sánchez, whose eyes have scrutinized every page of this book and whose love sees me through every day--gracias por todo.

Chapter 1

Poetic Resistance:
Laying Hands on the Harp

From October 1657 until August 1658, radical religious sectarian and shipwright's daughter Anna Trapnel sang and prayed, inspired by the Holy Spirit, before a mixed audience of supporters and detractors. An amanuensis from her millenarian group, the Fifth Monarchists, ultimately transcribed around 990 folia of her psalms, sermons, and prayers before her period of inspiration ended.[1] According to the transcription of one of Trapnel's lyrical performances, she locates herself in the tradition of psalmists following David. Suggesting that David's harp will be handed down to her, she sings: "If once that harp be in my hand,/ I'll stand against you all" (*Voice for the King* 66). Trapnel indicates that having this harp in hand will enable resistance on her part, but what kind of resistance could her lyrics represent? Against whom does she position herself? Because she performed her lyrics in public, there were immediate, material responses to them. Not only does she report that onlookers jeered at her sometimes, but in 1654, prior to the performances recorded in the thousand-page folio mentioned above, she was tried and imprisoned for her appearances in Cornwall. Just before this trial, there was some question among the religious and political leaders of Cornwall about whether Trapnel should be tried as a witch, an episode that she relates with fear and dread.[2]

Before she sang the above lines about David's harp, she had thus already demonstrated her willingness to stand up to psychological and physical punishment. The resistance to which she alludes, therefore, could signify her brave determination to sing what she feels is divine verse regardless of how she is treated: she will withstand a wide range of social punishments--from ridicule to institutionalized restraint--in order to voice her political and theological critique of the Protectorate. Yet her resistance

---

[1] These performances are recorded in *A Voice for the King of Saints and Nations* (1658) and a thousand-page folio in the Bodleian Library (Bod. S. 42. I. Th.).

[2] See *Anna Trapnel's Report and Plea* 21-2, 25, 28.

is still greater than this. Her gender made her performances even riskier than they already were because of their controversial content: her public appearances disrupted expectations for properly feminine behavior. As Anne Laurence and Phyllis Mack indicate, prophetic activity on the part of a woman was not necessarily controversial in and of itself, because a woman possessed by God, after all, could not be held responsible for her words or actions.[3]   However, as her account in *Anna Trapnel's Report and Plea* of her trial at Cornwall and her resulting imprisonment reveal, some of her contemporaries were not convinced that the Holy Spirit was behind her lyrical political and social critiques. As I discuss further in Chapter 3, if not legitimately controlled by divine powers, such a publicly outspoken woman was not a prophet, but instead an unruly and unfeminine woman. When Trapnel takes the harp in hand as a form of resistance, then, she does so not only to voice her controversial political and religious views, but also to confront the restrictions placed upon her because of her female gender.

Furthermore, her resistance involves more than the social realm, with its heated theological and political debates and its strict gender codes. Her lyrics also enable her to intervene in the literary realm. In the lines above, Trapnel specifically locates herself in relation to a particular poetic tradition. Although it would be easy to assume that a shipwright's daughter would have had insufficient formal schooling to place her own lyrics explicitly in relation to a specific poetic tradition, Trapnel does so: she presents herself as God's new psalmist. Because, as I will show in Chapter 3, Trapnel reshapes the parts of the Bible that become the subject matter for her psalms, the poetic resistance that she enacts operates on a literary level, as well as on a social one. Her lyrics ultimately allow her to reshape the parameters of possibility for her social role, while they revise the conventions for religious verse.

In reworking both social and literary conventions through her lyrics, Trapnel is not alone as a seventeenth-century woman poet. In this book, I examine the works of several women poets who similarly insert their revisions simultaneously into the social and literary realms. The poets whose works I analyze occupied diverse social stations in a very hierarchical society, had disparate educational backgrounds, and did not necessarily share one another's values and beliefs. Like the poets themselves, their lyrics differ from each other greatly; they vary significantly in technique, style, and purpose. Despite these many differences, however, these poets have something in common when they lay

---

[3] See Laurence 347, 363 and Mack 24, 25, and 33.

hands on the harp: their poetry becomes a form of resistance. Through their verse, they create the means to rethink or to reshape their positions in society, and they add their own innovations to the history of the lyric.

In this book, I examine how seventeenth-century women's composition of lyrics intersects significantly with the social experiences of those women. I analyze the widespread phenomenon of child loss poetry; the extemporaneous ballads, originally performed in public, of radical sectarian Anna Trapnel; and "Book M," a virtually unexplored commonplace book composed and compiled by Katherine Austen. I consider this unique configuration of texts because each represents a category of early modern women's writing that has been previously neglected in the writing of women's literary history. This selection of texts allows me to challenge assumptions that have limited the study of early modern women's writing (such as anachronistic gynocritical assumptions) and to reveal the power of lyrics in women's reconceiving or changing of their positions in society.[4]

Writing lyrics was thoroughly integrated into the routine social lives of the women whose poetry I examine in this study. That does not mean that they combined lyric composition with communal spinning or other domestic tasks or that they kept pen at hand during (or immediately after) social events in case the muse beckoned. Perhaps some of them did. However, by "routine social lives," I simply mean the usual, ongoing ways in which these women were positioned in relation to society at large, the ways in which they were assigned particular roles to play--elaborations on their basic gender identity--that imposed upon them specific self-conceptions and that made each of them legible to the rest of society as a certain kind of woman. For the mother-poets discussed in Chapter 2, for instance, writing child loss poetry was not only a conventionalized cathartic act meant to purge grief and guilt but also a means to resist the cultural pressures that so cruelly blamed them--specifically because they were mothers--for their children's deaths. For Anna Trapnel, who was legible to her followers as a holy handmaid of God, composing lyrics spontaneously

---

[4] Showalter specifies that "the program of gynocritics is to construct a female framework for the analysis of women's literature, to develop new models based on the study of female experience, rather than to adapt male models and theories" (131). For a brief description of gynocriticism and recent critiques of it, see Pacheco 2-3. For insightful explanations of the humanistic limitations of gynocriticism, see Moi esp. 75-80 and Jones 6-7. For a historicizing critique of this and related conceptions of women's literary history that cannot accommodate early modern texts, see Ezell, *Writing Women's Literary History*. On the general phenomenon of early women writers in relation to social change, see Burke, Donawerth, Dove, and Nelson, esp. xvii and xix.

and publicly was an essential part of her multiple, interrelated efforts both to keep an audience and to protect herself from hostile, punitive responses while she dramatically protested contemporary institutions of power: Cromwell's Protectorate and the Church. For Katherine Austen, a wealthy widow, writing lyrics was shot through with social implications: her engagement with the formal and thematic conventions associated with the transmission and preservation of verse in manuscript is intertwined with her sensitivity to the social conventions corresponding to the role of a woman of rank.

Given the vibrant interplay between these women's lyrics and their various social roles, it might seem surprising that their works have been underexamined or ignored. Although Trapnel has received some attention from historians and literary critics, scholars have overlooked her importance as a poet because they have concentrated on how transgressive it was for her, as a woman, to have her verse (and other writings) printed. Trapnel has sparked interest because she was a socially unconventional woman for her time, because she was a publicly outspoken radical religious sectarian whose anti-establishment psalms, sermons, and visions landed her, for a short while, in prison. The social unconventionality of Trapnel's entry into the world of print has directed attention away from the strategic construction of her poems. Reading her verse with the limitations constraining women's literary efforts during the early modern period strongly in mind, some scholars have treated Trapnel's lyrics as if they are actually outside systems of literary convention--as if they are, in fact, evidence of Trapnel's mental instability.[5] In Chapter 3, however, I will demonstrate that the complicated lyrics that have suggested the handmaid's madness to some scholars become comprehensible as skillful appropriations of contemporary poetic practices when examined closely in historical and literary context.

Women's child loss poetry has previously been relegated to the category of a female subgenre; characterized as the pure, transhistorical communication of primal, maternal emotion; and thereby rendered uninteresting as a form of cultural production.[6] These elegies have also been underexamined because of a trait that they share with Katherine Austen's poems: most of them were transmitted in manuscript. As Margaret J.M. Ezell observes, twentieth-century feminists grounded their literary theories largely in nineteenth- and twentieth-century texts because

---

[5] See Cohen esp. 425 and Greer, *Kissing the Rod* 177, 178.
[6] See Greer, "Introduction" 12.

they worked under the assumption that women writers only become interesting and important when they write for publication in a capitalist, commercial setting (*Writing Women's Literary History* 4, 32). She explains that:

> What all of these theoretical models of authorship in the past do, in spite of their differences, is to erase the notion of manuscript authorship that did not have as its primary aim a commercial readership and, likewise, any sense of a culture of reading and writing in which it was engaged. Instead the notion of an author found in these disparate studies tends to dismiss non-canonical texts as 'aristocratic,' 'amateur,' and 'vulnerable.' (Ezell, *Social Authorship* 17)[7]

Hence, women's manuscript compositions, such as mother-poets' child loss poems and Austen's "Book M," have been automatically excluded from the domain of valuable women's texts. By attending to texts circulated in manuscript, by resisting the assumption that only printed works have value, this study "attempt[s] to let the past exist as different from the present" (Ezell, *Writing Women's Literary History* 13). It also attempts to allow for historical difference in its emphasis on the social dimension of the lyric in seventeenth-century England. This focus challenges both the anachronistic gynocritical image of the angry woman writing in isolation and the conceptualization--fostered through the privileging of the printed word--of the early modern lyric as a primarily closed (fixed and impermeable) and generalizing (potentially universal in meaning and value) text.[8]

The three sets of texts that I examine seem at first glance to be consummately private, the products of isolation.[9] A mother's poem written in response to her child's death seems a purely domestic, self-enclosed moment of grief. Trapnel strategically characterizes her public activity as beyond the pale of her consciousness. Swept into the realm of the supernatural, she was supposedly impermeable to mundane reality during

---

[7] On the significance of women's manuscript writings, also see Burke 135.

[8] Moi observes that reading women's texts to discover "*feminist rage*" "in less sophisticated guises is perhaps the most recurrent theme of Anglo-American feminist criticism" and that it "manages to transform *all* texts written by women into feminist texts, because they may always and without exception be held to embody somehow and somewhere the author's 'female rage' against patriarchal oppression" (62). Ezell similarly notes the tendency to assume that "Society . . . silenced women, and where it could not, it drove them mad and characteristically infused their writings with bitterness and anger" (*Writing Women's Literary History* 25).

[9] For an example of a study that foregrounds how a seventeenth-century woman's poetry emphasizes privacy, see Masten.

her performances. Austen's commonplace book, prefaced with qualifying remarks specifying its personal, private nature, seems the epitome of an asocial document. However, social concerns are central to these works, and the composition of lyrics is instrumental to the negotiation of those concerns. These women poets were not the "isolated and unusual creatures" that feminists who have based their narratives of women's literary history on linear, evolutionary models have tended to assume (Ezell, *Writing Women's Literary History* 30).

To understand exactly how these women's texts intersect with the social lives of those women, it is first necessary to consider how scholars have begun to rethink the relationship between lyric poetry and the social realm of the early modern period more broadly. How are sixteenth- and seventeenth-century English lyrics social, and what difference does it make to think of them as such? Arthur Marotti's studies of Sir Philip Sidney's encoding of his social ambition as love language in *Astrophil and Stella*, of John Donne as a coterie poet, and of the competing cultures of manuscript and print in sixteenth- and seventeenth-century England have called attention to the occasional nature of lyric poetry during that period and to its significance as a form of social currency. By examining the differences between the transmission of lyric poetry in manuscript and print, Marotti has revealed that the critical focus on printed collections of lyrics has contributed to their conceptualization as stable, author-centered artifacts that are detached from specific historical circumstances.[10] As Marotti observes, however:

> In the system of manuscript transmission, it was normal for lyrics to elicit revisions, corrections, supplements, and answers, for they were part of an ongoing social discourse. In this environment texts were inherently

---

[10] Marotti explains that "Although some postmodern conceptions of literature would have us view literary works as textually unstable, literary studies are still dominated by an idealism that privileges the best, latest authorially sanctioned version of the text, the one reified in a modern edition that uses all the resources of sophisticated textual scholarship to produce the work in its 'purest' form--that is, its printed version that supposedly realizes the author's final intentions (whether or not he or she was conscious of them) . . . But the idealism that governs both the practice of modern textual scholarship and of much literary criticism generally ill suits not only the literature of a manuscript culture but also much of the literature of the early era of print" (*Manuscript* 137). In her insightful examination of the relationship between gender and Renaissance authorship, Wall demonstrates that "these common characterizations of the 'closed' printed work and the 'open' manuscript are . . . descriptions of particular textual interpretations that were socially constructed and perpetuated during this time period" (8).

malleable, escaping authorial control to enter a social world in which recipients both consciously and unconsciously altered what they received . . . In the manuscript environment the roles of author, scribe and reader overlapped. (*Manuscript* 135)

Lyric poetry was thus conceptualized as a medium for social interaction. Wendy Wall notes that "Even when writers do not represent poetic making as collaborative, they nevertheless assume that poetry is resolutely occasional, produced through channels of exchange rather than through the force of a seemingly autonomous creative energy" (36). In certain settings, lyrics could even function as a form of social currency insofar as, for courtiers for instance, they "were an extension of artful, polite behavior and, at the same time, ways of formulating actual or wished-for social transactions" (Marotti, *Manuscript* 9). A collaborative, social model for lyric production, transmission, and reception thus better fits sixteenth- and seventeenth-century contexts than does the later notion of the unique, isolated, autonomous author.[11]

While scholars such as Marotti, Ezell, and Wall have emphasized the social nature of the lyric during this period by calling attention to the circulation of lyrics in manuscript miscellanies, to coteries of poets in friendly competition with each other, and to lyrics as a form of socioeconomic currency in the patronage system, I focus on how the sociality of the lyric relates to women's writing when that writing seems especially insular and does not fit neatly into patterns of interaction predominantly followed by men. Thus, in examining the poetry of these particular women, I expand what might count as "social" verse. Some seventeenth-century women did compose lyrics to participate in the forms of sociality described above. The family, in addition to courtly and satellite-courtly environments, was a major locus for the circulation of verse in manuscript miscellanies. Similarly, a number of women poets--notably the women in the Aston-Thimelby circle and Katherine Philips--played central roles in coteries, and other women poets, such as Aemilia Lanyer, used lyrics as a form of socioeconomic currency in the patronage system.[12]

---

[11] For more on the social dimensions of the lyric during this period, see Marotti "'Love Is Not Love': Elizabethan Sonnet Sequences and the Social Order," *Manuscript* and *John Donne, Coterie Poet*; Wall esp. 1-22; Ezell, *Writing Women's Literary History* esp. 37-8, 56-7, and *Social Authorship* esp. 21-44.

[12] On the family as a locus for the circulation of lyrics, see Marotti, *Manuscript* 40-48; on the Aston-Thimelby coterie, see Marotti, *Manuscript* 45-6, 51-2, 165; on women's participation in the circulation of lyrics, see Marotti, *Manuscript* 48-61. On women in coteries (including Katherine Philips and the women in the Aston-Thimelby coterie), see

While the women's lyrics that I discuss in this study participate in these patterns of sociality to varying degrees (I include child loss poems from the Aston-Thimelby coterie, for instance), they are poems that are especially likely to be considered voices in a vacuum upon one's initial encounter with them, voices seemingly uttered in isolation that vanish instantly, voices subjected to scholarly assumptions that have effectively erased them from the greater continuities of mainstream English literary history. Despite the appearance of self-enclosure, (which, in some cases, is maintained deliberately as a protective illusion), however, those poems enable their various poets to reconceptualize or to change their positions in society, while adding their own innovations to the available Renaissance lyric traditions.

Chapter 2 examines familiar child loss lyrics, such as Jonson's "On My First Sonne" and "On My First Davghter" and Milton's "On the Death of a Fair Infant Dying of a Cough," alongside less familiar ones by women and men, parents and non-parental consolers. It focuses, however, on maternal child loss poetry as a special case. I argue that cultural anxieties surrounding childbirth and the frequent demonization of the mother in various sixteenth- and seventeenth-century English written artifacts, in conjunction with biological and theological notions of femininity linking a woman's mental activity to her physical creativity, made writing child loss poetry paradoxical for a mother-poet. The occasion of child loss constituted a culturally sanctioned opportunity for a woman to compose a poem, yet doing so necessitated the mother-poet's erasure of herself as creative agent. While child loss poetry involves a set of commonplaces with which any poet writing about a dead child would engage, a mother-poet's adaptation of these literary conventions relates to her precarious social position as a mother who has lost her child and who is, by writing a poem, engaging in an intellectually creative act to compensate for the failure of a physically creative one. A mother-poet writing upon the occasion of her own child's death thus tends to create the illusion of her own self-effacement as the intellectual agent behind her poem. While male and female poets who write verse for someone else's dead child embellish the conventions associated with the genre by using techniques and figures from dominant poetic trends, mother-poets avoid appropriations from mainstream poetic traditions and work towards what I call a maternal plain style. Thus, while child loss

---

Ezell, *Writing Women's Literary History* 48-57 and *Social Authorship*, esp. 25-8, 52-4. On Aemilia Lanyer's participation in the patronage system, see Lewalski, *Writing Women in Jacobean England* 219-26 and Woods, *Lanyer: A Renaissance Woman Poet* 43-54, 101-8.

poetry written by non-parental consolers can circulate, like any other lyric, as material for coterie competition, mother-poets' verse avoids the display of poetic self-consciousness typical of such competition, even if their poems circulate in manuscript. Despite the cultural pressure towards the erasure of miscreating maternal agency in mothers' lyrics, however, some mothers adhere strictly to the expected, acceptable commonplaces while nevertheless structuring their verse so that it interrogates simultaneously the literary and social conventions that focus such intense blame for the child's death on the mother.

In Chapter 3, I explore how Anna Trapnel's adaptation of the tradition of metrical paraphrases of and verse meditations on scripture, and her importation of that tradition into the battleground of dispute over the politico-theological issues of the revolutionary period constitute a fascinating intervention of literary convention in the social realm. While some scholars understand Trapnel's dramatic posturing as a prophet, at least in part, in terms of her successful manipulation of recognizable cultural codes, the focus on her socially disruptive, unconventional behavior has fostered an understanding of her and her works that undermines any serious attempt to analyze her lyrics as more than an incidental aspect of her overall performance as a prophet.[13] In other words, such approaches emphasize her status as God's handmaiden to the extent of erasing her creative agency as a poet. To counteract the tendency to categorize Trapnel unproblematically as a prophet, I demonstrate that the rhetorical and formal interplay among her transcribed songs and prayers enables her to speak publicly, not only as a prophet, but also at times as a preacher. Understanding her as a lyric preacher also provides a basis for examining her poetry--which has often been taken as a sign of madness or neglected in favor of analyzing her public role--in relation to traditions and contemporary practices. Having thus shown the instrumentality of Trapnel's lyrics in shaping her vacillating public role, I focus on a specific example of how she appropriates contemporary poetic practices and biblical subject matter to justify her public speech. By analyzing how Trapnel appropriates the tropes and themes of the Song of Songs and fuses her imitation of its repetitive, cyclical construction with the ballad meter and simple vocabulary common to metrical translations of David's Psalms in order to justify her public speech and to underwrite her poetic voice, I provide detailed evidence of the

---

[13] On the staging of the prophet's body, for example, see Purkiss. On the prophet's death-like trance, see Dailey esp. 453 and Mack 34. On Trapnel's singing as a sign of divine possession, see Hobby 35 and Smith 50.

handmaid's importation of adapted literary conventions into the social realm.

Chapter 4 examines "Book M," the commonplace book of Katherine Austen, a widow especially concerned with social propriety; "Book M" suggests that she was anxious to display the proper appearances associated with having a high social rank and that her anxieties about her social status were compounded by her status as a widow. Her manuscript reveals that when she became a widow, she became acutely aware of her gender as a liability because she discovered how it rendered her less capable of protecting her material holdings than her late husband was. While I do not claim that Austen, as a result of the changes that widowhood brought to her life, became actively conscious of the conflicts between her status (and her ambitions for ever higher rank) and her gender, I show that the inconsistencies engendered by this conflict underpin Austen's complicated, discontinuous self-representations, which she often presents in the form of lyrics. Despite the fact that Austen frames her commonplace book as a private document, for her, writing--both process and product--is inextricably linked to social life. As a Royalist and Anglican writing at the beginning of the Restoration, her investment in shoring up her status compels her to avoid revisionary political and religious ideas, especially those that disrupt social decorum. Hence, on one level, she makes her writing as socially acceptable as possible: she composes uncontroversial religious meditations in verse, which thank God for his providential blessings and pray for divine assistance, and occasional poems about her relatives, which commemorate dead loved ones and position Austen in relation to her family. Nevertheless, she experiments with reconceptualizing her position in society. She mobilizes simultaneously at least three discontinuous figurations of herself--as Penelope or assailed widow, as powerful prophet, and as amateur poet--to advance her interest in social status and personal power. Ultimately, Austen's verse performs the advance in social rank so important to her and so jeopardized, in her view, by her gender.

What difference do these women's lyrics make to our understanding of the early modern period?[14] The rewards of examining closely these three

---

[14] Some readers may also wonder whether the women's poems included in this study are any "good"; there is no short, simple answer to that question. I agree with two observations about aesthetics that Moi articulates especially well: (1) "aesthetic value judgements are historically relative and . . . they are deeply imbricated in political value judgements," and (2) "feminist criticism is about deconstructing such an opposition between the political and the aesthetic: as a political approach to criticism, feminism must be aware of the politics of aesthetic categories as well as of the implied aesthetics of political approaches

sites of overlap between women's lyric production and their social experience are as varied as the poets themselves. Analyzing child loss poetry in seventeenth-century England, for instance, reveals that gender does not inflect such verse in a simple, straightforward manner. Male and female poets writing poems to console parents write strikingly similar poems; mother-poets writing about their own child loss write the most distinctive verse. Examining the lyrical preaching of Anna Trapnel suggests that the range of ways in which early modern women claimed the right to preacherly authority is broader than has been previously assumed.[15] Trapnel's deep assimilation of biblical subject matter and intricate metrical interweaving of scripture with her critiques of contemporary political and ecclesiastical authorities, and the strategic interplay between her verse and prose constitute an especially complex, yet subtle, justification for her preacherly role. Attention to Austen's "Book M" brings to light a number of previously unknown, generically innovative lyrics composed by a woman and demonstrates her strategic self-representations in response to a wide variety of conventional delimitations of her social position. Several of Austen's poems also make specific contributions. Her transcription of a poetic fragment by Richard Corbett, for instance, emphasizes how lyrics during this period were treated as both malleable and permeable. Austen's recontextualization of this fragment--which in the context of other Cavalier

---

to art" (85, 86). From one point of view, the "implied aesthetics" of my project is that lyrics that enable women to reconceptualize or to alter social positions that seem restrictive or damaging to them are "good." Yet as we will see, the lyrics in this study differ significantly in technique, style, and purpose. The poets have different educational backgrounds and value different forms of knowledge. They would not have necessarily agreed with each other's politics or appreciated each other's aesthetics. Social elitist Katherine Austen, for instance, would almost certainly have scorned Anna Trapnel's public singing, even if Austen were to notice, begrudgingly, the powerful effect of her rhetoric. Trapnel had more of her verse printed and disseminated it more widely, both through print and her public performances, than most of the other women mentioned in the study. Likewise, Trapnel apparently had no trouble keeping an audience. While Katherine Philips had a lower social station than Lady Mary Carey, Philips, so comfortable with her role as poet in comparison to other mother-poets, may have been unimpressed by Carey's stark, wrenching maternal plain style. In 1681, however, Charles Hutton was impressed enough with Carey's writing to transcribe all of her child loss poems and approximately 200 pages of her prose into a leather-bound, gilded book that also includes transcribed writings by Thomas, Lord Fairfax. For more on aesthetics, see Moi; Guillory, *Cultural Capital*; Ezell, *Writing Women's Literary History* and *Social Authorship*, esp. 123-139; Felski; Waugh; Battersby; and Brand and Korsmeyer, "Introduction: Aesthetics and Its Traditions."

[15] Cf. Margaret Fell Fox's direct argument for women preachers in *Women's Speaking Justified, Proved and Allowed of by the SCRIPTURES*. See Mack on how Mary Cary and Katherine Chidley "insisted that they *were* ministers, not prophets" (91).

love lyrics would seem playfully bawdy--effectively rewrites it as one among many of Austen's strategies to represent herself as a chaste, helpless widow. Similarly, Austen's experimentation with the country house poem, which enables her ambitions to be a poet and to be a woman of rank to become mutually reinforcing, contributes an innovation to the genre through the exclusion of a feature conventionally central to it: the celebration of the patron/landowner as the origin of the bounty and goodness of the estate.

If we construe broadly "that harp" to which Anna Trapnel refers at the beginning of this chapter as signifying multiple seventeenth-century poetic traditions, then all of the women poets at the heart of this study take that harp in hand in the sense that they insert themselves into pre-existing poetic traditions and writing practices. This book concerns itself primarily with what those women do when they get that harp in their hands--when they exert poetic resistance by employing various lyric traditions to change or to reconceive damaging, restrictive conventions that shape their social lives.

Chapter 2

Despised Creatures:
The Illusion of Maternal
Self-Effacement in Seventeenth-Century
Child Loss Poetry

It is as though male writing were by nature procreative, while female writing is somehow by nature infanticidal. (Barbara Johnson 198)

The cultural context of seventeenth-century England brought women's physically creative abilities into a potentially dangerous association with their intellectually creative ones, thereby allowing a mother-poet's agency in writing a poem on child loss to be conflated with her supposed agency in ensuring (or not) the life of her child. The association of a mother's inappropriate intellectual activity with the death of her child makes writing a poem about that loss paradoxical.[1] Such a bereaved mother-poet encounters a culturally sanctioned opportunity to write a poem--a limited occurrence for a seventeenth-century English woman--but must use that occasion to renounce or disprove any seemingly improper attempt at creative intellectual agency.[2] She may write a poem but must erase herself as poet. This double bind, however, results in some mothers' composition of poems that resist the literary and social conventions blaming the mother for the death of her child by interrogating, and thereby invigorating, the commonplaces associated with elegies and epitaphs for children.[3]

---

[1] Lilley also notices competing tendencies in women's elegy (90).

[2] Phillippy notes "the unusual license to write and publish afforded to women in proximity to death, particularly to mothers mourning the loss of their children" (321).

[3] Miller's assertion that "early modern women's varying expressions of maternity . . . could not be contained within traditional generic boundaries" reinforces this claim on my part (6). However, as I discuss later in this chapter, some women writing poetry about their own child loss did adhere fairly strictly to the expectations of this especially severe, demanding genre. For a compelling discussion of how Gaspara Stampa and Sofonisba Anguissola rewrite female creativity--and thereby avoid some of the complications that ideas

In this chapter, I first discuss some anxieties surrounding childbirth and the frequent demonization of the mother--important aspects of the cultural context in which mothers composed their child loss poetry--in sixteenth- and seventeenth-century England. Next, I explicate the culturally and historically specific thematic conventions for composing upon the occasion of child loss in early modern England. Male and female poets, parents and non-parental consolers alike selected from these commonplaces. Third, I argue that mothers writing about their own experiences of child loss tend to choose a poetically self-effacing plain style. This maternal plain style--which creates the illusion that a mother's poem is not the product of a miscreating maternal mind--avoids the appropriation of conventions common to love lyrics that non-parental consolers use frequently when writing epitaphs and elegies for children. Finally, I use Mary Carey's poetry as an example to demonstrate how some mothers' rejection of dominant poetic trends created an opportunity for them to develop and to invigorate the conventions of child loss poetry by simultaneously borrowing from and interrogating them.

Miscreating Mothers

> Of her there bred
> A thousand yong ones, which she dayly fed,
> Sucking vpon her poisonous dugs, eachone
> Of sundry shapes, yet all ill fauored. (Spenser 1.1.15.4-7)

Few members of sixteenth- and seventeenth-century English society were more likely to be demonized than mothers.[4] Spenser's Errour, a mother

---

concerning biological procreativity had for the early modern female artist--through invoking the Virgin Mary, see Rose 29-48. For more on Anguissola's appropriation of the Virgin Mary as a model of proper female creativity, also see Yavneh 78. On Catholic and Protestant controversies concerning the Virgin Mary as a figure of maternal power, see Dolan 282-92. On Elizabeth Grymeston's use of convention in her maternal legacy to "[challenge] customary distinctions establishing gender difference in discourses of religion and education" (163), see Snook 163-75.

[4]   Francus observes that "In the West, the image of the fecund female has often been associated with monstrosity" (829). A notable exception--upon which Mack also comments (40-41)--to the pervasive demonization of the mother is Spenser's portrait of Charissa in child-bed; see *The Faerie Queene* esp. 1.10.29-34. Her "multitude of babes" (1.10.31.1) counterbalances Errour's foul brood from Canto 1. Yet Spenser's portrait of Errour's vileness is more thorough and detailed than the corresponding portrait of Charissa, the good mother. Also see Mendelson and Crawford 67-8; Miller 1, 6-7; Ehrstine 121; and

"Most lothsom, filthie, foule, and full of vile disdaine" (1.1.14.9), and Milton's Sin, who gives birth to Death, a "shape,/ If shape it might be called that shape had none" (*Paradise Lost* 2.666-667), frame the period and serve as telling measures of just how monstrous representations of mothers could become. Errour and Sin are not hideous merely because they personify spiritual depravity or because they bring men to their destruction. They are repulsive because they are mothers whose offspring reflect and multiply their evil and ugliness.[5] As Deborah Willis indicates, Renaissance depictions of witches similarly rely upon the demonization of the mother.[6] In Shakespeare's *Macbeth*, witch-like Lady Macbeth invokes hellish powers to replace her mother's milk with poison and incites Macbeth to murder by claiming that she could kill her own children had she sworn--as has Macbeth to kill Duncan--to do so.[7] In Jacobean pamphlets, such as *The Wonderful Discovery of the Witchcrafts of Margaret and Philippa Flower*, peasant women are represented as witches who not only conspired to kill the local nobleman's children and to render his wife barren, but who confessed to suckling satanic familiars at the very breasts that should nurture children.[8]

Dolan 282 on the idealization and criticism of mothers. See Steinberger 201-21, on the late seventeenth-century development of the figure of "the good mother" in French comedy. Also see Steinberger's discussion of negative depictions of mothers in French theater (esp. 203-4).

Miller emphasizes "the enabling spectrum of powers associated with maternity in the early modern period": "Combining the sexuality of generative wombs with the authority of generative words and roles, mothers and other female caregivers shared a potential for social influence that extended far beyond the boundaries of their immediate families, in association with emblematic power as well as actual political and cultural authority." As I show, the role of maternal power in relation to child loss poetry proves more vexed than it might be in genres such as the prose maternal legacy in which female procreativity is represented as successful (since such texts assume the survival of the children) and in which the display of female intellectual creativity is even more subtle than in the case of most maternal child loss poetry (since poetry arguably makes formal innovations more immediately visible than do most prose works). Despite the troubled relation between maternal power and child loss poetry, however, the verse of some mother-poets does "illuminate their own creative processes . . . [and] question the conventional parameters of domestic roles," as Miller observes generally of writing that plays upon the powers "associated with maternity in the early modern period" (14).

[5] See Spenser's *The Faerie Queene* esp. 1.1.13-26.109-234 and Milton's *Paradise Lost* esp. 2.648-889. For connections between Christianity and maternal demonization, see Francus 829, Blumenfeld-Kosinski 11, and Thickstun 10-13.

[6] Willis asserts that "Witches were--or were believed to be--mothers 'gone bad' " (ix). On associations between witches and mothers, also see Hayes 179-200.

[7] See *Macbeth* 1.5.40-54 and 1.7.48-60. For more on Lady Macbeth, see Staub 333.

[8] See esp. 372, 374-5, 377-8.

While one might assume that early modern mothers were represented as witches to express the degree to which those particular mothers were poor examples of proper maternity, Phyllis Mack observes the opposite: a foolproof method for making a horrible figure of any kind more horrific was to make it a mother. "In fact, the most potent image of woman's spiritual marginality," Mack asserts, "was not the deviant witch brewing potions or stroking her familiars but the ordinary mother" (35). Why could "the ordinary mother" seem like such a potentially threatening figure, and what does this dangerous potential mean in relation to her poetic efforts when writing about her own child loss? To respond to these questions, we must first consider the many anxieties surrounding childbirth in early modern England.

The cultural expectations surrounding childbirth made it a focal point for multiple, diverse anxieties related to women. While, as I discuss below, many of those anxieties arguably relate to a desire to control unruly femininity, at least one of them consists of a fear on behalf of women. David Cressy explains that the period immediately prior to childbirth was one in which a husband was likely to fear greatly for the life of his marital partner, as well as for the child who might prove an all-important male heir: "At stake was the woman's health and safety and her ability to continue as helpmeet and partner, as well as the economic, legal and emotional consequences of her bearing a child. At such a time a man might think of heirs and expenses, as well as the comfort of his marital companion, while a woman might dread the ordeal and wonder if she was going to die" (*Birth, Marriage, and Death* 44).[9] Interestingly, Cressy points out that early

---

[9] Cressy explains that historians have revised their ideas concerning early modern people's emotions: "Historians once advanced the notion that people in the past did not love each other and were coldly unemotional in the face of a death in their family. But the bulk of evidence indicates that love, pain, and grief were deeply rooted and widely experienced in early modern England. Even with death all around them, with mortality rates that a modern society might find numbing, the people of Stuart England displayed intense emotions when a child, a spouse, or a parent died" (*Birth, Marriage, and Death* 393). For Laslett's cautions about extrapolating attitudes towards children from what he sees as inadequate information, see 18-19. Stone, meanwhile, in the sort of statement to which Cressy and Laslett object, asserts that "The expectation of life was so low that it was highly imprudent to become too emotionally dependent upon any other human being . . . affective relations were widely diffused rather than concentrated on members of the nuclear family" (5). For Stone's views specifically on the degree of sixteenth- and seventeenth-century adults' emotional investment in babies and children, see 70, 82, 105-7, 112-17, 174-5, 193, 652. Stone allows for the possibility that some early modern mothers were more attached to their babies than were fathers; see 114. Stone also admits limitations to his approach to investigating emotions; see 93. Also see Phillippy's summary of the debate about early modern affect, 321.

modern fears of the mother's death in childbirth were exaggerated given the actual mortality rates of the time. "Fearful expectations abound in the records," he writes, "and examples of women dying in childbed are not hard to find. But it would be misleading to deduce from this evidence that childbed mortality was common. In fact the opposite is true. Most women survived childbirth without complications and most mothers quickly recovered" (Cressy, *Birth, Marriage, and Death* 30). Regardless of the statistical risks to the mother during childbirth, a husband might fear for his wife for reasons ranging from his love for her to his concern that she might die and leave him alone with a motherless child to raise.

Worry about a wife's well being was not the only anxiety related to childbirth. As a middle-class husband, for instance, fretted about his wife's survival, he was also likely to face significantly altered daily routines, in which he performed his wife's household duties himself, an inversion of gender roles that might have given him a taste of what life could be like--at least until he could find another wife or other form of domestic help--if his current partner were indeed to die in childbirth.[10] Furthermore, custom required him to keep his distance from the birthing room. A community of women controlled that domestic space, leaving the knowledge of the husband's future well being--as signified by the health of his wife and child --in the hands of those women, whose provisions he must supply.[11] "From the viewpoint of ministers and physicians, and perhaps too for many husbands," Cressy explains, "the gathering of women at childbirth was exclusive, mysterious, and potentially unruly" (*Birth, Marriage, and Death* 55). In discussing how birth attendants were expected to know whether the children they witnessed being born were legitimate or not (since women undergoing the trauma of childbirth were believed likely to reveal the truth about their children's fathers), Caroline Bicks articulates specifically-- beyond the general fear of communal femininity free from patriarchal

---

[10] See Cressy, *Birth, Marriage, and Death* 35, 44.

[11] For more on women's control over childbirth (to the exclusion of men), see Cressy, *Birth, Marriage, and Death* 55-7 and Miller 8. For an intriguing discussion of the case of Thomas Salmon, who cross-dressed as a woman in order to join the festivities after a successful delivery in the all-female birthing room, see Cressy, *Travesties and Transgressions* 92-115. For an engaging account of patriarchal anxieties surrounding the belief that midwives could shape (through cutting the umbilical chord long or short) male infants' future virility, see Bicks 53-61.

surveillance--why the dominance of women in the birthing room could foster anxiety among men:[12]

> The women of the birthroom . . . could compromise the physical and discursive sites of virility's production: they occupied the husband's marital bedchamber both during and up to a month after the birth, and reminded him of his inferior narrative powers when it came to telling stories about his wife and her offspring . . . Whether or not they knew more than the husband or the state, birth attendants witnessed and testified to what few men could lay claim to having seen or known. (50)

Cultural anxieties surrounding the birthing room were arguably widespread, not only due to its exception from patriarchal control over the household, but also because of how it represented a gap in patriarchal knowledge.[13]

Anxieties about childbirth extended from those centered on women and mothers in general to others focused specifically on the connections between mother and child. There were many concerns regarding how a pregnant woman's physical, mental, and spiritual states and experiences could affect her child. Cressy writes that:

> In traditional lore the womb-child was . . . threatened by evil spirits and myriad dangers that required specific action or avoidance. A pregnant woman might not attend funerals in order to avoid harmful influences; she might refuse to engage in winding or grinding activities for fear, sympathetically, of strangling the child; she should be shielded from the sight of monsters lest her foetus become deformed. (*Birth, Marriage, and Death* 46)[14]

Mack explains further that:

> From the onset of her pregnancy a woman was believed to enter a liminal and potentially dangerous spiritual condition, for the process of gestation, which doctors viewed as the fermentation of corrupt matter within the womb, placed her outside the pale of strictly human culture . . . A pregnant woman was also believed to possess intensified emotional energy and

---

[12] On the midwife's duty to determine the father of an illegitimate baby, see Cressy, *Travesties and Transgressions* 13. For more on the role of the midwife, see Cressy, *Travesties and Transgressions* 84-91.

[13] On the limited knowledge that even medical doctors had about childbirth, see Bicks 53.

[14] For more on dangers to the unborn child in the early modern period, see Cressy, *Birth, Marriage, and Death* 45-7.

imagination . . . Indeed, her essence had become so porous that the mere objects of her sight could permeate her body and distort the fetus. (35)

A pregnant woman's interaction with the world around her was believed to be so fragile and so subject to influence that "the mere objects of her sight" could shape--and potentially deform--her unborn child. So suspect was the female imagination that, according to Mack, "a prime explanation for the birth of a deformed child was that . . . a woman's volatile imagination, infused by evil forces, was sufficient to transform the fetus into a monster" (39).[15] Mendelson and Crawford indicate that these beliefs were not merely the abstract, distant theories of medical practitioners or the opinions solely of men: "Women recounted the popular lore to each other, believing that their behaviour, diet, and imagination could contribute to the outcome of their pregnancies" (151).[16] Given how fragile early modern people believed an unborn child to be and how many fears they had about how a pregnant woman could harm her child unintentionally, it is no wonder that there were also worries about the possibility that she might harm it on purpose:[17]

---

[15] Schwarz notes that "For medical texts from the period, the primary threat is perhaps an overindulgence of *thinking*: mothers may make their children effeminate by loving them too much after they are born, but they can make them monsters by thinking about them too much before. . . . If a woman looks at or thinks about the wrong thing, her child will become that thing" (299-300). Also see Cressy, *Travesties and Transgressions* for more on the belief "that a woman's imagination could have damaging effects on her offspring" (25). On early modern English interpretations of the birth of deformed or monstrous infants, see Cressy, *Travesties and Transgressions* 23, 29-50. He writes that there were "at least six lines of explanation [for monstrous births] that were not mutually exclusive but collectively and cumulatively reinforcing. They could be seen as freaks of nature or as manifestations of divine power; they could be interpreted as judgements and punishments against individual sinners, usually the parents, or as generalized warnings to the community at large; they could be seen as portents or prognostications, looking forward to some earthly catastrophe, or as precursors of the latter days, foresignals of the end of the world. And finally, for people who were moved by none of these explanations, the monster babes provided opportunities for freak-show entertainment, occasions for idle amusement" (Cressy, *Travesties and Transgressions* 36-7).

[16] Margaret Cavendish, in *A True Relation of my Birth, Breeding, and Life*, uses this logic implicitly in her description of herself and her siblings in order to emphasize her own mother's many perfections: "Also she was an affectionate mother, breeding her children with a most industrious care and tender love. And having eight children, three sons and five daughters, there was not any one crooked or any ways deformed. Neither were they dwarfish, or of a giant-like stature, but every ways proportionable; likewise well featured, clear complexions, brown hairs (but some lighter than others), sound teeth, sweet breaths, plain speeches, tuneable voices" (92).

[17] On fears of the mother as a deliberate threat to her unborn child, see Cressy, *Birth, Marriage, and Death* 47.

"Attempting to be rid of her womb-child a pregnant woman might reverse all the advice designed for its care, and subject her body to violent shocks and purges" (Cressy, *Birth, Marriage, and Death* 49).

Anxieties about an infant's survival and well being continued after a succcessful delivery. Lawrence Stone explains that there were far too many ways in which babies could be hurt:

> Infants in the Early Modern period were exposed to lack of attention by the mother in the first critical weeks; premature weening; accidental smothering in bed with their parents; the transfer of the infant to the care of a wet-nurse (with the high probability of death by neglect); abandonment in doorways; or deposit in parish workhouses or foundling hospitals, which were often almost equally lethal if less offensive to the public than dead babies littering the streets. (69-70)[18]

The younger a baby, the less likely it was to survive. Cressy explains that "one in every two conceptions ended in miscarriage . . . Miscarriage was a frequent occurrence and was often described with anguish," as is evident in my discussion below of Mary Carey's poem, "Upon ye Sight of my Abortive Birth ye 31th: of December 1657" (*Birth, Marriage, and Death* 47). Cressy also provides these figures: "Demographic estimates show that approximately 2 per cent of babies born in the Elizabethan period died before the end of their first day of life. Death claimed a cumulative total of 5 per cent within a week, 8 or 9 per cent within a month, and 12 or 13 per cent within a year, with slightly higher rates of infant mortality in the later seventeenth century" (*Birth, Marriage, and Death* 117).[19]

Not only were there good reasons to worry about a baby's basic survival; there were also ongoing concerns about the continued physical connection between mother and child through breastfeeding. As Naomi Miller points out, early modern Europeans believed that "breast milk was . . . a purified form of menstrual blood, which changed color as it passed back and forth between the breast and womb, bearing witness to the fluid materiality of women's bodies and their reproductive function" (4-5). Most importantly, early modern European culture linked breast milk with the maternal power to shape a baby's character and moral disposition: "Babies

---

[18] For more on dangers to early modern children, see Stone 77, 81.

[19] For a discussion of local statistics on infant mortality in a specific community (Clayworth), see Laslett 69. For birth rates in early modern England, see Stone 63-6. For mortality rates in early modern Europe, see Stone 66-73. Stone asserts that in the early modern period, the "infant and child mortality rate . . . [was] between thirty and fifty per cent" (651).

sucked in their mother's principles, both good and bad, along with their milk . . . " (Mack 36).[20]   Breast-feeding was so fundamental to determining a child's identity, in fact, that, according to Rachel Trubowitz:

> The Word is literally sucked in at the maternal breast--a perception that underscores the crucial role that lactating motherhood is mandated to play in the transmission of official discourse. To put this another way, maternal breastfeeding, as represented in the didactic literature on the English home, secures the shifting parameters of English national identity by interpellating children into the state as normative speaking subjects. (97)

Not only could a mother's breast milk define her child's future emotional, moral, and national identities, but her love for that child could also influence it strongly.   Edith Snook points out that "Humanists, such as Erasmus, Elyot, Vives, and Ascham, express fears that mothers and their love will turn boys from the rigours, reason, and discipline that they associate with scholarship and masculinity toward the life of delicacy, flattery, and foolishness that they attribute to women" (164).[21]   Early modern culture was so rife with anxieties over childbirth and the survival of infants and children that even the nourishment of a mother's breast-milk and the comforts of her love were understood to be potentially harmful.

Given the many, diverse fears surrounding childbirth and child-rearing--and especially given those directed at the important but precarious connection between mother and child--it is perhaps not surprising that the cultural meanings associated with the death of a child could be particularly negative.   The various anxieties about the mother's role in childbirth left plenty of room to blame her in the event of disaster.   As Mack puts it, "If even a normal childbirth was seen as a spiritually loaded event, the death of an infant might well be spiritually catastrophic, because the exhausted mother was instructed to interpret the death as punishment for her own sinfulness" (37).   Mendelson and Crawford provide an example of this logic at work: "Having a small child and a new baby, Susannah Bell had resisted

---

[20] For more on breast milk, also see Mendelson and Crawford 28-9; Cressy, *Birth, Marriage, and Death* 87-8; Francus 839-40; Vosevich 64; Luecke 242-3; Yavneh 67; and Trubowitz 84. For an intriguing argument about connections among "breast milk, blood, and the racialized construction of English national identity" (83), see Trubowitz 82-101. Also see Bergmann's compelling account of the relations among breast milk, language, and ethnicity in early modern Spanish texts 105-20.

[21] See Phillippy 319-332, for more on "maternity . . . as a unique site of affective and emotional license" (320).

her husband's desire to emigrate to New England."[22] The subsequent death
of her infant convinces her that her loss is punishment for her resistance to
her husband's wishes (Mendelson and Crawford 137). Mendelson and
Crawford likewise observe that "Sins, including failure to observe the taboo
on sexual activity during menstruation, could lead to miscarriage or
deformity" (151).[23] Mack's "ordinary mother" existed at the very center of a
web of cultural anxieties related to childbirth (35); ultimately, the death of a
child might reveal--even in the most seemingly perfect of mothers--some
secret, fatal sin, a lurking, potential threat actualized at the cost of another's
life, another who might well be his father's only heir and thus the symbol of
and means for patriarchal continuity. As I touched upon at the beginning of
this section, a wide range of early modern written cultural artifacts--from
Spenser's and Milton's epics to Shakespeare's *Macbeth* to Jacobean
pamphlets--play upon these anxieties about mothers through their
demonizing representations of maternal figures. Similar concerns manifest
themselves, however, in texts that do not portray maternal figures explicitly
as actual monsters or witches.

A prominent example of the female imagination's susceptibility to
spiritual misconception, for instance, is Milton's depiction in *Paradise Lost*
of Eve's vulnerability to Satan's influence when he whispers in her ear to
affect her dreams. Milton's poetic speaker explains that Ithuriel and Zephon
find Satan:

> Assaying by his devilish art to reach
> The organs of her fancy, and with them forge
> Illusions as he list, phantasms and dreams,
> Or if, inspiring venom, he might taint
> The animal spirits that from pure blood arise
> Like gentle breaths from rivers pure, thence raise
> At least distempered, discontented thoughts,
> Vain hopes, vain aims, inordinate desires
> Blown up with high conceits engendering pride.
>
> (*Paradise Lost* 4.801-810)

---

[22]   See Mendelson and Crawford 151-2 for additional historical anecdotes
illustrating the interplay between child loss and a mother's sense of her own sinfulness. Also
see Mendelson 196; Mendelson and Crawford 28; Cressy, *Birth, Death, and Marriage* 33;
and Stone 208-11.

[23]   On other taboos relating sexual activity to weak offspring, see Stone 495. On
links between monstrous births and sexual activity, see Cressy, *Travesties and
Transgressions* 37-8.

Milton makes Satan's first direct assault on the human couple in Paradise an attempt to manipulate Eve's "fancy"; the devil hopes to "raise [in her] . . . inordinate desires/ Blown up with high conceits engendering pride," as if to impregnate her with the sin of pride itself.[24]

Given the association of pregnancy with a woman's vulnerability to supernatural influences in early modern England, it is not surprising that the figure of the mother could be used to emphasize spiritual danger. In anti-puritan civil war propaganda, for instance, one frequently finds so-called bad mothers' inappropriate behavior conflated with their membership in radical sects. Anecdotes of women sectarians producing hideously deformed offspring reinforced the idea that those children were reflections of their mothers' spiritual waywardness.[25] Even the pervasive demonization of the Roman Catholic Church often involved figuring it as a grotesque mother, the Whore of Babylon. In *A Second Fiery Flying Roule*, for example, Abiezer Coppe, a Ranter, refers to "ripping up . . . the bowels of the wel-favoured Harlot, the holy Whore, who scorns that which is called prophanesse, wickenesse, looseness, or libertinisme, and yet herself is the mother of witchcrafts, and of all the abominations of the earth" (37). Fifth Monarchist Anna Trapnel's *Report and Plea*, meanwhile, depicts the Catholic Church as the whorish mother of a bastard--the Anglican Church. Trapnel chastizes England for, among other things:

> dressing the Scarlet Whore in new clothes, so as to blinde and deceive Cities and Countries, telling them, That it's the true genuine fruit of the

---

[24] See DiSalvo for an argument about the problematic relation between Milton's representations of his own divine inspiration and production of verse, and such depictions of "female" fancy. See Guillory's *Poetic Authority* for a general discussion of Spenser's and Milton's ambivalent relationships to imagination. Guillory's observation that Milton "deliberately seeks to evade tropes in representing himself at the moment of inspiration" suggests an interesting parallel between Milton's poetic self-effacement at his most authorizing moments and the similar illusion of poetic self-effacement in mother-poets' elegies for their children (*Poetic Authority* 154).

[25] Mack summarizes, for example, the case of Mary Adams, "a pious young woman of respectable family who converted from sect to sect, finally becoming convinced that she was pregnant with the Holy Ghost. She gave birth to a dead, deformed child in prison after a labor lasting eight days. Confronted with the child, whom she could not bear to look at, she asked the jailer for a knife to cut her nails, and, in her despair, disemboweled herself. The account was published and signed by ten town officials, who saw the monstrous birth as proof that she had given birth to a devil" (41-2). See *An Account of Mary Adams, the Ranters Monster* (London, 1652). For similar anecdotes about connections between "heretical" or "antinomian" women and their "monstrous" offspring, see Mack 42-3. On women who think they are pregnant with the Messiah, see Capp 42.

Womb of the Church, and spouse of CHRIST, when it will indeed be
discovered to be from the Harlots brood, and so a Bastard, which is
sentenced by the LORD . . . the LORD hath pronounced destruction to
Babylons Brats, as well as to *Babylon*. (*Report and Plea* A6)

A pitiless Mother, a sensationalist pamphlet, also conveys its anti-Catholic
message through an account of a supposedly bad mother: Margaret Vincent
falls prey to "Papism" and immediately kills two of her children as a
consequence of her "perverted" religious beliefs.[26]

Mothers' elegies for their dead children share this cultural context in
which the intellectual, spiritual, and moral shortcomings of mothers were
believed capable of replication in their offspring's bodies and destinies.[27]
Such mother-poets had to confront the idea that their children's early deaths
signified and were a form of punishment for their own sins. As a
comparison of male- and female-authored poems in this genre will
demonstrate, the cultural significance of the multiply miscarrying mother--
her spiritual and intellectual deformities manifesting themselves in the
physical monstrosity or premature death of her child--presented women
with a special challenge in composing such poems.[28] In this seventeenth-
century context, a mother writing poetry over the dead body of her own

---

[26] For more on Margaret Vincent, see Miller 7 and Staub 336-8. Also see Staub's
discussion of the similar depiction of motherhood in *Bloody Newes from Dover* 338-9. For
another example of a "bad" mother (Anne Hutchinson) in relation to anxieties surrounding
religious controversy, see Luecke 246.

[27] On the negative connotations of female "creative energy," also see Krontiris 18.

[28] Barbara Johnson's observations on much later child loss poems are illuminating:
"it is clear that a great many poetic effects may be colored according to *expectations*
articulated through the gender of the poetic speaker. Whether or not men and women would
'naturally' write differently about dead children, there is something about the connection
between motherhood and death that refuses to remain comfortably and conventionally
figurative [or, as we will see, comfortable with conventional figures, for that matter]. . . . The
indistinguishability of miscarriage and abortion in the [Lucille] Clifton poem ["the lost baby
poem"] indeed points to the notion that *any* death of a child is perceived as a crime
committed by the mother, something a mother ought by definition to be able to prevent"
(198).

Lilley describes general differences between male- and female-authored elegies:
"Masculine canonical elegy is dominated by the drive towards succession and self-placing,
and the construction of heroic genealogies. Its central narratives concern desire deferred, the
reification or elision of the elegized, and strategies of textual possession and inscription.
Women's elegy, at least in the seventeenth century, seems to partake of a logic of
renunciation and cancellation, expressly refusing the reification of the elegized" (87). As I
will demonstrate, child loss poetry presents a special case with special restrictions for
mother-poets; however, men and women poets write surprisingly similar poems for other
people's children.

child should use her composition as both a cathartic and confessional exercise. She should write verse to express grief and self-blame. In the most optimistic of scenarios, her poem should help her to acknowledge her fault in the child's death, and ultimately, to allow her to reconcile herself with her culpability, the child's absence, and God's will.[29] Given the notion of the female imagination as an entity that tends to misconceive, a mother's elegy for her child presents only restricted opportunities for attempting a display of virtuoso poetic technique during an age in which much verse was produced out of coterie competition that encouraged shows of imaginative, intellectual mastery and verbal skill.[30] Some mothers' child loss poetry resists these limitations, however, by adhering strictly to the expected, acceptable commonplaces of the genre on one level while on another interrogating the literary and social conventions blaming the mother for her child's death.

The Commonplaces

> Loneliness is loneliness, and anger is anger, we have assumed, whether it was felt by a thirteenth-century nun or a twentieth-century professor. (Ezell, *Writing Women's Literary History* 27)

In offering a critique of twentieth-century feminists' approaches to early modern and medieval texts, Margaret J. M. Ezell notes that the interest in creating a historically continuous tradition of women writers with whom modern women can identify replicates the traditional, masculinist, humanist process of canon formation insofar as it is assumed that women's experiences and emotions transcend historical and cultural differences. As Ezell argues:

---

[29] Mendelson writes: "Usually these maternal laments represented an attempt to bear the loss with Christian fortitude. Women tried to assure themselves that their own sins were to blame and that in any case their innocent children had obtained the joys of eternal life" (197).

[30] Marotti claims that "[i]n both manuscript and printed collections, answer poems, parodies, and other forms of competitive versifying testify to the status of poetry as a kind of social currency" (*John Donne, Coterie Poet* 12). He also asserts that "Difficulty, even magnificently unnecessary difficulty, was a valued commodity in the Inns-of-Court environment, the opportunity to exercise intellectual mastery that somewhat compensated for political and social vulnerability" (Marotti, *John Donne, Coterie Poet* 70).

Not only have women's literary histories confirmed the continuity of female experiences, but they have also tended to assert that emotional responses to landmark human experiences such as giving birth and psychological responses to social stress such as isolation or injustice have remained constant. (*Writing Women's Literary History* 26-7)

This overlooking of historical and cultural difference when it comes to representations of women's emotions is evident in the treatment of women's child loss lyrics. For instance, Germaine Greer, editor of *Kissing the Rod: An Anthology of Seventeenth-Century Women's Verse*, proposes that child loss poetry is one among several "female genres," a classification that tends to suggest that such verse approaches natural, spontaneous self-expression in response to a universal female experience ("Introduction" 12).[31] The relegation of women's child loss verse to a female genre makes it very easy to forget that canonical male poets such as Ben Jonson, John Milton, Thomas Carew, and Robert Herrick wrote poems occasioned by the deaths of babies or children. As I will demonstrate, such canonical authors borrow from the same set of specifically seventeeth-century English themes as do

---

[31] After discussing a child loss poem believed to have been written by a woman, Greer generalizes that "ladies were expected . . . to write out their own heartbreak in metrical form" (10). Wynne-Davies claims that women's child loss poems "are the most overtly autobiographical of all the poetry collected [in Wynne-Davies's anthology] and show that, while familial relationships might have enabled women to write, they were regarded as far more than an advantageous encouragement to literary production" (xxiii). I show that, while mothers' child loss poems do relate to those women's life experiences, their participation in the expected conventions of the genre complicates any autobiographical content and that, furthermore, child loss poems were at most a very ambivalent "encouragement to literary production." Mermin's observations concerning women poets' depictions of children in the Victorian Age, when considered in relation to my cultural and historical contextualization of seventeenth-century English women's child loss poetry, provides the kind of comparative information necessary to form a preliminary basis for a cross-historical, non-essentializing consideration of women's writing on such seemingly "primal" themes as child loss. Mermin asserts, for instance, that "[o]ne of the odder features of women's poetry, particularly common in Victorian England and America, is the presence of animals and children. When a woman looked for something to take the same relation to her within a poem that female figures take for male poets, the equation often reads: a male poet is to a woman as a female poet is to a child or animal" (74). In the seventeenth century, this equation sometimes holds in child loss poetry, but typically only if the woman poet does not write about *her own* bereavement. Thus, while in Victorian poetry, "A mother's lament for a dead child is the feminine equivalent of a man's lament for a dead beloved," in Renaissance verse, a mother-poet's project when composing about the death of her own child is to write a poem that attempts to erase its status as an act of intellectual creation (Mermin 74). This cross-historical comparison belies the notion that women everywhere and always write about child loss in the same way.

less known mother-poets in composing elegies for dead children. Broadly summarized, there are three main thematic concerns that almost any seventeenth-century English poet addresses when composing on the subject of infant mortality: the need for the parents to resign themselves to God's will; the child as lost property; and parental sin as the ultimate cause of the child's death.[32] While male and female poets alike engage with these themes, their poems demonstrate an array of gendered differences in treating them. To understand better both how those differences manifest themselves and the precise features of the commonplaces, it will be helpful to analyze a range of examples.

Child loss poems usually include an explicit formulaic assertion of resignation to God's will in accepting the death of the infant or child. Mary Carey's "Wretten by me att the same tyme [as her husband's similar poem]; on the death of my 4th, & only Child, Robert Payler" begins by asserting "My lord hath called for my sonne/ my hart breth's forth; thy will be done" (1-2). Carey's husband George Payler similarly engages with this theme in the opening couplet of his poem upon the same occasion: "Dear wife, let's learne to get that Skill,/ Of free Submission to God's holy Will" (1-2). But a gendered difference is already apparent in Carey's and Payler's treatment of this theme, for Carey directly addresses God in submitting her will to his ("thy will be done"), while Payler uses their son's death as an occasion to take a didactic stance towards her. Hence, he addresses his verse to her instead of God and speaks of submission as something that they have yet to learn, not as an immediate offering to God. Some poets push the necessary concession to God's power to the point of reasoning that it is better for the child to be dead. Parental grief and resignation thus transform into the joy of imagining the afterlife of the innocent in heaven.[33] Elizabeth Egerton's epitaph, "On my Boy Henry," begins by asserting maternal grief:

---

[32] Joshua Scodel delineates another significant theme of seventeenth-century child loss poetry that I do not examine here: the child "as little-but-great" (70).

[33] Scodel observes that "the majority of late sixteenth- and seventeenth-century English epitaphs that explicitly treat the afterlife of the soul situate it in heaven. The continuing strength of the pre-Reformation view of England, even among otherwise strong Calvinists, probably stems from its greater consolatory power" (81). For more on the consolation of imagining a dead infant in heaven, see Cressy 388 and Stone 113. On the many complex questions surrounding infant baptism and corresponding beliefs about the after-life of a dead baby, see Cressy 114-17.

Here lyes a Boy y[e] finest child from me
Which makes my Heart & Soule sigh for to see
Nor can I think of any thought, but greeve,
For joy or pleasure could me not releeve . . . (1-4)

But her poetic speaker claims to overcome this grief at the conclusion of the poem by asserting "But y[u] art happy, Sweet'st on High,/ I mourne not for thy Birth, nor Cry" (Egerton 9-10). No presumably secular "joy or pleasure" could comfort her, but the idea that her child is safely "on High" stops her tears with the last word in the poem. Jonson similarly employs this formulaic compensatory locution in "On My First Davghter," in which he implies that his daughter is better off in heaven.[34] This father finds himself glad because "shee parted hence/ With safetie of her innocence"; he imagines her in the afterlife occupying a place among those privileged to be part of the "virgin-traine" of "heauen's Queene" (*Epigrammes* 22.5-6, 9, 7).[35]

The second major theme of seventeenth-century English child loss poetry is that the dead child constitutes lost property. This theme inevitably engages with the Christian commonplace that all of creation is ultimately God's possession; hence, any perceived sense of human loss is actually a form of misprision, or even hubris.[36] Elegies for children thus often suggest

---

[34] Scodel also notes "Jonson's sense of death as a beneficent end": "he normally imagines children's deaths as removals--unhappy only for the living mourners--from the pains of the adult world" (72). See Scodel 75-85 for more on Jonson's "On My First Davghter."
[35] Katherine Philips uses a similar consolatory strategy in "On Little Regina Collyer, on the same tombstone [as her father's]." Regina

By death's fierce hand was snatched hence
In her state of innocence:
Who by it this advantage gains,
Her wages got without her pains.
                    ("On Little Regina Collyer" 3-6)

Philips appropriates many Jonsonian techniques in her child loss poetry. The consolatory logic that Philips and Jonson employ can be considered a variation on Jed's notion of "chaste thinking," which "follow[s] a narrative sequence of chastity, rape, corruption, and self-castigation" (7). Philips' and Jonson's celebratory variation on chaste thinking finds cause for relief in the deaths of the girls about whom they write because those girls have managed to pre-empt the sexual violation that chastity invites.
[36] See George Herbert's "The Dedication" and "The Holdfast" for a more generalized engagement with this paradoxical Christian commonplace. This notion seems a Christianized version of "the ancient commonplace of life as a loan requiring repayment by death" discussed by Scodel (79).

that parental consolation comes through acknowledging that it is an act of self-delusion--in Milton's terms "false imagined loss"--to consider the child one's own ("On the Death of a Fair Infant Dying of a Cough" 72). One cannot lose something that one never really had; the "lost" child was, at most, a temporary gift. Jonson thus consoles himself when his daughter dies by reasoning, "Yet, all heauens gifts, being heauens due,/ It makes the father, lesse, to rue" (*Epigrammes* 22.3-4). Jonson's "heauen" has a metonymical relation to God, and whatever comes from God returns to him. Jonson suggests that recognizing this theological reality minimizes his fatherly grief. Similarly, in writing about her late step-daughter, Katherine Philips advises other parents to "reckon children 'mong those passing joyes/ Which one hower gives them, and the next destroyes" and makes herself and her husband examples from which to take warning: "we were secure of our content,/ But find too late that it was only lent" ("In memory of F.P. who dyed at Acton 24 May 1660--13th of her age" 71-2, 73-4).

An alternative strategy for effecting the consolation expected of an elegy is to suggest that, even though in strictly theological terms God owns all creation, the parents actually "lost" their child through a fair barter with God. Loss becomes exchange: a human child is traded for God's only son, Christ.[37] A brief, anonymous poem from Arthur Scattergood's commonplace

---

[37] In "Evensong," Herbert addresses a similar idea: "But I have got his son, and he hath none" (8). Herbert represents a poetic speaker surprised at the seeming inequality of the exchange implied by the parallel structure of the line: God gives his son but receives nothing in return. In child loss poetry, the deceased child balances out God's gift. The parents (ideally) can feel that they have given something back to God, and therefore that their loss is worthwhile, even if, ultimately, it is impossible to give God anything that he does not already have.

A passage from Queen Elizabeth's translation of Margaret, Queen of Navarre's *Godlie MEDITATION of the inward love of the soule towards Christ our LORD* printed in Thomas Bentley's *THE MONVMENT OF MATRONES* (1582) provides additional context for understanding the potential relationship between spiritual exchange and material loss. In the third chapter of the translation, entitled, "*Of the Soules infidelitie or apostasie* from GOD," the young Elizabeth writes: "But heere is the worst, what maner of mother have I beene: For, after that I by faith had receiued the name of a true mother, I became verie rude vnto thee my Sonne: because that after I had conceiued and brought thee foorth, I left reason, and being subiect to my will, not taking heed vnto thee, I fell asleepe, and gaue place to my great enimie, the which, in the night of ignorance, I being asleepe, did steale thee from me craftilie, and in thy place she did put hir child, which was dead, and so I did leese thee, which was a sorow=full remorse for me. Thus did I loose thee my sonne, by mine owne fault, because I tooke no heed to keepe thee. Sensualitie my neighbour, I beeing in my beastlie sleepe, did steale thee from me, and gaue to me hir child, which had no life in him, named sinne, whome I said: I would not haue, but vtterlie did forsake him.

book (BL Add. 44963) plays with this idea through its exchange--at the
level of narrative--of a dead child for Christ. The poem inserts the child
into the story of Christ's nativity:

> Into this world, as strangers to an Inne,
> This Infant came guestwise, where when't had bin,
> And found no Entertamm^t long to stay,
> Hee only broke his fast, & went his way.

The child is a version of baby Jesus, who, instead of finding no room at the
inn, finds inadequate entertainment to detain him from his journey. The
fact that this child loss poem appears in Scattergood's commonplace book
grouped with three others, which are juxtaposed with a mock epitaph for the
Earl of Castlehaven, suggests that the compiler had a special interest in
clever epitaphs. That such a poem playfully incorporates the notion of loss
as exchange into its short narrative, with the dead child substituting for the
infant Christ, supports the notion that rewriting loss as exchange was
conventional for the genre. The poet's literalization of the convention flirts
with heresy: the dead child almost usurps Christ's role in a miniature
Christmas pageant, yet the poet abandons that narrative just before the
usurpation is complete. The child departs--instead of sleeping in a nearby
manger, for instance--when he finds "no Entertamm^t" in the inn that
metaphorically stands in for "this world." Conventional loss rendered
exchange becomes a joke befitting the taste of a verse compiler who would

---

She affirmed that he was mine owne, but I knew him to be hirs. For as soone as I
came to the light of grace, which thou hadst giuen me, then I knewe my glorie to be changed,
when I saw the dead child not to be mine. For the same which was aliue, whom she had take
awaie, was my child: so apparent was the change betweene Jesus and sinne. . . . O sweete
Jesus, thus hast thou proued me, how much I loued thee: yea and when by sinne I had lost
thee, yet didst thou returne unto me" (11-12). Elizabeth's translation conflates the theme of
exchange--here figured as the illicit act of a thief, with whom the mother's spiritual state is
complicit--with the theme of parental sin that I discuss above. Because Bentley's *THE
MONVMENT OF MATRONES* is effectively a religious conduct manual targeting a female
readership, these words penned by one queen, translated by another, and dedicated to a third
(Queen Katherine Parr) could have been quite influential. Beilin proposes that "Bentley's
apparent purposes were to educate women in their long spiritual history and to place the
women of his own time in a framework that authorized their pious utterances" (66). While
this celebratory reading of Bentley's motives could be partially accurate, the passage quoted
above also suggests that he published it to put contemporary women in their place.

categorize epitaphs for children side-by-side with a mock epitaph for the Earl of Castlehaven.[38]

Milton's "On the Death of a Fair Infant Dying of a Cough" makes more serious use of both of the above strategies of consolation that I have categorized as together constituting the second major theme of child loss poetry: the child as temporary gift and as item of exchange. Addressing the bereaved mother in the last stanza, Milton's poetic speaker concludes:

> Then thou the mother of so sweet a child
> Her false imagined loss cease to lament,
> And wisely learn to curb thy sorrows wild;
> Think what a present thou to God hath sent,
> And render him with patience what he lent;
>   This if thou do he will an offspring give,
> That till the world's last end shall make thy name
> to live. ("On the Death of a Fair Infant" 71-77)

The fact that Milton ends his elegy in this manner suggests the degree to which the notion that the mother receives something--Christ--out of the "false imagined loss" of her child was seen as irrefutable, if not the best consolation for parental grief: exchanging one's own child for God's is an offer that one cannot refuse. Like Milton, Mary Carey combines the strategies of recognizing the child as God's possession and conceptualizing loss as exchange:

> my all; that mercy hath made mine
>   frely's surendered to be thine:
>
> But if I give my all to the
>   lett me not pyne for poverty:
>
> Change wth me; doe, as I have done
>   give me thy all; Even thy deare sonne:
>
> > ("Wretten by me att the same tyme; on the death
> > of my 4th, & only Child, Robert Payler" 3-8).

---

[38] Variants of this poem appear in *Wit's Recreations*, 1640, Sig. Aa7; BM Add. MS 15227, fol. 76, "In Filim Secretarii Winwood"; MSS Ashmole 38, p. 198; Sancroft 53, p. 45; Tanner 465, fol. 71^v. Cited in Crum 471.

Despite Milton's and Carey's engagement with the same conventions in these two fragments, their treatments of them are strikingly different. Carey's poem, for example, represents the stakes in the exchange as being higher than Milton's implies. Contrast, in particular, her repeated figuration of her dead child as her "all" with his minimization of the mother's loss by using such terms as "present" and "lent" to describe the fair infant. Also, her poem voices, through its string of imperatives directed towards God ("Change," "doe," and "give"), a much more active role in the exchange than Milton's speaker suggests that the bereaved mother he addresses should take. That mother should "cease to lament," "curb [her] sorrows wild," and "render [God] with patience what he lent."

The final pervasive theme of child loss poems is particular to those composed by parents. Such elegies tend to associate the premature death of the child with parental sin; not surprisingly, given the frequent demonization of the mother in seventeenth-century England, mothers tend to wrestle with this idea with great seriousness.[39] Fathers address the notion that their sinfulness relates to their children's deaths but to a lesser extent than mothers do. George Payler attempts to console himself and his wife, Mary Carey, by concluding his poem on the occasion of their fourth child's death by suggesting God's moral pedagogy in depriving the couple of their heir. He asserts that his son's premature death does not cause him grief, "If by such Changes, God shall bring us in/ To love Christ Jesus, & to loath our Sin" (11-12). He thus loosely associates parental sin with his child's death, implying that he and Carey have not learned "to loath [their] Sin" enough if God must still call their attention to their unworthiness by taking away their child. Jonson, too, touches upon the issue of parental sin, when he states, "My sinne was too much hope of thee, lou'd boy" in "On My First Sonne" (*Epigrammes* 45.2). Jonson's treatment of this theme, however, minimizes the potential seriousness of the charge that parental sin had a role in his son's death. The fact that he admits the instrumentality of his own sin reveals the conventionality of the gesture precisely because he only admits his sin to reconceptualize it as a quality that seems unexceptionable in a good parent: Jonson's sin was investing too much hope in his beloved son. Although Jonson asserts in his final couplet, borrowed from Martial, that he will "[vowe]" that "what he loues may neuer like too much" (*Epigrammes* 45.11-12) and in doing so suggests that he has been guilty of loving the

---

[39] Lilley explains maternal self-blame in slightly different terms: "Frequently, in maternal elegies, the mother chastises herself for her involuntary expulsion of the child from the protection and integrity of her own body, and for 'selflove' . . ." (90).

creature more than the Creator, he does not explicitly confess. Hence, while Jonson's poem engages on different levels with the conventional acknowledgement of parental sin, it does not do so as seriously or as directly as do many mother-poets' elegies for their children.

Gertrude Aston Thimelby's "On the Death of Her Only Child" lays out the gendered dynamics between parents with a self-flagellating directness that is almost startling to today's reader. She begins her poem by distinguishing the mother's and father's roles in the physical and spiritual well-being of the dead child:

> Deare infant, 'twas thy mother's fault
> So soone inclos'd thee in a vault:
> And father's good, that in such hast
> Has my sweet child in heaven plac'd.
> (Thimelby, "On the Death of Her Only Child" 1-4)

Here "mother's fault" and "father's good" represent a strictly gendered dichotomy in which the mother ascribes all blame to herself and everything praiseworthy to her husband.[40] Mary Carey's ventriloquism of God in "Upon ye Sight of my abortive Birth ye 31th: of December 1657" makes the link between the mother's spiritual state and her child's physical state more than clear, while it also shows--through its contrast with poems like Payler's and Jonson's--the difference in how much mothers and fathers took the idea of parental sin seriously and personally.[41] In Carey's third elegy, she asks God to explain why her baby died. The answer that Carey puts in God's mouth is shocking in the thoroughness of its condemnation of her spiritual shortcomings:

> Methinkes I heare Gods voyce, this is thy [the] sinne:
>   And Conscience justifies ye same within:
> Thou often dost present me wth dead frute;
>   Why should not my returns, thy presents sute:
>
> Dead dutys; prayers; praises thou dost bring,
>   affections dead; dead hart in every thinge:

---

[40] While Thimelby may play upon the difference between the mother's association with bodily production (in which she has failed because her child has died) and the father's association with spiritual generativity (in which he has succeeded given Thimelby's certainty of her child's arrival in heaven), her use of this body-soul dichotomy overlaps precisely with the gender dichotomy she articulates.

[41] I borrow the notion of "ventriloquism" from Harvey.

>In hearing; reading; Conference; Meditation;
>in acting graces & in Conversation;

>Whose taught or better'd by ye no Relation;
>thou'rt Cause of Mourning, not of Immitation: (37-46)

Spiritual insufficiency on the mother's part--in every conceivable devotional duty appropriate to a seventeenth-century Protestant woman--becomes implicated in Carey's physical miscarriage. These lines highlight the cruelty of the cultural context that makes Carey so efficient in anatomizing her own spiritual "deadness" upon the occasion of her spontaneous abortion.

An elegy in Katherine Austen's virtually unexplored manuscript miscellany "Book M," which I discuss more fully in Chapter 4, demonstrates a special case in which a mother can confront the role of her sins in her child's death without flagellating herself: the child's unexpected recovery from a life-threatening disease. Austen's poem is unusual in its comparison of the death of someone else's child to her own son's harrowing escape from the same seemingly terminal illness. The title that she gives her poem calls attention to the comparative nature of its subject matter: "Dec[ember] 5: 1664 Upon Robin Austens recovery of the smal pox and coronal popoins son John diing of them: a Youth of a very forward growth their ages the same. pop: 3 yeares for growth more." Like Carey, Austen uses her poem to question God's ways. "Why was mine spar'd," she asks, while "one so strong" and "judg'd to live long . . . <did> dye"(15, 16, 20)? Reasoning further, she asks, "Was it his Sin, or my <our> desert,/ Made mine to live and him to part" (23-4)? That the trajectory of her questions leads her to consider the role of parental sin in a child's death supports the notion that doing so is a cultural and generic commonplace, while it also exposes a particular case in which the mother-poet can minimize self-blame. My return later in this chapter to Austen's poem, along with Carey's, will explicate mothers' dramatic revisions of the potentially one-dimensional, simplistic themes common to elegies for children.

Maternal Plain Style

When seventeenth-century English poets composed elegies on behalf of other people's children, they not only engaged with the conventional themes described above, but they also appropriated tropes from the dominant poetic trends of the period. In particular, they borrowed with striking consistency from figures used commonly in Elizabethan love lyrics and from the newer manifestations of those figures in metaphysical and Cavalier seduction poems. Like cruel, fair beloveds and coy mistresses, dead children are typically associated figuratively with precious jewels and beautiful flowers.[42] In his poem "Epitaph on S(alomon) P(avy) a Child of Q. El(izabeths) Chappel," Jonson, for instance, characterizes the dead boy actor as "[t]he stages iewel" (*Epigrammes* 120.12).[43] An anonymous epitaph entitled "On an Infant Being Dead" makes the child-as-jewel image the structuring conceit for the entire poem:

> Here in this Tombe enclosed lies
> A precious Jewell of great price
> W^{ch} nature in ye world's disdaine
> But shew'd & put it up again. (BL Add. 44963)

Gertrude Aston Thimelby in "To Sir William and My Lady Persall, Uppon the Death of their Little Franke" advises the "Happy Parents" to "mourne no more,/ You this jewell but restore" (1-2). Thomas Carew uses the same image in his "*Epitaph on the Lady* Mary Villiers" when he warns any onlooker who "posses[es] a gemme,/ As deare to thee, as this to them" to sympathize warmly with the bereaved parents lest that onlooker discover, upon returning home, his or her own child dead (7-8). Like Carew's epitaph, Thimelby's "An Epitaph On a Sweet Little Boy of Sir William Persall" invokes the compassion and identification of other parents specifically through the image of the child as a jewel: "If you be loving parents, here's/ A jewel richly worth your teares" (9-10). Male and female poets alike thus use the lost-child-as-jewel image when writing about other people's children. Similarly, male and female poets consoling parents frequently appropriate the image of the female beloved as a flower in their elegies for children. Milton begins "On the Death of a Fair Infant Dying of a Cough" with such a comparison:

> O fairest flower no sooner blown but blasted,
> Soft silken primrose fading timelessly,
> Summer's chief honour if thou hadst outlasted
> Bleak winter's force that made thy blossom dry . . . (1-4)

---

[42] For more on flowers, female beloveds, and the dead, see Deming 99-102.

[43] Scodel sees Jonson's figuration of the young actor Pavy as a jewel as part of the poet's effort to show how his own "art raises lowly Pavy" (73).

Anne Bradstreet writes of "Three flours, two scarcely blown, the last i'th' bud,/ Cropt by th'Almighties hand" in "*On my dear Grand-child* Simon Bradstreet, *Who dyed* on 16. Novemb. 1669. *being but a moneth, and one day old*" (3-4). Katherine Austen, writing "On the Death of my Neece Grace Ashe. 4 years," calls the lost child a "Sweet blooming bud/ Cropet from its stud" (1-2). The child in Carew's generic "*An other*," "'Twas but a bud, yet did containe/ More sweetnesse then shall spring againe" (7-8), while Herrick describes "a pretty bud,/ Lately made of flesh and blood" in "*Upon a child that dyed*" (H-310.1-2). These dead children are represented as flowers--in some cases mere buds--that fade before they can flourish.

Why do these poets figure dead children through the use of images that are typically associated with the conventionally female beloved in the love lyric tradition? While at first glance this overlap in figuration may seem incongruous, it makes sense on a number of levels. Flowers and jewels make sense as metaphors for the poetic object, in particular, because their various resonances have similar functions in both kinds of verse. Whether representing a coy mistress or a dead baby, a flower emphasizes the destructive effects of time on the natural world. In love poetry, beauty fades all too quickly; in child loss lyrics, frail life passes all too soon. Similarly, in both cases the comparison of the poetic object to a jewel reinforces the value of that object. While elegies for children presumably help to console the bereaved parents, such compositions also provide an opportunity to display one's own poetic prowess (mother-poets, however, prove exceptions to this notion). The incorporation of as many techniques and figures as possible from dominant, fashionable poetic trends into child loss lyrics could thus render those poems occasions to engage in coterie competition.[44] Images of flowers and jewels could therefore serve as symbolic currency, shoring up the cultural value of the poet's elegy.

Mothers, however, almost entirely exclude images borrowed from amorous verse when they write poems about their own dead children. For example, while all of Thimelby's poems concerning child loss ("To Sir William and Lady Persall Upon the Death of Their Little Franke," "An Epitaph on a Sweet Little Boy of Sir William Persall," and "Mrs. Thimelby, on the Death of Her Only Child") engage in the commonplaces detailed above, only the two poems that concern *other people's children* figure the lost child as a jewel. In contrast, the third poem is virtually an exercise in developing the plainest style possible. Given that several of Thimelby's poems on topics other than child loss are in direct imitation of Donne, the

---

[44] For more on coterie competition, see Marotti, *John Donne, Coterie Poet.*

absence of figurative language in her elegy to her child suggests that its achievement, paradoxically, is in its refusal of self-consciously poetic figures. When Thimelby's "Mrs. Thimelby, on the Death of Her Only Child" (which I include in its entirety following my discussion of the fragments) is compared with her three verse fragments below, Thimelby's rejection of mainstream seventeenth-century poetic techniques in writing about her own experience of child loss becomes apparent:

> Nature, nor art, (should both contest)
> Can help me now, my thoughts fly higher
> Then the rash Phaetons request,
> Or bold Prometheus for his fier. ("To H--T--" 1-4)

> Some froward heretickes in love ther bee,
> Wilfull abusers of his diety;
> Whose weake opinions, and whose feavorish flame,
> Pretend his right, but doe abuse his name.
> ("No Love Like That of the Soule" 1-4)

> Past is the winter absence of the sunne,
> The welcome embleame of your joys begunne,
> Your sonne's returning, to make good the trope,
> Tis he presents this new-years horiscope.
> ("To The Lady Elizabeth Thimelby on New-Yeares-Day, 1655, Looking Dayly for Her Sonne from Travaile" 1-4)

These excerpts provide a glimpse of the ways in which she locates her verse on topics other than child loss with respect to dominant poetic traditions. For instance, her references to Phaeton and Prometheus in the first example indicate her familiarity with Christian humanism, as well as with the commonplace figuration of Nature and Art in creative competition with each other. The second fragment echoes Venus's speech in Donne's "*The Indifferent*" (23-7) and recalls Donne's particular style of mixing the secular and sacred in poems such as "*The Canonization*" and "*The Relic*."[45] The third excerpt calls attention to Thimelby's self-consciousness as a poet: here she at once employs a traditional figure (the coming of spring sunshine

---

[45] Thimelby's poem "Upon the Lady Persalls Parting With Her Daughter Without Teares" plays directly upon Donne's "*A Valediction: of weeping*." Likewise, she and her brother exchanged poems on the topic of self love ("To Mr E--T, Who Holds Selfe-Love in All Our Actions" and "Self-Love Mentayned to the Faire Self-Denyer, My Sister"). Cf. Donne's "*Selfe Love*." On the Tixall group's engagement with Donne, see Burke 139.

signifying the arrival of joy), puns on that figure (sunne/sonne) and so exposes that her technique is constructed. While the poet suggests that the return of Lady Elizabeth Thimelby's son adds significance to and improves upon the arrival of spring, and thereby "make[s] good the trop[ing]" of the seasons, Thimelby also calls attention to the effectiveness of her figurative language through this reference. The poet and her poetic object both "make good the trope."

As these examples make clear, Thimelby was a practiced poet. It is thus all the more striking that her poem for her dead child does not self-consciously call attention to her poetry:

> Deare infant, 'twas thy mother's fault
> So soone inclos'd thee in a vault:
> And fathers good, that in such hast
> Hath my sweet child in heaven plac'd.
> I'le weepe the first as my offence,
> Then ioy that he made recompence:
> Yet must confesse my frailty such
> My ioy by greife's exceeded much:
> Though I, in reason, know thy blisse
> Can not be wish'd more then it is,
> Yet this selfelove orerules me soe,
> I'de have thee here, or with thee goe.
> But since that now neyther can be,
> A vertue of necessitie
> I yet may make, now all my pelf
> Content for thee, though not myselfe.

Thimelby's poem engages predictably with the commonplaces detailed above, with the exception that as much as Thimelby admits her "mother's fault," she refuses to rewrite her grief as joy. Wrestling with the conventional requirement of a statement of resignation, Thimelby pragmatically declares herself "Content for thee, though not myselfe." Hence, she challenges the commonplaces of child loss verse, but she does not signal the poem's relationship to a fashionable poetic trend, as she does in constructing her poems that borrow from the metaphysical tradition. While she structures her meditation on child loss through the use of rhyming couplets, iambic tetrameter, and balanced syntax, she prefers fairly straightforward statements to figures or images, and she avoids altogether the deliberate self-referentiality evident in the three fragments above. Her elegy to her own child tacitly refuses the display of creative agency typical of her other poems: it attempts to remove any glaring marks of a miscarrying mother's brain.[46] While Thimelby acknowledges her "mother's fault" as her "offence" and "confesse[s] [her] frailty" in succumbing to "selfelove"--thereby voicing perfectly appropriate, commonplace sentiments--on another level she resists blame for her child's death by excluding from this poem the displays of skill that she employs elsewhere.

The two child loss poems in Katherine Austen's commonplace book (one comparing her son to another boy of the same age and one concerning her niece) similarly highlight a dissociation of the display of poetic technique from the composition of verse upon the occasion of her own child's brush with death. Her elegy for *her niece* calls unusual attention to her poetic technique. In fact, Austen's "On the Death of My Neece Grace Ashe 4 yeares" is atypical among the poems in her commonplace book in its complex meter. It consists of two stanzas of eight lines, each of which is divided into four dimeter and four tetrameter lines:

> Sweet blooming bud
> Cropet from its stud
> When growing up
> Vnto faire hope
> Thy preety sweetnes time hath hid
> As soone as showne we are forbid
> To gaze upon that Lovely hue
> On which Times shady Curtaine drew
>
> Yet when we know
> The best manyt grow
> In this dark vaile
> Where ills stil Aile
> The great disposer sets them free
> Whose better character doth see

---

[46] Scodel's description of Jonson's relation to his epitaphs for children indirectly supports my reading of Thimelby's (and other mothers') resistance to self-referential poetic techniques when it comes to writing about her own child: "As a creature made rather than self-made, the child also becomes analogous to the small poem Jonson 'makes' in honor of the child. Jonson has both the child and the brief epitaph implicitly demonstrate that the little can yet be great. His brief, tender epitaphs on children thus also assert the power of his epigrammatic art" (72). The line between the created objects child and poem is very thin. Scodel also claims, however, that "Jonson the father restrains the proud maker's claims" when he wrote his "masterpiece of expressive brevity": "On My First Davghter." "Its twelve lines," Scodel asserts, "are nevertheless a triumph of compact implication. The epitaph is, as Jonson surely knew it to be, the first major poetic epitaph in English upon a child" (75).

> And earely in their none age place
> Where there chiefest part wil grace.

The variation in meter underlines the brevity of Grace Ashe's life--the first four lines of each stanza appearing by contrast with the last four to be visually and metrically cut in half--while it also calls attention to Austen's poetic technique.   Writing upon the occasion of *another mother's loss*, Austen constructs the entire first stanza around a conceit based on the commonplace elegiacal figuration of the child as flower.

By comparison, Austen's second child loss poem, "December 5: 1664 Vpon Robin Austen's recovery of the smal pox and coronal popoins [?] son John diing of them," attracts less attention to Austen as a poet: she does not trope her own child as a flower or jewel.[47] Instead, she reserves this kind of figuration for "coronal popoins" son John, who fell ill at the same time as her own son and who never recovered. John was:

> . . . one so strong
> Whose lively health, judg'd to live long
> A verdant Youth, in's growing Spring
> The prime of all the schollars. Him
> A Jewel in his parents eye
> And this so lov'd a youth <did> dye . . . .(15-20)

Yet Austen's references to her own son, who ultimately survived his illness, are bolder than Thimelby's references to hers. Instead of comparing him to a jewel or flower, Austen dramatizes his brush with death while referring to him directly as "My child" and thereby highlighting her relation to him:

> My child lay sicke while darts of death
> Was ready to exhale his breath
> A dangerous infectious Dart
> Might have seized vpon his heart
> Expeld his vital powers in haste
> And early in his none age waste. (3-8)

---

[47]   Stevenson and Davidson include a transcription of Austen's elegy in their anthology; see 314-15. Presumably in the interest of recording Austen's final intentions in their transcription of her poem, they eliminate her marks of revision, which I include and interpret here. Ambiguities in Austen's handwriting have also resulted in differences between my transcription and theirs. For instance, they read "coronal popoins" as "General Popams" in the title and "prime" in line 18 as "Prince." They also transcribe the poem's date as "1644," after noting in their introduction to Austen that she dates her book from 1664.

In the same manner in which Austen dramatizes events in her own life throughout "Book M," usually in order to set in relief her rescue by divine providence, she figures her son's small pox as "darts of death" and "A dangerous infectious Dart." The survival of her son despite those dramatic darts, however, frees Austen from identifying with the cultural figure of the demonized mother whose inappropriate thoughts and behaviors result in her child's death. Austen dramatizes her son's ambush by death because she is in a position to ask: "Was it his Sin, or my <our> desert,/ Made mine to live and him to part" (23-4)?   Austen pushes the thematic commonplace of parental sin to its logical conclusion: if parental sin causes a child's death, then parental merit, or "desert," must be responsible for a child's recovery from death's most aggressive attacks.

Austen thus challenges the restrictive conventions of maternal child loss poetry. She follows the logic of motherly blame to its extreme conclusion and finds herself consequently liberated from guilt; in fact, she discovers reason for self-congratulation. However, the need to remain obedient, to retain the spiritual "desert" that she implies saved her son, overrides her poetic daring. She immediately retreats from her question in the lines that follow, answering it negatively and asserting that she is not one to question God. More importantly, her manuscript indicates that she made three significant revisions to her poem:

> Was it his Sin, or my <our> desert,
> Made mine to live and him to part
> O noe my Lord with <my> handes <I doe> vphold
> It was thy will, nor dare be bold
> To Search thy Secrets or Ask why
> My week Son liv'd, a strong did dye
> Thy glory, and thy mercy too,
> As well in death as life in sue. (Austen 23-30)

In the first version, Austen takes all the credit for her son's survival; upon reconsideration, however, she changes "my desert" to "our desert" and takes the emphasis off the importance of her own spiritual state in determining her son's fate. While her first revision minimizes her positive role in her son's survival, her second clarifies her self-depiction as God's supplicant. She indicates that the "handes uph[e]ld" are hers and that she raises them actively: "<I doe> uphold." Austen's revisions thus downplay her agency in affecting her child's welfare and emphasize her active obedience to God. Nevertheless, while these revisions reinforce her retreat away from her bold challenge to the commonplace admission of parental sin, they still register some resistance: Austen trades one kind of agency for another. If she relinquishes a controlling hand in her son's destiny, she asserts self-control, paradoxically, in subjugating herself to God. Although this seems a dubious trade, it exposes Austen's attempts to negotiate the fundamental contradiction underpinning child loss poetry: child loss provides women a culturally sanctioned opportunity to compose poetry, while it simultaneously requires a mother-poet to suppress any display of intellectual, creative agency.

Katherine Philips' child loss poems constitute an instructive exception to my argument that mother-poets writing about their own children create the illusion of their self-effacement as poets. In "In memory of F.P. who dyed at Acton 24 May. 1660--13th of her age," for instance, Philips uses extensive flower imagery to represent her stepdaughter. In response to the child's death, her poetic speaker exclaims, "Ah beauteous blossom! too untimely dead!" (7) and proposes:

> As well we might enquire, when roses dye,
> To what retirement do their odours fly;
> Where do their vertues and their blushes hast,
> When the short triumph of their life is past,
> Or call their perish'd beauties back with teares,
> As add one moment to thy finish'd yeares. (19-24)

One can speculate that her social role as Frances Philips' stepmother did not restrict her poetic efforts because her biologically creative powers were not under scrutiny and were therefore less likely to be conflated with her poetic display of intellectual agency. Likewise, her stepdaughter's survival until age 13 may have diminished the need for a show of motherly self-blame. It is also possible, however, that Philips could better resist the cultural pressure towards self-effacement because she and her verse had the approval and support of several men recognized publicly for their creative activities.[48] Henry Vaughan and Henry Lawes, for instance, were among

---

[48] The ornate sonnets (ca. 1584) on the theme of child loss by Anne Cecil de Vere, written much earlier than Philips', serve as indirect evidence supporting the notion that Philips' network of supporters enabled her to resist the cultural pressure towards the maternal plain style. Wynne-Davies notes that "Anne Cecil could count amongst her family eight women writers . . . It would, therefore, have been perfectly acceptable, even expected, for Anne Cecil to write poetry, or perhaps to follow her mother in translating verses . . ." (352). Philips and de Vere thus both wrote their poetry in contexts that would have helped them to resist the idea that women's intellectual creativity was not only undesirable but dangerous. For more on de Vere's child loss poetry, see Phillippy 322.

her supporters, and in 1651, Vaughan wrote the first poem to celebrate Philips publicly as a poet. Philips' first poem to appear in print also came out in 1651 in a collection of verse by a number of her associates.[49] Her ability to expose her verse, with patriarchal support, to an audience larger than that accessed through manuscript transmission might have enabled her to resist the cultural restrictions surrounding the creative efforts of mother-poets.

Philips even resists self-blame and poetic self-effacement when writing about her late son, Hector Philips. In "EPITAPH. ON HECTOR PHILLIPS. at St Sith's Church," she neither flagellates herself in response to her son's death nor strives toward the maternal plain style to which Thimelby and others turn (cf. esp. lines 15-22). Likewise, she employs a self-consciously poetic technique in "On the death of my first and dearest childe, Hector Philipps, borne the 23^d Aprill, and dy'd the 2^d of May 1655. set by Mr. Lawes." For example, she associates her son with flower imagery: "I did but see him, and he disappear'd,/ I did but touch the Rose=bud and it fell" (5-6). Although she compares her son to a "Rose=bud" in a particularly indirect fashion, allowing the parallel syntax of these juxtaposed lines to imply an analogy between child and flower, for a mother-poet to employ this kind of comparison at all, as we have already seen, is rare. Similarly, Philips writes: "Tears are my Muse, and sorrow all my Art,/ So piercing groans must be thy Elogy" (11-12). On one level, these lines dramatize a particularly explicit erasure of the mother as poet by figuring Philips' verse as natural, spontaneous utterances. On another, however, they call attention to their artistic constructedness: this mother-poet has a "Muse" and an "Art" of her own.

Philips' conclusion to her "Elogy" responds to Jonson's "On My First Sonne," in which he calls "BEN. IONSON [his son] his best piece of *poetrie*" (*Epigrammes* 45.10). She writes:

> An Off'ring too for thy sad Tomb I have,
>   Too just a tribute to thy early Herse;
> Receive these gasping numbers to thy grave,
>   The last of thy unhappy Mother's Verse. (17-20)

While this conclusion seems far from enacting the kind of self-effacement evident in other mother-poets' child loss lyrics, it arguably performs and overcomes a greater renouncement of creative agency than do poems

---

[49] See Thomas, "Introduction" esp. 1:6-13.

written in the maternal plain style. Philips concludes her elegy for her first-born son by articulating the death of her poetry; the final line claims to be "The last of thy unhappy Mother's Verse" (20). While Jonson refers to his son as his "best piece of *poetrie*," Philips suggests that the death of her son marks the end of her poetry. This self-referentiality makes the mother-poet's renouncement of poetry sound like all the greater a refusal of intellectual creative agency. While Philips' verse is "Too just a tribute to [her son's] early Herse," in that those personified "gasping numbers" follow the infant to the grave, her verse is also "Too just a tribute" in that a mother-poet's physically and intellectually creative powers are so closely associated as to be intertwined. According to the logic of seventeenth-century English culture, Philips' assertion that she lays to rest her poetic talent alongside her first son makes perfect sense.   Philips' elegy, however, belies her renouncement of poetry. By explicitly inscribing into it such a close relationship between her child and her verse, Philips appropriates the traditional figuration (usually by male poets, such as Jonson) of poems as offspring. Hence, although her poem seems to be an elegy to poetry as well as to her son, it nevertheless becomes an occasion to challenge the likes of Jonson on his own terms. If Philips resists the cultural requirement that a mother's child loss poem undo itself as poetry by subtly inserting her poetry into dominant traditions, then Mary Carey directly confronts the restrictions a mother-poet faces with no recourse to those dominant trends. Instead, Carey resists the literary and social conventions blaming the mother for the death of her child by interrogating, and thereby invigorating, the commonplaces associated with epitaphs and elegies for children.

Mary Carey's Poetics of Exchange and Possession

> What birth is this; a poore despissed creature?
> A little Embrio; voyd of life, and feature.
> (Carey, "Upon ye Sight of my abortive Birth ye 31th:
> of December 1657 1-2)

No other mother-poet in this study appears to have had the misfortune to write as many child loss poems as Mary Carey. Carey also stands out in the starkness of her plain style; in her 114 lines of verse, she uses only one image that might be considered metaphysical ("Upon ye Sight of my abortive Birth" 23-4). Most of her poems either avoid conventional figurative language altogether or borrow images strictly from the Geneva

Bible. Without infusing the conventional themes of child loss poetry with figures from dominant poetic trends, however, Carey manages to invigorate these potentially flat commonplace sentiments by borrowing from them while simultaneously questioning and complicating them through her subtle combination of simple diction and rhymes, and indeterminate syntax.

Carey progressively negotiates and challenges the conventional themes of child loss poetry across her three poems about her own dead children. For example, in her first poem, occasioned by the death of her son Robert, she undermines her immediate, straightforward claim to submit to God's will:

> My lord hath called for my sonne
>   my hart breth's forth; thy will be donne:
>
> my all; that mercy hath made mine
>   frely's surendered to be thine:
>
> But if I give my all to the (5)
>   lett me not pyne for poverty:
>
> Change wth me; doe, as I have done
>   give me thy all; Even thy deare sonne:
>
> Tis Jesus Christ; lord I would have;
>   he's thine, mine all; 'tis him I crave: (10)
>
> Give him to me; and I'le reply
>   Enoughe my lord; now lett me dye.

At first glance, her statement of resignation in line 2 in the face of her child's death could not be more formulaic. However, she reclaims her child through her multivalent references to possessed objects in the poem and through her indeterminate play with possessive pronouns. In the first line, she refers to "my sonne"; in the second, he becomes "my all." Carey mitigates this reference to her son as her "all"--a reference that raises the stakes of her experience of child loss above those suggested by the conventional notion of the child as a specific gift (out of many divine gifts for which one should be grateful) or as an isolated item of exchange--by qualifying her possession of him as that which "mercy hath made mine." By indicating that her child (as her "all") is a divine gift, Carey satisfies the commonplace that all creation is ultimately God's. Her renaming of "my sonne" as "my all," in fact, could be taken as an acknowledgment of the idea that the loss of her son signifies that she can own nothing herself. Yet her repetition of "all" in the four internal couplets calls attention to the magnitude of her loss (3, 5, 8, 10). That Carey equates giving her "all" with the possibility of having to "pyne for poverty" further conveys just how much she must give to God (6). After Carey's first equation of her son with her "all" in the second couplet, she continues to complicate and question the idea that everything belongs to God. Although she claims that her son is "[freely] surendered," the perfect rhyme of "mine"/ "thine" and their syntactic similarity suggest that they are of equal weight. The merest shade of difference separates them, and while the slippage of "mine" to "thine" across the couplet fittingly demonstrates the seeming ease with which a true believer's illusion of personal ownership should give way to an acknowledgment of the deity as absolute possessor, it also blurs the boundaries between the poet's property and God's.

In the second section of the poem (the third and fourth couplets, which constitute the poem's pivotal moment), the speaker participates in the convention of reconceptualizing loss as exchange. Yet instead of representing the transformation of loss into exchange as an act of re*conceptual*ization--the intellectual and spiritual recognition that one has all along had the gift of God's son--Carey literalizes the convention by demanding a trade with God. Boldly addressing God in the fourth couplet, she asserts, "Change wth me; doe, as I have done/ give me thy all; Even thy deare sonne." Although the speaker demands that which is, in very orthodox Christian terms, already hers, her use of imperative verbs in speaking to God ("Change . . . doe . . . give") strain under the thematic requirement of total, submissive acceptance. She even repeats her demand in the final couplet: "Give him to me." After thus transforming her relinquishment of her son into a demand for God's, trading "my all" for "thy all," the speaker refers to Christ in the fifth couplet as "thine, mine all." At first glance, Carey's play with the word pair "mine"/ "thine" performs the conventional exchange of her child for God's: in the second couplet, the speaker makes what is hers God's ("mine" becomes "thine"), and in the fifth couplet, the speaker renames that which is God's hers ("thine" becomes "mine"). Carey loses her child but gains Christ: the generically expected trade is complete. Yet Carey destabilizes this reading by consistently calling attention to the similarity of the two words. If their status as end-rhymes and their parallel syntax highlight their likeness in the second couplet, their juxtaposition in line 10, such that they seem to slide semantically and aurally into each other, does so even more. The second appearance of the pair completes a chiasmus, which further unsettles the issue of who owns what. The proximity of "thine" and "mine" in line 10 suggests a kind of joint ownership, which, due to the previous coupling of these possessive pronouns as rhymes in lines 2 and 3 in reference to Robert, seems to extend to him. Not only does Carey call attention to the similarity of the "thine"/ "mine" pair and blur the distinction between them, but her first-person possessive is the final word. After all of this unstable exchanging, the speaker is left with that which is "mine." Carey complicates the conventional exchange with God to such an extent that it becomes a kind of shell game, and it is not unambiguously clear in the end that the poem enacts the generically required acceptance of death.

Carey's second poem on child loss, "Wretten by me at the death of my 4th sonne and 5th Child Perigrene Payler," continues to negotiate terms of ownership with God:

> I thought my all was given before
> But mercy ordred me one more:
>
> A Perigrene; my God me sent
> him back againe I doe present
>
> as a love token; 'mongst my others,
> One Daughter; and hir 4 deare Brothers:
>
> To my Lord Christ; my only bless;
> is, he is mine; and I am his
>
> My Dearest Lord; hast thou fulfill'd thy will,
> thy hand maid's pleas'd, Compleatly happy still:

Carey explicitly links her first two poems together by beginning the second with the assertion: "I thought my all was given before" (1). Her repetition of "my all" supports my suggestion above that she chooses it because it magnifies her loss, while it remains within the circumscribed expectations of child loss poetry. Her use of "my all" here actually resists those generic requirements even more boldly than in her first poem, for in this case, it implies that God has crossed the line. Although the speaker thought that she had already been stripped of all her possessions, God still manages to take more from her. Carey highlights how much God has taken by enumerating her dead children in the second and third couplets. She has given God "A Perigrene. . . . One Daughter; and her 4 deare Brothers" (3,

6). This inventory of her "all"--6 dead children by the sixth verse--calls into question the terms of her exchange with God.[50]

In this second elegy, Carey again uses simple diction in combination with very subtly sophisticated syntax to destabilize her concessions to God as the ultimate possessor. In fact, the speaker assumes more agency in relinquishing her child than she does in her first poem. There she writes that her "all" "frely's surendered to be thine" (3-4). She represents her role in trading with God as one of absolute passivity: she surrenders. While "mercy ordre[s]" her to give "one more" in the second poem, she assumes a more active role in the exchange; she "presents" the child to God herself: "A Perigrene; my God me sent/ him back againe I doe present/ as a love token" (3-5). While the speaker takes a more active stance towards God by "present[ing]" her child to him instead of merely "surender[ing]" her son, the slippery syntax of these lines demonstrates resistance to the loss. The enjambment of the lines allows for semantic slippage across the object "him," the exchanged child, whom God sends to the speaker and the speaker returns to God. The construction of these lines suggests not only the immediacy of the exchange (Carey returns her son the very instant that she receives him), but it suggests a degree of contestation over exactly whose object Perigrene is. The boy Perigrene, like the word "him," seems suspended between two possessing subjects: "God" and "I." This poem, like the previous one, resists the conventional show of accepting loss. Perhaps it is because this poem so boldly challenges the restrictions of child loss poetry that Carey contains those challenges so forcefully at the end of the poem. In the final couplet, Carey reinscribes her verse firmly within the acceptable parameters of the genre. As if to counterbalance the signs of opposition demonstrated in the first three couplets, she concludes by asserting, "My Dearest Lord; hast thou fulfill'd thy will,/ thy hand maid's pleas'd. Compleatly happy still:" (9-10). The only space for potential resistance in Carey's submissive closure is in her implied conditional: *if* God has "fulfill'd [his] will," *then* his "hand maid's pleas'd, Compleatly happy still." Carey's opening line ("I thought my all was given before") implies that God has overstepped the terms of their exchange: he takes from a mother who is emotionally and spiritually in the red. Given this beginning, one can read the conditional ending as if Carey will submit and be happy in serving God *only if* God is now satisfied--if he will stop exacting from her spiritual payments in the material form of her children.

---

[50] She counts "Perigrene" twice in these lines, once by name and once along with his brothers.

Even so, Carey's assertion of absolute joy in child loss at the end of this poem seems an act of self-policing, a self-imposed harnessing of her subtle poetic resistances.

"Upon ye Sight of my abortive Birth ye 31th: of December 1657," the third of Carey's elegies, builds upon the previous poems but turns into an altogether more complicated meditation on the social and spiritual implications of child loss.   In it, Carey repeatedly undermines conventionally acceptable forms of closure in a protracted interrogation of the culturally determined significance of miscarriage. She begins in this interrogatory mode, asking, "What birth is this; a poore despised creature?" and answering herself, "A little Embrio; voyd of life, and feature" (1-2). This child, unlike the others she has lost, marks her doubly as a miscarrying mother: the child is not only dead, but featureless-- potentially a deformity or monster in the eyes of society. It is not surprising that Carey at first seems compelled to defend herself as a mother. She refers to her "Seven" successful deliveries of "living:/ Stronge, right- proportioned, lovely Girles, & boyes" to establish her credentials as a good mother (3, 4-5). These seven children were not only born alive, but they are far from being "voyd of life and feature"; they are healthy, strong, and attractive. Her reference to the "Seven tymes [she] went [her] tyme" both implies that she has a significant record of successful childbirths and draws a parallel between God's original act of creation across seven days and those seven births (3). Emphasizing God's creative powers, Carey indicates that those "lovely Girles, & boyes" successfully reflect not their mother's image, but God's. Their births represent "great wisdome, goodness, power love praise/ to my deare lord; lovely in all his wayes" (7-8). Her use of "lovely" to qualify both her children (5) and God's "wayes" underlines the idea that those children are reflections of God, mirrors of his loveliness. Carey thus builds up her qualifications as a good, successful, self-denying mother-- leaving out the fact that most of those seven "lovely Girles, & boyes" died early in childhood--and constructs a strong link between God's creative powers and image and her offspring in order to defend her miscarriage. She explicitly calls attention to God's role in *all* of her childbirths: "This is no lesse," she writes, "ye same God hath it donne" (9).

Yet there is significant tension around issues of possession, submission, and agency in this elegy. It is certainly to Carey's advantage to erase her own agency and creative power as much as possible given her bodily production of a "poore despised creature" (1). Hence, it is not unexpected when she says she "submits [her] hart, thats better than a sonne" and that she claims "his will's more deare to [her]; then any Child" (10, 14).

In the sixth couplet, however, she emphasizes the extent of the spiritual violence (and its material manifestations) to which she must submit, while she again uses possessive pronouns to question the notion of God's total agency and absolute ownership: "In giveing; taking; stroking; striking still;/ his Glorie & my good; is. his. my will" (11-12). Although Carey begins by referring to God's "giveing," she does not celebrate his bountiful gifts. Instead, she juxtaposes "giveing" with "taking," thereby highlighting the ephemerality of earthly possessions, even if bestowed initially by God. This "taking" acquires increasingly violent overtones in its role as a semantic and aural bridge between God's "giveing" and his "stroking; striking still."[51] The partial alliterative similarity between "taking" and the perfectly alliterating words that follow it reinforces their semantic association. The complement to God's giving, his taking, turns into blows. He not only "strik[es]," but he does so continuously, or "still," and he "strik[es]" dead or "still"-born, too, as evidenced by Carey's "poor despissed creature" (1). This line recalls Donne's Holy Sonnet 14, "BAtter my heart, three-perfon'd God," in its accumulation of violent terms, the relentlessness of which is emphasized through alliteration: Donne's speaker asks God to "bend/ Your force, to breake, blowe, burn and make me new" (3-4). Carey's and Donne's poems are also similar in their suggestion that spiritual violence may be necessary to ensure the welfare of the individual believer's soul.[52] The occasion of Carey's poem, however, calls attention to the physical manifestations of God's spiritual violence: God's "stroking; striking still" can and does literally kill.

Nevertheless, the cultural ascription of blame to the miscarrying mother complicates Carey's portrait of God's violence. God's agency and the speaker's are intertwined here, as they are in Carey's previous poems. In the second half of the above couplet, Carey again uses a play of possessive pronouns to question the relationship between God as subject and herself

---

[51]   Timothy Billings' helpful observation to me (via personal communication) that it is possible to read "stroking" (which recalls and embraces the violence of its noun form) as a parallel to God's "giveing" and as a positive complement to God's violent "striking still" emphasizes Carey's view of the vertiginous extremes of human relations to the divine and highlights the nuanced movement of the line.

[52]   I am obliged to Heather White for the suggestion (via personal communication) that the multivalent "stroking" also has an erotic resonance, which seems all the more significant when analyzed in relation to Donne's eroticization of spiritual violence. The erotic potential of "stroking," especially in conjunction with the poetic speaker's ecstatic requests that God quicken her in the final third of the elegy, suggests that Carey does borrow --albeit more subtly that do non-parental consolers troping dead children as flowers--from the amorous tradition in this elegy.

as subject. In the first half of line 12 ("his Glorie & my good"), she uses parallel syntactical structure and alliteration to suggest that whatever glorifies God is good for her. In juxtaposing the possessives after the caesura, however, ("is. his. my will") Carey undermines the differences between the very possessives that she holds apart structurally in the first half of the line. On one level, she obliterates the distinction between her will and God's, thereby representing perfectly the abject submission to divine authority typical of child loss poetry. But in a sequential reading of the line, "my" displaces "his;" the line ends with an assertion of the speaker's will.

The tensions and indeterminacies of this couplet represent Carey's attempt to negotiate the culturally scripted contradictions surrounding the bereaved mother's elegy to her child. While a seventeenth-century English mother should acknowledge the role of her own sin in her child's death, Carey's miscarriage potentially signifies such grave spiritual faults on her part that she attempts, through her poem, to find a way to admit some guilt while distancing herself from society's implied accusations. While a mother in this cultural context should submit herself entirely to God's will and contrast her own utter powerlessness to God's omnipotence, ascribing to God the ultimate responsibility--even if only by implication--for an occurrence so antithetical to creative power as the production of a "poore despissed creature . . . voyd of life, and feature" (1-2) would seem highly inappropriate. How can the speaker confess responsibility for her child's fate when her posture should be one of abject submission to God? How can the speaker celebrate God's will as the agent behind a failed act of creation? Whose fault is this "poore despissed creature"? The special case of child loss poetry and its contradictions leads Carey to grapple with the fundamental paradoxes generated, and glossed over, by the strict binaries underpinning Calvinism: the total depravity of humans versus God's absolute, perfect goodness; the absence of human free will in opposition to God's omnipotence.

Carey's speaker offers herself a full range of culturally acceptable and generically conventional consolations to smooth over the contradictions that seem so uncomfortably exposed by the occasion of an abortive birth. She affirms that God's will is unconditionally, unquestionably good; she expresses "joy, that God hath gain'd one more/ To Praise him in the heavens" (15-16). She expresses thanks that she's "made Instrumentall" to "God's praise, babes blesse" (19, 20). She speculates that perhaps God wants her to be more thankful for the children that she already has (21-2). She even repeats, virtually verbatim, the self-denying, submissive lines with which she ends her second elegy: "And if heere in God hath fulfill'd his Will,/ his hand-maides pleassed, Compleatly happy still" (31-2). With these lines, one expects closure. The speaker has rattled off the necessary commonplace sentiments of the genre and represents herself as having achieved acceptance of her loss. Instead, however, the speaker returns to the interrogatory mode with which "Upon ye Sight of my abortive Birth ye 31th: of December 1657" begins:

> I only now desire of my sweet God
>   the reason why he tooke in hand his rodd?
>
> What he doth spy; what is the thinge amisse
>   I faine would learne; whilst I ye rod do kisse: (33-6)

Given that this poem appears in the anthology *Kissing the Rod*, the reader (unfortunately) is especially ready to associate the invocation of the rod with what Greer characterizes in her editor's note as the transhistorical, transcultural patriarchal requirement that women approve the instrument of their affliction (xvi). Yet in the context of the cultural expectations surrounding child loss poetry, Carey's request is surprisingly bold; she asks God to justify his ways to *her*. Her question's juxtaposition with the conventional claim that she is "Compleatly happy still" belies that claim, exposing its artificiality. Its conventionality is highlighted further, in fact, by her previous use of it in her second elegy.

Carey's imaginative project expands with her direct questioning of God. While Katherine Austen retreats after asking God why some children die and not others, Carey dramatizes a divine response to her question. She projects God's voice into her poem. Carey's God explains "the reason why he tooke in hand his rodd" (34):

> Thou often dost present me wth dead frute,
>   Why should not my returns, thy presents sute:
>
> Dead dutys; prayers; praises thou dost bring,
>   affections dead; dead hart in every thinge . . . (39-42)

God presents the culturally scripted interpretation of miscarriage as a sign of maternal spiritual insufficiency, emphasizing the magnitude of Carey's failure through the repetition of "dead": "dead frute . . . Dead dutys; prayers; praises . . . affections dead; dead hart . . ." Carey wrestles with the horror of this interpretation of miscarriage. While representing God as her spiritual accuser satisfies the generic requirement that she acknowledge the role of her sinfulness in her featureless child's demise, her approach to this commonplace theme is unusually dramatic. Rather than confessing spiritual inadequacies in her own voice, she represents them as judgments coming directly from God. Although this can seem cruelly self-flagellating, since Carey's pen animates God's mouth, it can also be seen as a strategy to escape self-punishment. The speaker confirms God's words when she acknowledges that "Conscience justifies ye same within" (38), but Carey distances herself from the terrible logic of parental sin by having God present that theory of child loss.

Carey undermines her participation in the thematic commonplaces of child loss poetry precisely at the moment that she presents her first-person acceptance of God's harsh judgment. In the midst of asking forgiveness, the speaker exposes the double bind that constrains her efforts to find a means through which to achieve consolation:

> My dearest Lord; thy charge, & more is true
> I see't; am humbled & for pardon sue;
>
> In Christ forgive; & henceforth I will be
> what, Nothing Lord; but what thou makest mee;
>
> I am nought, have nought, can doe nought but sinne. (53-7)

Carey pleads for God's pardon and begins to promise that she will improve in the future. Yet she interrupts herself mid-promise: "henceforth I will be/ what, Nothing Lord; but what thou makest me." The speaker unveils the contradiction in the idea that she must thank God for exposing her sins and, as a consequence of this divinely granted self-knowledge, promise to amend, yet her agency can manifest itself only *as* sinfulness. She pointedly highlights this contradiction by asserting her subjectivity, her "I," only to undo herself: "I am nought, have nought, can do nought but sinne" (57). Carey's speaker claims that she is and has nothing, effecting a complete erasure of her asserted agency. Her resistance to this self-undoing is not merely the dramatic emphasis of her repetition of "nought," but her juxtaposition of lines 56 and 57. It is precisely after she claims to be "what thou makest mee" that she declares "I am nought." Her self-undoing renders her as "voyd of life, and feature" as her own "poore despissed creature" (2, 1), and God is ultimately the creative agent--the miscarrying mother--behind her negated state of being.

While I do not claim that Carey, a strict Calvinist, would have consciously accused God of miscreating, I do suggest that this is the textual effect of her poetic interrogation of the cultural conventions that so cruelly ascribed blame for the deaths of her children to the mother. Ultimately, Carey finds a new logic of consolation in the abject self-negation she expresses in response to the Calvinist paradox that holds totally depraved humans responsible for their sins while only the omnipotent deity has agency to change anything. Returning to the familiar, assertive imperative with which, in her first poem, she commands God to exchange his son for hers and which belies her utter negation of self, Carey requests that God "quicken" her--that the one, true creative agent take action. Carey's poem effectively ends with the rapturous blossoming of life, conveyed through her repetition of variations on the terms "life" and "quicken."[53] Having interrogated the conventional themes associated with child loss poetry, Carey invigorates them without recourse to figures from dominant poetic trends. She simultaneously meets and surpasses the restrictive terms of the maternal plain style, subtly recuperating her creative agency in the intellectual sphere as she disavows miscreating in the physical sphere.

---

[53]   See esp. couplets 39-45. Cressy's description of the early modern understanding of "quickening" reinforces the idea that Carey here asks God both to give her a living baby (in her womb) and to make her a proper believer: the moment of "quickening . . . [is] when the mother could feel her baby moving in her womb. It was also a time, some moralists argued, when the woman should 'quicken' to repentance, as religious and physiological concerns became fused" (45).

Chapter 3

Anna Trapnel as Holy Poet
and Lyrical Preacher

Those who know Anna Trapnel's texts best probably think of her first as one of the many prophets to emerge on the scene of theological-political debate during England's revolutionary period. Her capacity to play the role of a prophet was instrumental to her ability to access a public forum--a notable feat given the cultural prescriptions against seventeenth-century women's interventions in the emerging public sphere. The current scholarly interest in women prophets has unquestionably called significant attention to Trapnel; in fact, two widely known undergraduate teaching anthologies-- *The Longman Anthology of British Literature* and the seventh edition of *The Norton Anthology of English Literature*--include passages from Trapnel's texts. Her prophetic role-playing has enabled her to brush shoulders with this century's assembly of canonical authors.[1]

Despite this particular success, however, I would propose that the recent scholarly emphasis on Trapnel's prophetic role downplays how her texts use other strategies to enable her both to proclaim her theological-political opinions and to construct a culturally legible lyrical voice. Acknowledging that she played multiple social roles and that these disparate roles relate differently to her textual production opens the conceptual space that allows us to see the value of her poetry, in particular. Understanding Trapnel at least in part as a preacher--a role enabled by her production of poetry--serves both as a corrective to an analytical trajectory

---

[1]   Both anthologies include selections from *Anna Trapnel's Report and Plea*, the document in which she gives her account of her trial at Cornwall. Although the scholarly interest in Trapnel as a prophet seems to have influenced the inclusion of her texts in mainstream undergraduate teaching anthologies, *Anna Trapnel's Report and Plea* is not primarily a prophetic text. Rather, it is Trapnel's brief account of some trances (that she does not remember fully, being under the control of the Holy Spirit at the time) and of her trial, where she speaks as a regular citizen. The inclusion of her text in these anthologies signifies increased awareness of her and her works, but it does not imply recognition of her poetic talent (since there is no verse in *Anna Trapnel's Report and Plea*) or the promotion of her works to canonical status.

that tends to inscribe her into a passive position with respect to her works and provides a basis for examining the construction of her poetic voice in relation to contemporary traditions and practices. As we will see, her preacherly and poetic roles are so intertwined with each other that it is almost impossible to understand one without analyzing the other. To arrive at a point where it makes sense to discuss Trapnel in detail as an intriguing, sophisticated lyricist, it is thus necessary to examine closely the complex relations between her roles as preacher and poet. Because these roles themselves overlap in complicated ways with her status as a radical sectarian who many believed to be a prophet and with her gender, it is also important to consider how these features of her social identity relate to her poetic composition. Ultimately, I hope to show that, for scholars invested in the project of recovering the works of early modern women writers and inscribing them into a revised literary history, it is crucial to recognize Trapnel as a poet.

As I discuss first, the focus on Trapnel as a prophet attempts to fix the slippage--evident both in twentieth-century scholarship and in seventeenth-century cultural products--around definitions of "prophets," and in doing so, places Trapnel into a theoretically passive role. Next, I move beyond the well-established significance of the use of prophetic discourse as an authorizing strategy for women otherwise forbidden access to public venues of communication to call attention to Trapnel's indirect claim to participation in the ministry, a particularly dangerous implication, mediated by her verse, that is related to her later imprisonment and that resists the complete evacuation of personal agency associated with prophets. Finally, I use Trapnel's reworking of Canticles in *A Voice for the King of Saints and Nations* as a model to show how she constructs a culturally legible lyrical voice by responding to contemporary poetic traditions and practices. Locating her appropriation of Canticles first with respect to traditions of writing metrical paraphrases of or verse meditations on David's Psalms and the Song of Songs, and second with respect to the verse of her fellow radical sectarians highlights simultaneously how she produces a sophisticated lyrical voice by responding to poetic practices of her day, and how she uses her appropriation of the Song to legitimate her public speech and to underwrite her poetic production.

Witch? Subversive? Prophet? Preacher? Poet?

> I am forc't out of my close retired spirit, by Rulers and Clergy, who have
> brought me upon the worlds stage of Reports, and Rumors, making me the
> worlds wonder, and gazing-stock: and some have said, they thought I had
> been a Monster or some ill-shaped Creature, before they came and saw,
> who then said, they must change their thoughts, for I was a woman like
> others that were modest and civill . . . . (Trapnel, *Anna Trapnel's Report
> and Plea* 49)

Although Anna Trapnel is not known primarily as a poet to scholars today,
she occasionally represents herself as one--specifically as a psalmist. On
Dec. 15, 1657, she challenged her audience to produce a better song than
hers:

> Alas, Brethren, can you think that
> Any creature on the earth
> Can bring out such a glorious Psalm,
> Or can with it come forth?
> Can you think any thing from the creature (5)
> Can be so large and high;
> Can have Doctrine and Application too,
> With so much sweetness and glory?
> Can you think any thing from a creature?
> Let all your Poets you tell, (10)
> Whether they can frame such a Psalm,
> Or come forth with such a knell.
> Call your Scribes, and all your Poets,
> And all your Wise-men too;
> And all your Astrologers together, (15)
> To frame a song so new.
> O do you inquire round about,
> See if they can appear
> With a note and tune for Jesus Christ,
> That is so divinely clear. (20) (untitled folio 221)

Enumerating the strengths of her "glorious Psalm," Trapnel suggests that no
other song could be "so large and high" or could yoke "Doctrine and
Application" together with "sweetness and glory" (3, 6, 7, 8). Her song, she
contends, is the loudest, the newest, the most "divinely clear," the best (12,
16, 20). No effort from any representative of the traditionally masculine
regimes of knowledge--no poet, no scribe, no wise man, no astrologer--can
compete with her psalm (13-16); in fact, she implies that poets, who should
be especially apt judges of verse, will agree with her (10-12). However, she

also suggests that discriminating listeners will recognize the divinity of her song and will understand that she, a mere "creature" herself, could not possibly be the agent behind its production (1-9). In other words, at the same moment in which she seems to assert herself as a psalmist, she calls attention to her role as a prophet; she is merely the weak vessel through which the Holy Spirit produces its lyrics. This textual complexity makes it necessary to examine very closely the relationship between Trapnel's role as prophet and as psalmist.

As a prophet, she is perhaps most widely known as the Fifth Monarchist who sang and prayed, apparently entranced, before an audience of political and military leaders and their wives at Whitehall in the winter of 1654.[2] *The Cry of a Stone* relates how Trapnel accompanied Vavasor Powell, a Welsh preacher, to a hearing before the Council of State in which he was to "account before them of some things by him delivered in his publique Exercises in *London*."[3] Trapnel then collapsed into "a Spirit of Prayer and Singing" from which she did not recover for twelve days and during which she lay prone and rigid, eating almost nothing (*The Cry of a Stone* 1). Powell had been arrested and brought to Whitehall for asserting "that the Protectorate would be short-lived" (Greer, *Kissing the Rod* 175) and that Cromwell was "the dissemblingest perjured villain in the world" (qtd. in P.G. Rogers 41). As *The Cry of a Stone* relates, Trapnel, through her prayers and songs, also explicitly chastised Cromwell and his Army; she even predicted Cromwell's death. Yet even though she, too, spoke publicly against the nation's leader, she did so without being arrested--for the

---

[2]   The Fifth Monarchists were radical Protestants active from the revolutionary period into the Restoration. They were millenarians who believed that Jesus's reign on earth, which would constitute the fifth monarchy by their count, was imminent. Some Fifth Monarchists favored violent means to prepare for Jesus's reign, and some were involved in revolts against Cromwell's Protectorate. Some plotted to assassinate Cromwell in 1657, and others later organized into military groups (P.G. Rogers 81, 112). Also see Hill, *The English Bible* 306-7 and Capp 14, 20, 131-4. Capp indicates that many Fifth Monarchist ministers, including Vavasor Powell, had been army officers first (80). Trapnel appears to have ceased public activity with the Fifth Monarchists before physical violence broke out.

On Trapnel's "distinguished visitors," see Capp 41. Mack specifies that Trapnel sang for "members of Parliament, members of the aristocracy, and the future Lord Mayor of London" (77).

[3]   Elaine Hobby writes that "[Trapnel's] outpouring was provoked by recent events in the government. The Barebones Parliament (Parliament of Saints), a nominated assembly which had included twelve Fifth Monarchist leaders among its 144 members had been dissolved on 12 December 1653. The arrests of certain Fifth Monarchists (Christopher Feake, John Simpson and Vavasor Powell) had swiftly followed, as they began to prophecy and preach against Cromwell" (32).

moment.[4]   Many historians and literary critics would explain Trapnel's success in voicing her opposition to Cromwell's Protectorate as a result of her ability to play the role of prophet. Such investigators of seventeenth-century texts have recently paid much attention to her claims to divine inspiration; to her self-figuration as a mere, weak vessel of the Holy Spirit; to the significance of her female body, the biology of which could, paradoxically, make her words suspect but could also make her a more believable prophet; and to her approximation of a death-like trance, which also added credibility to her claim to prophetic gifts.[5]

Why does Trapnel's prophetic role make her seem passive in relation to her texts, and why does this passivity complicate analysis of her verse? The premise behind Trapnel's works that include lyrics--*The Cry of a Stone* (1654), *A Voice for the King of Saints and Nations* (1658), and an untitled folio of 990 leaves that contains, according to one early critic's estimate, over 200,000 lines of verse--is that she is dead to the world when she sings.[6] The contents of these texts were transcribed from Trapnel's oral, extemporaneous performances by other Fifth Monarchists.[7] When taken

---

[4] P.G. Rogers relates that on Jan. 19, 1654, "an ordinance was issued making it a treasonable offence to write, print, teach, or preach that the Protector's authority was tyrannical, usurped, or unlawful" partially due to the activities of radical sectarian leaders like Powell, Feake, and arguably, Trapnel (42). Trapnel was eventually arrested for preaching in Cornwall. P.G. Rogers specifies that "on 2 June 1654 the Council of State had ordered her to be sent to Bridewell . . . where she was kept till 26 July" (47).

[5] For discussions of Trapnel's divine inspiration, see, for example, Berg and Berry 48-50; Burrage; Cohen esp. 422-7; Hobby 31-6; Mack esp. 92-8; and Wiseman 186-90. On Trapnel as a weak vessel, see Mack 32-4. On relevant notions of female biology and the prophet's body, see Mack 24-34; Purkiss; and Wiseman 192. On the prophet's trance, see Dailey esp. 453 and Mack 34.

[6] The notes of Bertram Dobell, the bookseller who sold the untitled folio of Trapnel's verse to the Bodleian Library in 1901 for four guineas, provide the basis for this estimate (29).

[7] Scholars have sufficient reason to believe that Trapnel had a significant hand in the production of her lyrics: she was literate, as she indicates in *The Cry of a Stone* (3), and her non-prophetic works, *A Legacy for Saints* and *Anna Trapnel's Report and Plea*, which do not appear to have been transcribed, are very similar in content to her prophetic works. I have found that analyzing Trapnel's songs in relation to the poetic practices of her day not only lends credence to the idea that she had significant control over the production of her lyrics but that doing so also helps to shape our understanding, more broadly, of issues of authorship, authority, and agency in relation to seventeenth-century texts. Mendelson and Crawford offer useful insights into the biases against and the importance of taking seriously women's oral contributions to cultural production: "Historians, like their seventeenth-century male counterparts, have tended to assume that women were culturally impoverished because of their exclusion from élite literate culture. In some respects women certainly were disadvantaged by their illiteracy . . . But in a plebian society based on sociability, neighborliness, and mutual interdependence, oral genres were often more useful and effective than literature skills" (218). Given the practice of recording confessions of faith and

alone as examples of Trapnel's works, these "prophetic" texts raise questions about the extent of Trapnel's agency in their composition and production. In contrast, in Trapnel's conversion narrative, *A Legacy for Saints* (1654), and in *Anna Trapnel's Report and Plea* (1654), in which she explains the events that lead to her imprisonment, she writes as saint and citizen, instead of performing as prophet, and questions about authorial agency become less relevant. When Trapnel writes as saint and citizen, however, she includes no verse.

Sue Wiseman articulates the problem that, for feminists who model their analyses on traditional humanist criticism, complicates discussions of female prophets like Anna Trapnel as early modern women writers: "Where, if anywhere, is the authority, or the voice of authority, in seventeenth-century prophetic discourse by women? . . . Where does the voice of the female prophet 'come from'--the Bible? God? A fixed subject position?" (176). Reading Trapnel's texts according to the theological significance that she, her supporters, and friendly audience members probably would have ascribed to her prophetic claims, Wiseman explains that:

> the language of 'prophecy' as constituted in these texts permits them to encode in Biblical language a criticism of the present which is offered as underwritten by God. Meaning does not rest in a patriarchal order but with the great patriarch in the sky: there are no intermediate steps. God is the law, word, father. The authority of the text is not located in any subject with attendant socio-economic conditions; access to the logos liberates it from this. (189)

Trapnel's claim in her prophetic texts that her words originate with God and her rendering of her body a sign of her possession by the Holy Spirit empty

---

conversion narratives delivered orally (and publicly) at church meetings, the transcription of Trapnel's prayers and songs is also not unusual. John Rogers' *Ohel or Beth-shemesh. A Tabernacle for the Sun* (London 1653), for instance, includes a chapter of transcribed oral presentations to the church congregation (392-439; this includes twelve inserted pages used to correct an error in pagination). Rogers presents his editorial principles on 392 and 417-19. Interestingly, he records the spiritual experiences of many women: Elizabeth Avery, Elizabeth Chambers, Ruth Emerson, Anne Hewson, Dorothy Emett, Anne Bishop, Tabitha Kelsall, Frances Curtis, Mary Turrant, Elizabeth Marrow, Rebecca Rich, Mary Burrill, Mary Barker, Margaret Fanshaw, Ann Hanly, Sara Barnwell, and Ann Megson. Capp indicates that Henry Walker published a similar transcription of congregational meetings (94). For another compelling contemporary instance of transcribed, extemporaneous speech, cf. the Putney Debates.

Geoffrey Nuttall observes that the "extempore nature" of prophesying eventually had a stylistic influence on preaching (82).

her utterances of human creative agency.[8] When Trapnel speaks as a prophet, she does not speak as a Fifth Monarchist; she does not speak as a shipwright's daughter who paid taxes to support the Army and who sold her "Plate and Rings, and gave the mony to the Publick use"; and most significantly, she does not speak as a woman (*Anna Trapnel's Report and Plea* 50).

Although reading Trapnel's works from within the parameters set by seventeenth-century prophetic discourse exposes the vulnerability of a feminist criticism that looks for and celebrates a direct, intentional relationship between the woman author-as-whole-self and her text (such a feminist criticism cannot accommodate the widespread seventeenth-century phenomenon of female prophets in its account of literary history), I would contend that it is also necessary to consider how Trapnel's works, taken together, cannot be confined within those parameters.   There *are* intermediate steps between Trapnel's utter emptying out of her own subjectivity and her location of absolute meaning and authority in the divine utterances that she conveys. As Wiseman points out:

> radical Protestant theology and the revival of the new age of prophecy never quite delivered the potential it had to actually degender speaking, and even as they claim the "free space" offered by speaking with the grace of God female prophets negotiate the material and ideological constraints of their circumstances. (178)

In Trapnel's case, her texts reveal that contemporary civil and religious authorities held her personally responsible for some of the most subversive writing attributed to her. "The authority of the [prophetic] text" as an ideally functioning strategy might not be "located in any subject with attendant socio-economic conditions," but it did not necessarily function ideally.   That prophetic authority was subject to scrutiny, as was the "subject with attendant socio-economic conditions" most closely associated with it (Wiseman 189). Trapnel relates in both *A Legacy for Saints* (56) and *Anna Trapnel's Report and Plea* (25) that government officials in Cornwall tried to make her take credit for the contents of *The Cry of a Stone* [or an

---

[8] Wiseman elaborates on this "prophetic" authorizing strategy: "Trapnel talks to God, sees visions, and . . . constantly draws on Biblical intertexts. But the question of who, exactly, speaks shifts: the authority of her text is in the relationship between her and God" (193).

Purkiss demonstrates "that the visibility of the woman prophet's body was a means by which she negotiated a space to speak within the constraints of a seventeenth-century religious discourse, and hence a way for her to threaten established orders and hierarchies" (141).

abbreviated version of it called *Strange and Wonderful Visions from White-hall* (1654)]. She provides this account of the interrogation at Cornwall that ended in her imprisonment:

> Then *Lobb* said, *Tender her the book which was written from something said at* White-Hall: so the book was reached out to me: and Justice Lobb said, *What say you to that book? Will you own it? is it yours?*
> A.T. *I am not careful to answer you in that matter.*
> Then they said, *She denies her book.* Then they whispered with those behinde them. Then spake Justice Lobb again, and said, *Read a vision of the horns out of the book*: So that was read then Justice Lobb said, *What say you to this? is this yours?*
> A.T. *I am not careful to answer you in that matter, touching the whole book, as I told you before, so I say again: for what was spoken, was at* White-hall, *at a place of concourse of people, and neer a Counsel, I suppose wise enough to call me into question if I offended, and unto them I appeal* . . . (*Anna Trapnel's Report and Plea* 25)

Trapnel the citizen, participating in a public forum without using prophetic discourse, employs rhetorical ambiguities both to protect herself (she faces physical punishment) and to ensure the logical consistency--and therefore the credibility--of her prophetic role. Despite repeated, direct questioning, she sidesteps the issue of authorship. Her use of the passive voice in referring to the contents of the book--*"for what was spoken, was at* White-hall"--not only distances her from the subversive text under dispute, but it also reinforces the premise behind her prophetic performances: whenever she is possessed by the Holy Spirit, she is unconscious of her actions. The closest she comes to "own[ing]" "her book" is at the end of the passage, where she indicates that she is aware of the incident to which her interrogators refer. Yet she admits only to knowing the physical setting of the event and does so only to suggest that her present judges abuse their authority by applying it outside their jurisdiction. Trapnel the citizen covers for Trapnel the prophet. It is very clear that acting as a prophet constitutes a particular kind of self-figuration for Trapnel and that, as such, it does not represent all of her creative and political interventions in the public sphere. It is less clear, however, exactly what it meant for her to act as a prophet during the period of upheaval in which she did so and how that relates to the other parts that she played in her public--usually controversial, often dangerous--interventions.

The crisis of authority that permeated the social order during the English Revolution was inextricably linked to uncertainties and conflicting views concerning how to read divine signs--from God's word in scripture to the movings of the indwelling spirit to the world itself, which was seen by some as replete with divine meaning.[9] That many people claimed to have direct access to God's intentions and wishes during this period and that some of them called themselves prophets is not surprising given the fusion of politics and religion and the instability of the social hierarchy. A prophet who confirmed the beliefs of a particular group was sure to find an audience, and those in the highest echelons of political power paid attention to the utterances of God's vessels.[10] Whereas a visionary, male or female, could secure an audience if he or she were inspired to utter statements in support of the beliefs or political agenda of that audience,[11] he or she could also encounter threats to life and limb. Women entering the public arena to make religious claims were at especially great risk. Female preachers, missionaries, and prophets faced not only ridicule, humiliation, and imprisonment, but also restraint by iron bridle, whippings, and death threats.[12] Yet certain public roles that women assumed were better received than others. Mack suggests that seventeenth-century notions of female biology, which characterized women as particularly susceptible to supernatural possession and as more emotionally than rationally inclined, made the figure of the female prophet arguably not only more acceptable than a female preacher but more tenable than a male prophet (24, 25, 33).[13] The most inappropriate religious role for a seventeenth-century woman to assume was that of preacher, a role believed to be specifically forbidden to

---

[9] Berg and Berry observe that "The years between 1640 and 1660 might . . . be described as a period which opens with an excess of revolutionary activity on both the physical and verbal planes, a period characterized not only by Civil War, but also by a fierce and bitter debate over the possession of meaning, of the logos" (51).

[10] For a discussion of the confusion caused at all levels of society by the seriousness with which a prophet's words could be taken and by the difficulty in determining who was inspired by God, who was inspired by demonic forces, and who was a fraud, see Mack 79-83. Also see Nuttall 34-47 and Richey 1-3.

[11] Mack recounts, for example, the positive reception of Elizabeth Poole's instruction in 1648 by some parliamentary soldiers "because it agreed with Cromwell's policy" and the Council's later questioning of "the authenticity of her visions" once her inspirations no longer supported their political interests (78, 79). [Poole's offending divine advice was "[urging] the Council to spare the king's life" (Mack 79).]

[12] See Hinds esp. 216-17. Men who expressed their religious convictions also faced serious risks. Powell was imprisoned for speaking publicly against Cromwell. In an extreme case, Quaker James Nayler, who rode into Bristol on an ass in imitation of Christ's arrival at Jerusalem, was whipped, branded, and had a hole bored through his tongue (Mack 198-9). The significant difference between treatments of male and female radical sectarians was that there was a general cultural prescription against women's participation in the emerging public sphere, which meant that women's public appearances could theoretically attract hostility regardless of what they said or how they conducted themselves.

[13] Also see Hobby 26.

women by the Pauline injunctions in I Corinthians 14:33-5 and I Timothy
2:11-12 against women speaking in church.[14]

For a seventeenth-century woman in England, claiming to be a
prophet could be a less controversial means to gain a public audience than
claiming to be a preacher would be.   And although it is important to
understand a woman who claims that she is a prophet according to the
implications of that role, the emphasis on Trapnel as a prophet in recent
scholarship has had damaging ramifications in the worst instances and has
met its limits in the best.   Alfred Cohen, for example, takes the phenomenon
of women prophets seriously in order to argue that such women, including
Anna Trapnel, were actually insane (425).   Even more damaging is the less
obvious implication on the part of the editors of *Kissing the Rod* that
Trapnel was crazy.   Although they anthologize a verse fragment from *The
Cry of a Stone*, the editors seem neither to take Trapnel's claims to prophetic
authority seriously, as Cohen does, nor to allow for the possibility that
Trapnel's lyrics respond to contemporary poetic traditions and practices.
Their description of her verse as "rhapsodic utterances" is generous in
comparison to their later reference to her poetry as "ravings" (177, 178).[15]
Given *Kissing the Rod*'s project of calling attention to the works of
seventeenth-century women poets and making them accessible in a modern
edition, it seems self-defeating to downplay the efforts of Trapnel, who may
rank among the most prolific of female poets of that century.[16]

Most feminist scholars seem to have emphasized Trapnel's role as a
prophet partially out of respect for her religious convictions, the specifics of
which constitute significant historical differences between her and those
who study her writing today.[17]   Trapnel might have sincerely believed that

---

[14] For instance: "As in all churches of the saints, the women should keep silence in
the churches. For they are not permitted to speak, but should be subordinate, as even the law
says. If there is anything they desire to know, let them ask their husbands at home. For it is
shameful for a woman to speak in church" (I Corinthians 14:33-5).

[15] Richey claims that Trapnel "disclose[s] her feminist perceptions in an ecstatic,
irrational mode of utterance" (212). When Richey refers to Trapnel's songs, she does so
primarily to emphasize their theological significance: "Christ's song, then, is one with the
song of the handmaids and one with Trapnel's own" (211). Wiseman notes that "Trapnel's
recorded spoken text reads, with some interjections from the transcriber, like a polished and
finished piece of poetry" (177). Yet Wiseman does not elaborate. Rare references to Trapnel
as poet, rather than as a prophet, or to her poetic works primarily as such include Atwan and
Wieder 359-60, Hageman 196, and Stevenson and Davidson 295-301.

[16] An almost one thousand page book of Trapnel's verse is in the Bodleian Library
(Bod.S.42.I.Th.).

[17] Even if a modern scholar studying Trapnel shares her basic beliefs, that scholar
would not share the particular historical inflections of those beliefs. In other words, the
context of England's civil wars and the proximity of the Reformation, as merely two

she was divinely inspired and that her life was part of a continuing biblical narrative. It is thus understandable that Elaine Hobby, for instance, attempts to demonstrate the importance of Trapnel's religious beliefs to her successful performance as a prophet. Yet in Hobby's treatment of Trapnel, the prophet overshadows the lyricist to the extent that the question of her verse as participating in and responding to contemporary literary traditions and practices all but disappears. Hobby explains at one point that Trapnel "had already experienced her inspiration to versify as proof of [God's] control over her" (35).[18] Taking Trapnel's poetry as proof to Trapnel of her prophetic vocation, Hobby respects Trapnel's spirituality while foreclosing analysis of her verse in its mundane, contemporary context. If Trapnel's verse is primarily proof of divine inspiration to her, why should it signify anything beyond that to us? Although Mack points out that "Trapnel found a public voice that was as much the fruit of her own intelligence and political activism as it was the product of a disembodied trance state," (119) she accepts the theoretical position that all seventeenth-century audiences would have been hostile to a woman asserting herself in an active, ministerial role. She makes Trapnel the particular example to prove her general assertion "that beliefs about the traditional and quite familiar qualities of passivity, irrationality, and passion that had justified women's *absence* from the political arena were used to justify their visionary activities as well" (106). Although this statement applies to Trapnel to some degree, Mack's firm adherence to the theoretical boundaries around women's public speech leads her into overlooking the considerable, important slippage that Trapnel's texts demonstrate with respect to prophetic and preacherly roles--roles that do not prove mutually exclusive.[19]

The ineffectuality of recent scholarly attempts to distinguish between women prophets and preachers reflects the confusion that women who publicly participated in the politico-religious conflicts of the 1640s and 1650s caused at least in part because women prophets and preachers were

---

significant examples, are too important to Trapnel's religious views and manner of expressing them to overlap precisely with today's scholar's spiritual convictions and rituals.

[18] Smith makes an almost identical claim: "Singing was a form of particular spiritual liberation for her and a sign of the nature of what she was prophesying" (*Perfection Proclaimed* 50).

[19] Although Mack indicates at one point that "Trapnel actually preached to mixed audiences of Fifth Monarchists and Quakers" (147), she does not explore the implications of her representation of this instance of Trapnel's public speech as preaching. Hobby also describes Trapnel as "travelling and preaching" without considering the significance of the "prophet's" preaching (32). In contrast, Nuttall, apparently because he only considers *A Legacy for Saints*, refers unproblematically in 1947 to Trapnel as a preacher (88). My goal is to take both roles into consideration, while addressing the imbalance in recent scholarship that privileges the more passive alternative in discussions of Trapnel.

not necessarily easy to tell apart.[20]   Anne Laurence presents a thorough categorization of religious behaviors (including writing and speaking practices) that were acceptable for women, as well as those that could distinguish a woman as a preacher.[21] Writing but preferably not publishing books of prayers, spiritual advice, and meditations; acting as "the teacher of godly precepts in the household"; prophesying, especially through relating dreams and visions; and acting as moral "examples to others" were in and of themselves uncontroversial behaviors for women (Laurence 346-7, 363).[22] Within a church community, it was acceptable for a woman to be involved in the "procedures for church administration"; to speak before the congregation to confess her faith or repent; and to help found a congregation (Laurence 348, 351, 352).

According to Laurence's analysis, however, a woman should not administer the ordinances or sacraments, and "women might not preach the Gospel as part of a teaching ministry with an authoritative position in the congregation" (351, 352).[23] Considering the environment of rampant and controversial lay preaching during the 1640s and 1650s, Laurence asks:

> If ministers were not required to be specially educated or to have some visible qualification . . . what was the difference between the ministry and a member of the congregation exercising his or her gifts, other than that the whole congregation had assented to the person being called? (360)

Her answer is that "The critical point seems to have been the exercise of personal authority over members of the congregation" (Laurence 360). But what constitutes "the exercise of personal authority over members of the congregation"?   As Dorothy Ludlow notes, "The distinction between women teaching at home and their preaching in public was often blurred,"

---

[20]   Ludlow highlights how Trapnel resists categorization by calling her, for example, a "prophetess-preacher" (101), a "prophetess/mystic/preacher" (107), and "a seer . . . a writer and an evangelist" (107).   Nuttall discusses the slippery status of prophecy--it was difficult to determine when and whether a person was possessed by the Holy Spirit--in relation to preaching; see 75-89.   He explains that "It is not difficult to see how this conviction of the right not only of ministers but of all, *ex ipse plebe*, to 'prophecy' would develop into the conviction that not only ordained pastors but laymen might also preach in the more formal sense" (Nuttall 78). Also see Richey 1-3.

[21] For more on the "theology of gender" in relation to women's status as believers and the religious rules available to them, see Mendelson and Crawford 31-4.

[22] Ludlow specifies that women prophets were "Less threatening, perhaps, but still viewed with some trepidation" (99).

[23] Radical sectarians either opposed the administration of the traditional, "formal" sacraments (Ranters, Quakers) or prioritized gifts of the spirit (Fifth Monarchists, including Trapnel) to such an extent that only Laurence's second main restriction was a concern.

as were the distinctions among "interruption, exhortation, and actual preaching" (95, 97).

Diane Purkiss's attempt to define the seventeenth-century sense of prophecy suggests that a prophet was no less difficult to identify than a preacher. In fact, Purkiss's effort to clarify prophecy implies an association between the woman prophet and woman preacher that could have alarmed a seventeenth-century patriarchal audience:

> For the radical sects in the seventeenth century, prophecy was any utterance produced by God through human agency. Hence the prophecies of women discussed in this essay include hymns, general moral exhortations, scriptural exegesis, prayers, spiritual autobiography and mystical revelations, as well as predictions . . . acceptance of a woman prophet depended on the belief that her utterances were divinely inspired . . . divine inspiration was uncomfortably similar to its supposed opposites: diabolical possession, witchcraft, and madness. (139, 140)

Purkiss indicates that defining a text as "prophetic" or a person as a "prophet" was contingent on an audience's belief that the words on the page or tongue were divine--not human, certainly not gendered--products.[24] Although accusations that Trapnel was a witch or was mad attest to the accuracy of Purkiss's observation that "divine inspiration was uncomfortably similar to its supposed opposites,"[25] Purkiss's statement leads to the question of whether and how one can tell if a so-called prophet is inspired at all--a question that is not isolated to the mind of today's scholar but that occurred to seventeenth-century commentators as well.[26] The

---

[24] Purkiss subsumes a wide range of speaking and writing practices and genres under "prophecy." Although this is appropriate given that men and women used the claim to prophetic gifts to justify a variety of behaviors, Purkiss's statement also illustrates how women's distinct speaking/writing practices can become eclipsed by the "prophetic" quality of those practices.

Mack also notes that "the status of visionary or prophet was not a fixed social definition analogous to that of the minister or magistrate; it was one end of a very slippery contiuum, the other end of which was the polluted whore or witch" (120).

[25] In trying to pre-empt arguments against her divine inspiration, for example, Trapnel asserts in *The Cry of a Stone* that "Oh, you cannot abide to think it comes from God; for then you would tremble; they say, we will not own it to be from God, but from some evil spirit, some witchcraft some design or hiring of men; But oh! says God, though you would not acknowledge it, yet you shall acknowledge it" (69-70). She also exclaims, "They will say the spirit of madness and distraction is upon her, and that it is immodesty" (*The Cry of a Stone* 67).

[26] Nuttall explains that "The claim advanced by the more radical party within Puritanism that the Spirit which was in the apostles, as manifested in the written word, was also in themselves led inevitably . . . to the further question, how men could discern God's Spirit within them from their own fancies" (35). For more on the controversy surrounding

newsbook *Mercurius Politicus*, for instance, reports in reference to Trapnel's Whitehall performance that "There seem to be two convincing Reasons against her Spirit; the one is, that it withdraws from Ordinances, and the other is, that it is Non-sensical." The article does not suggest that Trapnel is a witch rather than a prophet. Rather, it suggests that her claim to the gift of the Holy Spirit is fraudulent: her utterances do not accord with the traditional ordinances, and they make no sense to the writer of the article. The implication is that Trapnel may be misguided or silly, but she is certainly not extraordinarily inspired. The article concludes that her behavior is mundane and political: it is designed to "disaffect the people to the present Authority" (166). Trapnel's epistle to "The Church sometimes meeting at AL-HOLLOWS" provides an account of a similar accusation of political subversion. In her letter, she specifies that the clergy not only accuse her of being a witch, but also call her "deluder, Imposter . . . [and] further said I stirred and provoked the people to Rebellion against powers (*A Legacy for Saints* 49).[27]

As we have seen, a prophet might not only be a witch possessed by the devil instead of the Holy Spirit; even worse, a prophet might be an ordinary woman attracting an audience to listen to her own beliefs, opinions, teachings, and scriptural interpretations. She might be a preacher and a politically subversive one at that. Contemporary texts such as *A Discoverie of Six women preachers* (London, 1641) and Thomas Edwards' *Gangraena* (London, 1646), both of which provide mocking, demeaning accounts of the women preachers of whom they purport to give true descriptions, exhibit concern about a virtual epidemic of women preachers. "On a Puritan maide," a bawdy, anti-puritan lyric from a manuscript (BL Add. 44963) belonging to Arthur Scattergood (1611-1687), makes the fruition of a "Puritan maide['s]" hypocritical licentiousness the occasion to put the mere idea of a female preacher back in its place:[28]

---

the question of how to "discern God's Spirit," the source of prophetic inspiration, see Nuttall 34-47. Nuttall indicates that "the question of discerning of spirits" did "not [arise] with urgency" until the radical sectarians "allow[ed] what they believed to be the Holy Spirit's motions to lead them into eccentric or fanatical sayings or behaviour" (44).

[27] For Trapnel's accounts of similar accusations, see *A Legacy for Saints* 58 and *Anna Trapnel's Report and Plea* 18, 19, 21, 49.

[28] Crum indicates that the same poem appears in MS Rawl. poet. 26, fol. 8[v] and lists a number of manuscripts that record variants on it: MSS. Don. d. 58, fol.35; Eng. poet. e. 14, fol. 89[v] rev.; Rawl. poet. 31, fol. 3[v]; Rawl. poet. 172, fol. 12. Its many appearances in various forms suggest its popularity.

> On a Puritan maide.
> A Puritan maide by one of hir societie
> Being gott wth child did pray in Christian pietie
> The child she might conceive might be a Preacher
> Because so learned a man had overreach'd her
> Hir time now come, & all hir paine being past,
> She ask'd ye mid'wife, what God had sent at last
> The Midwife said in more then halfe a laught'r;
> The child you have brought forth is prov'd a daugt^r
> But be content, it is a pretty baby,
> And hath a Pulpit, where a Preacher may bee. (64)

The "Puritan maide['s]" overzealous desire to produce an offspring who would be a preacher gives the poet the opportunity to remind his audience what--in his reductive, misogynist view--stands between women and the authority of a true spiritual leader. While the "Puritan maide" and those of "hir societie" are the butt of the joke, the poem betrays an anxiety, expressed through association, about the proximity of a woman's unruly desires to ministerial authority. The January 15, 1646 delegation of London Aldermen and the Common Council who petitioned against women preachers before the House of Commons probably would have enjoyed the joke; their petition constituted real opposition to the possibility that women might desire the public authority that preaching entails, and worse, that they might actually gain that authority (Ludlow 97). Although Trapnel's claim to prophetic gifts is an important aspect of her attempt to speak publicly with impunity, she implicitly equates her role with a ministerial one. By strategically playing her prayers and songs off each other, she constructs a pulpit--a conceptual space from which she can speak with authority--in which *she* can be the preacher.

Lyrical Preaching

> The spirit in a Sermon-Psalm
> (Trapnel, *Voice for the King* 61)

> A verse may find him, who a sermon flies,
> And turn delight into a sacrifice.
> (Herbert, "Perirrhanterium" 5-6)

Lay preaching is central to *The Cry of a Stone*. Not only does the text indicate that Trapnel came to Whitehall to show support for Vavasor Powell, a Fifth Monarchist preacher called to task for his public denouncements of the Protectorate, but it also directly addresses the questions of who can be a preacher and who has the authority (or more significantly, does *not* have the authority) to decide. The prefatory letter to *The Cry of a Stone*, written by a group of Fifth Monarchists, states their position with regard to lay preaching:

> far be it from us, who are and shall yet be named the Vally of Vision, to bind up the goings forth of the most free and Eternal Spirit at any time, especially in these last dayes, within any Law, custom, order, or qualification of man, how antient or accustomed soever. (a2)

This statement presents the Fifth Monarchist belief that Jesus's earthly rule is imminent and that the Holy Spirit is therefore working directly in the world in the way that it did in the days of the apostles. That this declaration pertains to the controversial contemporary issue of lay preaching is evident in the authors' opposition to the notion that they--or, by implication, any human--should "bind up" the Holy Spirit "within any Law, custom, order, or qualification of man, how antient or accustomed soever."[29] Although the statement could indicate that the authors do not believe they can decide who is a prophet, this is not its only implication. Because the role of the prophet--unlike that of the preacher--was not institutionalized, there would be no reason to deny the relevance of "any Law, custom, order, or qualification of man" in discerning who was a prophet.[30] The claim that no particular earthly legal or social requirements should interfere with a person's use of his or her gifts for the benefit of God's people thus supports the uninstitutionalized phenomenon of lay preaching. The implication is that anyone who has the "Eternall Spirit" working in her or him could be a preacher. As we will see, Trapnel makes the best of this implication, and her lyrics are instrumental to her doing so. Analyzing the contrast between Trapnel's songs and prayers in *The Cry of a Stone* will help to illuminate how her verse enables her to speak as a preacher as well as--and at times instead of--a prophet.[31]

---

[29] Also see Capp 188.

[30] See Mack 120.

[31] Beilin examines the writing strategies of several earlier (late sixteenth- and early seventeenth-century) women writers who also assumed preacherly roles; see esp. xxi, 48, 50-1, 81-2, 94, 109-10, 116. Trapnel shares with these predecessors the Reformation notion "that verse could convey doctrine in a direct and pleasing way" (Beilin 81). However, Trapnel's lyrical preaching was arguably more subversive and put her at greater risk than did the activities of any of the women writers in Beilin's study simply because Trapnel made public appearances in addition to writing and because the context of the revolutionary period elevated the stakes of religious controversy in general. See Cope on how Lady Eleanor Davies, like Trapnel, used prophetic discourse not just to gain a public audience but to shape

Trapnel's account of a vision that she had two days before the formation of the Protectorate is especially useful in delineating the differences between the contents and tone of her prose and verse. Describing her vision, Trapnel relates how she saw a group of oxen, one of which had Cromwell's face. "[H]e run at me," she explains, "he run at many precious Saints that stood in the way of him, that looked boldly in his face; he gave them many pushes, scratching them with his horn." Soon, there was a "great fury coming from the Clouds, and [the oxen] presently were scattered, and their horns broken, and they tumbled into Graves" (*The Cry of a Stone* 13). Although what Trapnel predicts in this narrative is the failure of the current political establishment, as figured in the physical destruction of the oxen, the articulation of her prediction as a vision--a particularly acceptable medium through which a female prophet can receive divine information (Laurence 347, 363)--helps to protect Trapnel despite her transgression into the public sphere. Because she recounts this controversial, supernatural message as a vision that must be read figuratively, she also makes it more difficult to hold her, the weak vessel of its transmission, responsible for its significance. The figurative nature of the vision, in fact, makes it ambiguous enough to provide Trapnel an extra margin of safety as its conduit. The oxen's falling "into Graves," for instance, need not symbolize the actual deaths of the men that the oxen represent; it might merely foretell the end of their power in its present form.

Although Trapnel may sound fairly direct in her opposition to the Protectorate in this vision, she can be even more baldly critical of Cromwell and his followers in her poetry because when she sings she is supposed to be completely under divine control. Active creativity, after all, should be beyond her female abilities.[32] The Fifth Monarchist (known as the "relator") who transcribes Trapnel's divine utterances calls attention to the special status of her singing. Describing her physical appearance during her possession by the Holy Spirit, the relator notes that "the effects of a spirit caught up in the Visions of God, did abundantly appear in the fixedness, and immoveableness of her speech in prayer, but more especially in her songs" (*The Cry of a Stone* 13). The words that the relator transcribes issue from the mouth of a woman, but they are too stable to have come from an unruly female tongue or to have been produced by a woman's brain. Lest Trapnel's singing, in particular, be mistaken for her own creative effort, the

---

a certain social role for herself. Cope explains how Lady Eleanor "designat[ed] her call to prophecy an office" (208).

[32] As Mack notes, "the successful female prophet was invariably described, paradoxically, as dumb; 'dumb' meaning both stupid and mute, empty of everything but God" (32).

relator indicates that it is "especially" with regard to the "fixedness and immoveableness" of her songs that one can discern that she did not produce them. A contemporary commentator known as "B:T:" agrees with the relator's theory:

> If she did continue in it but for one or two dayes, I should be apt to thinke she might do it when she would, in the strength of parts, save for two things. 1st. she is so stifned in hir Body that were she not warme[e?] one would thinke hir dead. 2ly. Because (she saith) she cannot make a verse when she is hir self. (qtd. in Burrage 532)

Trapnel's versifying is a special case: it is the surest mark of her divine possession, and therefore, it is the best reason not to hold her responsible for the contents of her songs. The prophetic premise underwriting Trapnel's utterances in *The Cry of a Stone* thus undeniably enabled her prolonged, public appearance in 1654. However, we must not allow the significance of Trapnel's versifying to overshadow the meanings of her verse or to veil the importance of the manner in which she plays her prayers and songs off each other--both of which help her to assert herself as a minister.

Given the special status of Trapnel's singing, it is not surprising that her lyrics are, at times, scathingly direct. In the song that corresponds to her vision of the oxen in *The Cry of a Stone*, for example, she says:

> *Write how that Protectors shall go,*
> *And into graves there lye:*
> *Let pens make known what is said,*
>   *that,*
> *They shall expire and die. (19-20)*

If there were any doubt that the graves into which Trapnel's figurative oxen fall signify the actual deaths of the persons to whom she refers, her verse removes that doubt: "Protectors shall . . . into graves there lye . . . They shall expire and die." In her lyrics, Trapnel saves Cromwell the trouble of guessing. The juxtaposition in *The Cry of a Stone* of a song and prayer in which Trapnel attempts to convince Cromwell not to accept the title of "Protector" similarly highlights how her lyrics allow her to be especially direct in her political critiques. In her song, she ventriloquizes "what the Lord holds forth," bluntly relaying the divine command that Cromwell not accept the title of Protector:

> *. . . hearken to sound words which come,*
> *From him that is so rich;*
> *O listen what the Lord holds forth,*
> *And what he thee doth teach.*
>
> *That thou shouldst not assume to*
> *thee*
> *Higher power then Christ doth give*
> ....
>
> *O do not thou aspire, for to*
> *So high a title have;*
> *As King, or Protector: But oh*
> *Unto Christ that do leave.* (*The Cry of a Stone* 28-29)

The verse allows Trapnel to address Cromwell directly in the second person and to tell him what to do; the shipwright's daughter becomes political and spiritual advisor to the nation's leader. In contrast, in the prayer that follows Trapnel's lyrical warning to Cromwell not to accept the role of Protector, she reiterates her opposition, but much more indirectly:

> Therefore Father teach him, let him know that he may reign as one of thine: oh, is it not a sweet thing to be crowned by thee? and that is sweeter then to be crowned by man: O says *Gideon*! I will not be your King, the Lord shall reign over you: O it is enough for him to be one of thy Kings! Oh let him now deny, and cast it down, and say; without these Dignities and great Titles, I will serve the People and Commonality; and then wilt thou say to him, thou art my *Gideon*. (*The Cry of a Stone* 29)

She addresses her words to God, not to Cromwell, and she uses the form of a prayer to suggest what Cromwell should do, asking God to "let him know . . . " and to "let him now deny . . . " Her rhetoric is more persuasive than commanding in this prose passage: she proposes what a true Gideon would say in this situation, offering Cromwell a script that would enable him to avoid God's wrath while keeping his dignity. In fact, Trapnel fantasizes and plays both parts in a dialogue between Cromwell and God, suggesting that if Cromwell says what she tells him to say, then God will claim Cromwell as his Gideon. Although the indirect, persuasive style of this prayer seems potentially less disturbing to Cromwell and his followers than Trapnel's verse might have been, Trapnel's subtle scripting of the interaction between two patriarchs--God and England's leader--reveals Trapnel's rhetorical sophistication perhaps more than do her juxtaposed songs in this case.

While the premise that Trapnel was a prophet no doubt helped her to intervene in the political and religious controversies of the moment, the rhetorical and formal complexity of the interplay between her prayers and songs was also essential to her ability to continue those public interventions without incurring immediate hostility.[33] As we will see, those same features of her texts allow her to make an indirect claim to a ministerial role. This prayer, in which Trapnel claims that she is merely God's voice, clarifies how her mobilization of the differences between her prayers and lyrics relates to her subtle preacherly positioning:

> Oh thy Servant (speaking of her selfe) must now come forth against the great Rabbies of the world: Oh, thou knowest that thy Servant had often wrastled with thee that thou wouldst employ some other, but thou has over-ruled her, and hast put her to silence? and shall I not be willing to do or suffer thy Will? And thou givest strength unto her, and bearest up the Spirit of thy servant to go thorow with the Work, thy Servant is not any enemy to these men, thou knowest, but a friend. Oh, it is for thy sake, and for thy servants sakes, that thy Servant is made a voyce, a sound, it is a voyce within a voyce, anothers voyce, even thy voyce through her . . . and when thy Servant has done thy work, she shall be willing to lock up her selfe in her Closet againe, and not to be seen of men; Oh Lord, thy servant knows there is no self in this thing. (*The Cry of a Stone* 42)

In this prayer Trapnel carefully prefaces her attack on the clergy, "the great Rabbies of the world," by indicating that she has long resisted God's insistence that she be the particular person to make this attack.[34] She also

---

[33] The relator's frequent interventions between Trapnel's prayers and songs in *The Cry of a Stone*--well-timed reminders that a rational, male witness constantly monitors her-- also highlight the strategic significance of their interplay. Two medieval women's texts, Julian of Norwich's *Showings* and *The Book of Margery Kempe*, similarly suggest that a woman's participation in the production of her own text appears to necessitate a foregrounding of patriarchal containment. These texts are similar to Anna Trapnel's works in that they demonstrate how a woman's active involvement in her own spiritual representation requires a compensating display of patriarchal survcillance in proportion to the degree to which the woman exerts control over her text. Whether Trapnel's relator was the amanuensis *The Cry of a Stone* claims him to be, the narrator himself, or Trapnel's own invention in a text that she authored does not change the effect of the text's reminders that he is *there*, overseeing her interactions with God and her engagement with the public sphere. See Lynn S. Johnson for an argument suggesting a similar phenomenon in *Showings* and *The Book of Margery Kempe*.

[34] Trapnel's use of the term "Rabbies" to refer to spiritual leaders probably relates to what P.G. Rogers calls the Fifth Monarchists' "strong Hebraic tendencies and sympathies": "The lengthy and laborious efforts of the sect to interpret the Bible in accordance with their preconceived ideas, and their insistence on the necessity of the conversion of the Jews,

figures her relationship to God as indisputably appropriate for a woman. Her whole being "is made a voyce, a sound"; not only does her female body not taint or interfere with God's message, but it seems to disappear, dissolving into a divine voice. To emphasize that God's "servant knows there is no self in this thing," she refers to herself primarily in the third person. Likewise, she does not address the crowd that observes her but directs her statements to God.[35] Her words constitute a prayer that her audience should understand as part of a conversation between a divinely controlled, attenuated version of herself and God. The audience is eavesdropping; she does not realize that her conversations with God have become a public spectacle.

Shortly after Trapnel delineates her perfectly acceptable relationship to God and indicates her reluctance to chastise the clergy, however, she begins her divine versifying. Directly addressing her human audience instead of God, she asserts that:

> *For human Arts and Sciences,*
> * because you doat on them,*
> *Therfore the Lord wil others teach*
> * whom you count but Lay-men.*
> ....
> *Christs Scholars they are perfected*
> * with learning from above,*
> *To them he gives capacity*
> * to know his depths of love.* (*The Cry of a Stone* 42)

Trapnel immediately raises the issue of lay preaching in her critique of "the great Rabbies of the world." Because the institutionalized clergy "doat" on "human Arts and Sciences," Christ will educate his own chosen "Lay-men"; he will give them spiritual "learning from above." Trapnel emphasizes that

---

resulted in many Fifth Monarchy Men [sic] developing strong Hebraic tendencies and sympathies; and opponents sometimes commented caustically about this" (149).

[35] Although Trapnel characterizes herself as the ideal, weak vessel in her appeal to God, the form of her prayer actually corresponds to preacherly behavior that George Herbert recommends in *A Priest to the Temple, or The Countrey Parson His Character, and Rule of Holy Life*. In a chapter entitled, "The Parson preaching," Herbert explains that a good parson will "[turn] often, and mak[e] many Apostrophes to God, as, O Lord, blesse my people, and teach them this point; or, Oh my Master, on whose errand I come, let me hold my peace, and doe thou speak thy selfe; for thou art Love, and when thou teachest, all are Scholers. Some such irradiations scatteringly in the Sermon, carry great holiness in them" (233-4). In this context of analyzing how Trapnel postures herself not only as a prophet, but also as a preacher, it is compelling to note Herbert's observation that "The Prophets are admirable" in performing the kind of apostrophe that he recommends parsons include in their sermons (234).

lay preachers are indeed educated; they have all the spiritual knowledge anyone could need because they "know [Christ's] depths of love." Trapnel similarly figures the knowledge that one gets through the right belief as a kind of public schooling in *A Legacy for Saints*. In her conversion narrative, she asserts, "the creature can never learn the lesson of humiliation and self-denial till it hath been in the School of free grace, that is, the free School, where the best of learning is to be had" (*A Legacy for Saints* 15). That free education does not need to satisfy human requirements or standards, and a "creature" apparently need not have particular social characteristics to be admitted to "the free School."[36]

Although Trapnel refers to "Lay-men" at the beginning of her anti-clerical lyric, later in her poem she undermines the notion that a preacher must be male.[37] Chastising the official clergy, she sings:

> Oh you because have not kept in
> within your bound and Sphear,
> Therefore the Lord hath declared
> he'l put you in great fear.
>
> Though learning it be very good,
> when in its place it stands,
> But when it gaddeth forth thereout
> it looseth its great bands. (*The Cry of a Stone* 42)

Trapnel accuses learned men of not remaining within their proper "bound and Sphear"; she chastises them according to the same terms that they would use to disparage a woman for speaking in public, for over-stepping *her* "bound and Sphear." Trapnel also throws the gender-marked term "gaddeth" back at the clergy. As Mendelson and Crawford explain, "the technical term 'gadding'" was applied to women who attended "lectures and

---

[36] For more on radical sectarian attacks on formal education, see Nuttall esp. 83-4.

[37] Mack claims that "the mentality of the most eminent female prophets was not, in their view, radically dissimilar to that of male ministers . . . Indeed, in a different world, some of these women might have become ministers" (91). Mack does not, however, explicitly acknowledge Trapnel as a preacher along with "Katherine Chidley and Mary Cary [who] actually insisted they were ministers, not prophets" (91).

Ethyn Morgan Williams shows how much the question of women's preaching was intertwined with the issue of lower class, "uneducated" preaching. Also see Laurence: "Lay preaching was something that taxed the government, and on 26 April 1645, partly as a result of reports of soldiers preaching in the armies, Parliament passed an ordinance prohibiting preaching by laymen . . . The preaching of John Biddle, the Socinian, provoked the ordinace of 2 May 1648 to punish blasphemies and heresies, and the preaching of Abiezer Coppe and other Ranters the ordinance of 9 August 1650 against atheistical, blasphemous, and execrable opinions" (357).

sermons outside their own parochial boundaries." This behavior "was taken as a critique of the establishment doctrine expounded in their parish churches" and "was perceived as politically threatening." Such women who thus gadded about could be "punished in the ecclesiastical courts" (390-1). By using this term to refer to the institutionalized clergy, Trapnel therefore associates them with a specifically female-coded form of religious impropriety. She can chastise the clergy in this manner because she has already proven that she knows her place. The juxtaposed prayer in which she declares that she is merely "a voyce within a voyce, anothers voyce" ascribes to her the exact (passive) characteristics that Mack's analysis shows to be expected of and desirable in a female prophet.[38] It is only after indicating how perfectly she knows her own place--"when thy Servant has done thy work, she shall be willing to lock up her Selfe in her Closet againe"--that she accuses learned men of not knowing theirs and asserts that "Learning" is only "very good/ when in its place it stands." In indicating who may speak with authority on spiritual issues, Trapnel thus negates the importance of a university education and being male, and emphasizes the value of knowing one's proper place in the divine order.

Her implicit comparison of her own behavior with that of the clergy further suggests that she is a more genuine spiritual instructor than they:

> *O you have been so gallant, and*
> *   you have in silken walk'd,*
> *O you in dainty food have been,*
> *   that hath made you to talk;*
> *But when they cease putting in*
> *   to your wide mouthes that gape,*
> *O then you'll cease speaking that, which*
> *   before you did relate,*
> *Concerning the sweetness of Christ,*
> *   your studies had drawn out,*
> *O Christ I'm sure he wil you try,*
> *   Whether you truly spoke out.*
> *For your triall wil be, when that*
> *   your Revenues shal goe,*
> *Then it shal be manifest*
> *   whither your wind shal blow;*
> *But I wel know that those that are*
> *   true Prophets of the Lord,*

---

[38] Mack explains that "The ultimate manifestation of the prophet as a passive and entirely purified receptacle of divine energy was the maiden who preached prone, holding forth from a sick bed, or one who actually surmounted the death of the body, returning briefly from the grave with a message from the underworld" (34).

> *Wil live upon that pay which he*
> *declared in his Word. (The Cry of a Stone* 43)

Trapnel charges the clergy with living an extravagant lifestyle off the tithe: they wear silk and eat "dainty food." She also suggests that there is an inappropriate economy of exchange between the official preachers and their flock. It is only because the people keep "putting in/ to [the clergy's] wide mouthes that gape" that those preachers speak "Concerning the sweetnesse of Christ." She claims that, in the absence of the tithe, those spiritual leaders inappropriately invested in the material world would lose their inspiration to speak about Christ, but "those that are/ true Prophets" can "live upon that pay which he/ declared in his Word."[39] That *The Cry of a Stone* refers repeatedly to Trapnel's ability to fast for days while speaking almost constantly on behalf of God suggests that she, not the official clergy, is a "true Prophet," which her verse implies should be able to substitute for the clergy.[40] She comes as close as she safely can--and it is safer to make such an assertion in verse--to declaring herself a "true Prophet of the Lord" in the context of arguing that lay preachers are legitimate spiritual instructors.[41] In the prayer that follows her anti-clerical poem, Trapnel attempts to control and limit the poem's meaning. Addressing God once more instead of the clergy, Trapnel makes this request:

> Oh let not men thinke that thine doe cry down the Ministry of them that are full of the Ministerial Office, and of thy Spirit, and does speake from thee; but there are that are called Ministers, that doe deny Jesus Christ his

---

[39] According to P.G. Rogers, the Barebones Parliament (whose dissolution Trapnel protested and which had included influential, male Fifth Monarchists) had attacked the tithe on July 15, 1653, and "It was proposed that no tithe should be paid as maintenance for ministers after 3 November 1653: No decision was reached; instead the issue was sent to committee" (36).

[40] Wiseman observes that "Both Trapnel and Cary are at pains to establish the high status of prophecy in relation to the ministry of the gathered churches" (192). Smith seems more precise in his observation that "Trapnel seems intent on validating her own role as 'seer' alongside the spiritually gifted who occupy ministerial office" (*Perfection Proclaimed* 51). Yet the important point is rather that Trapnel blurs the roles of prophet and preacher together.

[41] In Trapnel's *A Legacy for Saints*, she similarly writes in a genre that is more acceptable for a woman--a combination of spiritual autobiography and conversion narrative-- to make a space for participating in a less acceptable genre. After she relates the stock events of her conversion narrative, she presents and interprets a "similitude" that, to her, expresses the truth of the trinity, and she performs scriptural exegesis (*A Legacy for Saints* 33-5). Satisfying the conventional expectations of the conversion narrative appears to make her brief sermon less transgressive. Trapnel's strategic use of genre is especially important in *A Legacy for Saints* because it is not one of her "prophetic" texts; the premise that God speaks through her does not apply in this case.

coming to set up his Kingdome, O thine would have them throwne downe before thee, the Lord wil not let there be a famishing of the Word in the Land, and he will take care of them; let there not be a cry among them, that if maintenance go downe, the Ministry wil down; let them looke into the Scripture, and there see what is the true Ministry, and what is their pay; let them see what those were who were thy true Ministers, were they such as did pamper their bellies, and their backs? (*The Cry of a Stone* 44)

Speaking in a manner that suggests that she is entreating God, not chastising the clergy on her own behalf, Trapnel reasserts what her poem claims: *real ministers do not need the benefits of a national church tithe.* She also equates being "full of the Ministerial Office" with being full of "thy Spirit," and she calls upon scripture to validate her equation.[42] Having "Spirit" is what distinguishes a real minister, not institutional approval or being paid to preach. Elsewhere, Trapnel also claims that educated men "have the form without the power" (*The Cry of a Stone* 57) and challenges her listeners to ascertain that she does have "the power," or Spirit, by checking her utterances against scripture. Her audience will know that her words come from the Holy Spirit "by the language of it, by the Rule through which it comes: how is the written Word carried forth in it!" (*The Cry of a Stone* 67). Trapnel has the form and the power: she speaks from scripture, and she speaks from inspiration.

Although she belittles herself when she asks the lord if he "wilt make a poor silly Creature to come out against [the learned men] because they have acted so sillily," she continues to imply that she not only knows the words of a good minister when she hears them but that her own utterances qualify. "What is become of your Zeal and Exaltations of Christ, have you ever a New-Covenant-Sermon to bring to your great ruler?" she asks her audience, "Are they like to the Sermons of the Saints formerly, to the Apostles Sermons which the Lord Jesus brought forth?" (*The Cry of a Stone* 69). Trapnel, like the apostles, does emphasize the covenant that promises Christ's return, and like the apostles, her words are "brought forth" by "the Lord Jesus." Answering her own questions, she tells God, "more of their own heads and fancies are in it, then of thy dainties; of their flowers, then of thine; Thou doest not, Lord, look at the curious decking of the

---

[42] See Ephesians 3:7-8 where Paul explains that "Of this gospel I was made a minister according to the gift of God's grace which was given me by the working of his power. To me, though I am the very least of all the saints, this grace was given, to preach to the Gentiles the unsearchable riches of Christ."

dishes" (*The Cry of a Stone* 69).[43]   The official ministers' sermons are
tainted by the intervention of their own creative impulses. Whereas Trapnel
is direct and plain-speaking in her inspired verses, the official ministers
impose their own prideful creativity on the divine text. Their knowledge is
"their own understanding, their own apprehensions, their own light": the
clergy's professions of faith are egocentric (*The Cry of a Stone* 57).[44]

While Trapnel makes her disapproval of the institutionalized clergy
very clear, she also indicates her approval of certain kinds of ministers.[45]   In

---

[43]   Trapnel sings explicitly about the inferiority of figurative language in
representing the sacred in these lines about Christ's crucified body from *A Voice for the King
of Saints and Nations*. She asserts that Christ's body was

> . . . not as Beaumont reports,
> For he doth allegorize,
> The body was with Deity,
> But not as he describes.
> The body prepar'd before time,
> Was in the deities sight;
> But notionisers of the body,
> They do not speak aright.
> The spoyl great mysteries because,
> They cannot bring them out;
> But by an allegory, or by
> A high speculative mouth;
> But O the crucified Christ,
> Teacheth us mysteries here,
> And O he bringeth down a Psalm,
> Which is most pure and clear. (*Voice for the King* 60-1)

Herbert, of course, also wrestles with the problem the use of figurative language
poses for religious verse. Cf. esp. Herbert's "Jordan (I)," "Jordan (II)," "A True Hymn," "The
Posy," and Sonnet I.
[44]   Mack argues that "The characterization of the female visionary as an empty
vessel reflected an attitude that was far more complicated than simple misogyny, for the
defects of rationality and the attuned intuition of visionary women were actually viewed with
respect, even envy, by those philosophers who felt alienated from God by their compulsive,
prideful reliance on the power of their own reason. Indeed, in this respect all women had a
clear spiritual advantage over men, for the static resulting from their weak and intermittent
surges of intellectual energy was less likely to interfere with their capacity to act as receptors
for the divine, spiritual energy emanating from heaven" (33). Trapnel takes advantage of this
cultural notion of gendered interactions with the divine and aggressively turns it back on the
clergy who oppose her.
[45]   John Proud and Caleb Ingold's prefatory letter to Trapnel's *A Legacy for Saints*
suggests that civil and religious leaders certainly noticed Trapnel's accusations against the
clergy. Among the three main points that they make in her defense is the claim that she only
opposes clergy who act like bishops. She blames the clergy for setting the civil authorities
against her in her prefatory letter to *Anna Trapnel's Report and Plea*. In fact, she relates in
this defense how the clergy use the advantage of their official positions to speak against her

A Legacy for Saints, she celebrates particular clergymen to prove that she does not oppose them all. She calls Mr. Greenhil, for example, a "Minister of God" and Mr. Simpson a "Trumpeter of *Israel*" and "Embassador of Christ" (*A Legacy for Saints* 29, 32). Of course, in doing so, she also suggests that the ministers sympathetic to the Fifth Monarchist agenda are the true ones. In *Anna Trapnel's Report and Plea*, for instance, she shows her approval of Fifth Monarchist preachers in her commentary about her arrest:

> it was that Messenger that took hold of Vavasor Powell, and carried him before the Councell . . . I said, though I was troubled at him for his taking Mr. Powell, yet for taking me . . . I was no whit troubled at him . . . I was had to my Chamber, which was Mr. Feaks prison first, so that I was quickly raised in my Joy. (37)

Her "Joy" seems to derive at least in part from her sense that the governmental authorities effectively treat her as they have other well-known Fifth Monarchist leaders: the "Messenger" who made Powell appear before the Council of State arrests her, and her prison room formerly housed Christopher Feake. Although Trapnel seems delighted at the implicit analogy between herself and these male Fifth Monarchist leaders, she models herself in particular on the apostle Paul. At the end of *A Legacy for Saints*, she includes epistles much in the manner of Paul, in which she addresses her congregation publicly, and she even writes a variation on Paul's well-known speech on love from I Corinthians 13:4-7 (52). Making her comparison with Paul explicit, she writes "*Paul* met with beasts at Ephesus, I may say also I have met with beasts in *Cornwell*" (*A Legacy of Saints* 54). In *Anna Trapnel's Report and Plea*, she relates that when she resists her friends' and God's wishes for her to go to Cornwall, God himself compares her to Paul. God tells her:

> *as truly do I thy Lord call thee to Cornwal by this vision* [as he called Paul to Macedonia]: then I answered, and said, *Paul was to preach there, what is that word to me?* then reply was, *But as sure as his was a vision from the Lord to go to Macedonia, so as sure had I a call and true vision to go to Cornwal.* (*Anna Trapnel's Report and Plea* 3)

By having God make an analogy between her and Paul that, ironically, undercuts Paul's injunction against women's speaking in church, Trapnel justifies, in advance, the activities in Cornwall that result in her trial and

---

from their pulpits, and she implies that they feel threatened because she does their job better than they do (*Anna Trapnel's Report and Plea* 25).

imprisonment. God's comparison of Trapnel with Paul implies that she should go to Cornwall specifically to preach, which she does, much to the envy of the local ministry. Trapnel so impressed her audiences at Cornwall that "some said afterwards, *Which of all our Ministers can hold out thus many hours without a cordial?*" (*Anna Trapnel's Report and Plea* 18). In Trapnel's narration of the events leading to her imprisonment, her audience's comparison of her to their local ministers inspires the hostility of those spiritual leaders. Trapnel comments that "when their Ministers thought they should lose their fleece, they began to stir" (*Anna Trapnel's Report and Plea* 18). She goes to prison because the official clergy fear that she will take their audiences--and not even charge *her* new congregation a fee.

Trapnel does not merely frame her account of her imprisonment so that it implicates the clergy; she ascribes the ultimate blame for the existence of the Protectorate to them, while she implies in yet another way that she is a truer minister than they. She sings:

> *Oh Clergy that you should so*
>   *wrong,*
> *And extenuate your joy,*
> *By bringing unto proud man*
> *That which God doth not covey.*
> *Oh that you should so Nurture them,*
> *And chear them in their sin,*
> *I tell you that Christ for this*
>   *will*
> *Not make your souls to sing.*
> *You shall not hear Sions song so sweet,*
> *Nor their mirth which draws nigh,*
> *But when it cometh forth to*
>   *light,*
> *You suddenly shall dye.*
> ....
> *For they that Zealous have been*
>   *for*
> *A Christ as Lord and King:*
> *He will himself open their mouth,*
> *And make them for to sing*
> ....
> *Oh he will rend you throughout,*
> *That Lyon which is strong,*
> *He will you trample under foot,*
> *Who is my joy and Song.* (Trapnel, *The Cry of a Stone* 71, 72, 73)

Trapnel's song performs and proves her own inspiration, while calling into question that of the clergy. They have not only supported "proud man" and have "[cheered] them in their sin," but they have not been "Zealous . . . for/ A Christ as Lord and King." As a consequence, Christ will neither "make [their] souls to sing," nor will they "hear Sions song so sweet" (71). If they were true ministers, Christ would "himself open their mouth,/ And make them for to sing"--as he does for Trapnel (72). Trapnel's singing becomes the sign of her ministerial office. Not only does Trapnel predict the violent death of the clergy, torn apart by Christ the lion for their misbehavior, but she also ends by asserting that Christ "is my joy and Song" (73). Although in one sense, Trapnel emphasizes that Christ is the pervasive subject of her singing, she also inverts the agency behind the song that she often attributes to the Holy Spirit. Here she "owns" her song, much as Justice Lobb later wants her to do in the case of her vision of the horns at her trial in Cornwall.[46] She implies that her song is her creation: it "is *my* joy and Song" (73, my italics). And *her* "joy and Song" participates in and responds to contemporary poetic practices and traditions.

The Radical Spouse

> O let God put his harp in hand,
> Then I'le challenge you all,
> And I do know, I shall stand sure,
> And you will crumble and fall,
> If God doth put his harp in hand,
> Then no man shall it break.
> No weapon form'd shall prosper against,
> What Christ shews from his seal,
> If once that harp be in my hand,
> I'le stand against you all;
> Do what you can, yet this weapon
> Shall not at any time fall. (*Voice for the King* 66)

In these lines from *A Voice for the King of Saints and Nations* (1658), Trapnel figures her relationship with the Holy Spirit as her possession of a harp; the Spirit has materialized into a musical instrument subject to the creative manipulation of God's lyricist. By invoking this image of the harp, the shipwright's daughter implies her comparison to David the psalmist and thus locates herself in the tradition of inspired poets. Here Trapnel is not

---

[46] See the discussion of *Anna Trapnel's Report and Plea* in the introduction to this chapter. Also cf. *Anna Trapnel's Report and Plea* 25.

simply the empty vessel--devoid of human agency yet replete with the divine word--that she claims to be as part of her strategic self-fashioning as a prophet; instead of emphasizing her role as God's instrument, she claims to wield God's instrument. And God's harp not only makes divine music, but it also acts as a "weapon" that will protect Trapnel physically if necessary.

Because many scholars have addressed how her performance as a prophet bears upon issues of agency, authority, and authorship in her texts, here I put aside questions centering on her prophetic role to examine her poetic appropriation of the Song of Songs, a text which, according to Barbara Kiefer Lewalski, "was declared the most excellent of all the thousand and five songs supposedly written by Solomon but not now extant, and indeed the most exquisite of all the songs and hymns in the scriptures" (*Protestant Poetics* 67). Before showing how Trapnel adapts Canticles so that it justifies her public speech, however, it will be helpful to gain a better understanding of how her verse relates to contemporary religious lyrics. By contextualizing Trapnel's verse in this manner, I hope both to reinforce the credibility of its extemporaneous nature and to highlight Trapnel's skill and facility in shaping her biblical subject matter.

One can best understand many features of Trapnel's songs--which she frequently calls "psalms," regardless of content, regardless of relationship to sacred or secular matters--through their connection to the traditions of rendering David's Psalms and the Song of Songs in metrical paraphrases and writing meditations on isolated aspects of or verses from them. Paraphrasing Psalms was such a widespread practice that Christopher Hill declares that "It is difficult to find a notable poet from Wyatt to Milton who did not try his [sic] hand at a version of the Psalms" (*The English Bible* 358). To Wyatt and Milton, one can add George Herbert, Henry Vaughn, Thomas Carew, Richard Crashawe, Henry King, Elizabeth I, James I, and Mary and Philip Sidney (Hill, *The English Bible* 359). Lewalski summarizes the biblical theory of poetics pertaining to the Psalms that seems to have contributed to the popularity of this kind of versifying, especially, as Hill notes, among "would-be poets" who "cut their teeth on paraphrasing the Psalms or the Song of Songs" (*The English Bible* 338):

> On all sides the Book of Psalms is seen as a compendium of all theological, doctrinal, and moral knowledge; of all the modes of God's revelation--law, prophecy, history, proverbs; of all the emotions and passions of the human soul; and apparently, of all the lyric genres and styles appropriate to divine poetry. (*Protestant Poetics* 50)

Given this understanding of the Book of Psalms, it is not surprising that Trapnel tends to classify her poems as "psalms" whether they chastise Cromwell or rework parts of the Bible.

How could Trapnel have gained the skills and knowledge necessary to compose--extemporaneously--sophisticated lyrics appropriating sacred texts? As Lewalski has shown, when analyzing the poetry of classically trained Protestant male poets who paraphrased Psalms and the Song of Songs, one must consider how they negotiated the differences between classical and biblical theories of versification (*Protestant Poetics* 31). However, Trapnel builds her poetic authority exclusively through reworking biblical subject matter, which is not surprising since she would have had ample opportunity to saturate herself with scripture. "We should not think of the Bible just as a book to be read, or to listen to," Hill asserts:

> It was everywhere in the lives of men, women and children. Not only in the church services they had to attend, but in the ballads they bought and sang, and in their daily surroundings . . . Biblical texts were very often painted on walls or posts in houses . . . In addition, walls were covered with printed matter--almanacs, illustrated ballads and broadsides, again often on Biblical subjects. (*The English Bible* 38)

Hill relates that even Oliver Cromwell "interrupted his pursuit of the defeated Scots after Dunbar to sing Psalm CXVII" (*The English Bible* 356). The likelihood that Trapnel was not only surrounded by scripture in her everyday life, but that, like other sectarians, she also avidly attended congregational meetings and studied the scriptures on her own explains the facility with which she manipulates biblical texts. As Mendelson and Crawford explain, "by ranging beyond their own parishes, even the illiterate could procure a sophisticated education in political as well as theological issues" (391). Trapnel's poetry, instead of being unintelligible and illiterate as her earliest critics called it, is difficult for today's reader to comprehend at the immediate level because it requires not just a high degree of familiarity with the Bible, but a deep assimilation of its various parts.[47]

---

[47] Richey makes a similar claim about the degree to which Eleanor Davies' prophecies were legible to her seventeenth-century audience (175). In 1914, the bookseller Dobell, who speculates that Trapnel was the "first woman preacher of whom we have any record," comments in reference to her verse, that "It need hardly be said that the lady's verse is very wretched stuff, the rime and reason of which are about equally defective." Furthermore, he asserts that *The Cry of a Stone* and the untitled Bodleian folio both consist of "illiterate and incoherent religious rhapsodies" (Dobell, "A Unique Book: Anna Trapnel" 222, 221).

After commenting on the biblical saturation of Milton's writings, Hill asserts that "Scarcely less Biblical are the writings of Levellers, notably Lilburne, of Gerard Winstanley,

Although Trapnel did not have access to a classical-humanist education at a university, her verse indicates that she was indeed highly educated: she was very practiced in biblical study during an age in which the Bible was pervasively understood as the highest authority on all subjects. "By the mid-seventeenth century," Hill writes, "English men and women had experienced a quarter of a millenium of emphasis on the sovereignty of the Scriptures as the unique source of wisdom on all subjects, including politics, and a source which must be open to everybody" (*The English Bible* 18). And the Psalms, as noted above, theoretically embraced in lyrical form all scriptural wisdom.

Lewalski asserts that "By 1640 there were well over three hundred editions (in several versions) of the complete psalter in English verse" (*Protestant Poetics* 39). The Sternhold-Hopkins psalter, composed mostly in ballad meter and printed in editions of varying price and quality, was the most widely used and was the psalter with which Trapnel was most likely to be familiar.[48] The cultural legibility and intricacy of her verse become simultaneously evident in light of its relationship to that found in the Sternhold-Hopkins psalter. Formally, for example, Trapnel's verse has much in common with it. The ballad meter that Trapnel uses is also used in most of the metrical translations in this most popular of psalters.[49] The rhymes that both employ also depend upon simple, monosyllabic words that were probably considered easier to sing and to remember than more complicated rhymes. Likewise, the psalter and Trapnel's lyrics share a tendency towards repetition (thematically, structurally, and in vocabulary) that was probably intended to render them as accessible and memorable as possible to the widest possible audience.

Noting the formal similarities between the Fifth Monarchist's songs and the Sternhold-Hopkins psalter calls attention to the interesting

---

of Ranters and especially of Fifth Monarchists" (*The English Bible* 21). Trapnel's verse would seem more approachable and more impressive if it were printed in a modern edition with the kinds of exegetical aids used in editions of Milton's works. Interestingly, Dobell also sees reason to compare Trapnel's verse with Milton's: "In one of her discourses she reports a dialogue between the Father and the Son, in which they discuss the question of the Fall of Man and the means of his redemption. This might have been thought to approach pretty closely to blasphemy, had not Milton followed in the lady's example--of course, in verse infinitely superior to hers, but not (if I dare to say so) with much more success in point of good sense or good taste" (Catalogue 30).

[48] On the popularity of the Sternhold-Hopkins psalter, see Hill, *The English Bible* 341 and Lewalski, *Protestant Poetics* 39. For more on the Psalms, in general, see Hill, *The English Bible* 351-61 and Lewalski, *Protestant Poetics* 39-52.

[49] The Sternhold-Hopkins psalter, however, does include some formal variation; see esp. Psalms CXI, CXX, CXXII, CXXI, CXXXVI, and CXLVII. All references to particular Psalms in this section are to the 1653 edition of Sternhold-Hopkins.

possibility that Trapnel sang her psalms in a manner similar to the selective, cyclical way in which a congregation might move through a psalter. Trapnel's poetry seems like a veritable "avalanche of language"--and therefore potentially evidence of insanity or fradulent transcription--if one forgets that she sang across several hours each day, taking breaks, and that some of her works represent weeks of singing (Hobby 34). The cramped format of her verse on the page, especially in the cases of *A Voice for the King of Saints and Nations* and the untitled folio, can suggest that her words came forth with as little time between them as there is little physical space on the page between each line.[50] The visual similarity of the distribution of type in Trapnel's books of verse and a 1653 edition of the Sternhold-Hopkins psalter, however, serves as an important reminder that Trapnel's verse may look like an avalanche of words because it was necessary to print as many lines as possible per page to reduce costs. The likelihoods that the psalter was an important model for Trapnel and that congregations and individuals who used Sternhold-Hopkins would have selected particular psalms to read or sing suggests that Trapnel composed, song by song, her own version of a specifically Fifth Monarchist psalter.

There is also significant stylistic overlap between Sternhold-Hopkins and Trapnel's songs. Trapnel's use of water imagery, for instance, especially images of the sea and floods, could have been influenced by the Psalms, as might her occasional cataloguing of God's creations and of creatures praising God.[51] Most significantly, however, the indeterminacy of the speaking position in Trapnel's poetry has a precedent in the Psalms. The poetic speaker in the Book of Psalms shifts from using "I" as singer and God's messenger to ventriloquizing God and impersonating other speaking subjects. The poetic personae in the Psalms directly address God and also warn and chastise human listeners, claiming, as does Trapnel, to teach, preach, and publish God's word.[52] Trapnel's songs also have much in

---

[50] Reacting, apparently, to the cramped visual format of *The Cry of a Stone*, the editors of *Kissing the Rod* explain that it "consists of a narration describing Trapnel's visionary behaviours, interspersed with transcriptions of her ravings, taken down as she uttered them extempore, hundreds of lines at a time, as far as one can gather without drawing breath" (178). While I am aware that *The Cry of a Stone* implies that Trapnel often spoke so quickly that her amanuensis (called the "relator") admits an inability to transcribe everything she says, I would contend that the relator's comments about the conditions of transcription ("the lownesse of her voice, and the noise of the people"; "the press of the people in the Chamber") are, in part, a rhetorical strategy to augment the realism, credibility, and drama of the scene of Trapnel's prophesying (58, 19).

[51] For water imagery, cf. Psalms XLVI, CVII; for the practice of cataloguing, cf. Psalms VIII, XCVIII, CIV, CXLVIII.

[52] For the use of "I" as singer and God's messenger; direct addresses to God; warnings to the audience; and the claim to teach, preach, and publish, cf. Psalms VI, IX,

common with the Sternhold-Hopkins psalter thematically. Trapnel appropriates the psalter's references to wicked, ungodly men, for instance, in order to chastise Cromwell and his followers, and she adapts the psalter's language of political subversion to fit the Fifth Monarchist agenda. The Psalms include material corresponding perfectly with the Fifth Monarchist claims that only Jesus is king and that God will replace all earthly kings.[53] Likewise, the Psalms share the Fifth Monarchist interest in economic concerns and Trapnel's particular interest in divine voices.[54]

The significant thematic differences between Trapnel's lyrics and the Sternhold-Hopkins psalter, however, also indicate that the shipwright's daughter did not simply borrow from it uncritically; she shaped its themes to fit her needs. For instance, while the psalter sometimes claims that God will save the poor, it also occasionally suggests that the poor are sinners who have received their proper reward and those who are rich and generous are the most godly.[55] While the Psalms express millenarian beliefs, they also thank God for securing David's earthly kingdom; the psalmist displays a very explicit will-to-power on his own behalf.[56] While Trapnel and the psalmist both use military imagery, she does not--as he does--indicate a personal intention to fight physically to secure the proper kingdom.[57] The political language invoked in the Psalms could easily be used to support the divine right of earthly kings, the justification of royal lines of succession, the requirement of passive tolerance for evil kings, and other attributes of absolute rule.[58] Trapnel filters out these aspects of the Psalms that contradict her political and theological beliefs.

Trapnel's songs also gain legibility and significance in their tangential relationship to the lyric compositions of several leaders of the

---

XIX, XXII, XXXI, XXXIV, XXXVIII, XLIII, XLIX, LI, LVII, LXX, LXXCIIII, LXXXVI, XCII, CVIII, CXIX, CXLV, CXLVII. For the Psalmist's ventriloquization of God and impersonation of other speaking subjects, cf. L, LXXXI, LXXXII, LXXXIX, XCI.

[53] For references to wicked, ungodly men, cf. Psalms I, XXI, XXXII; for politically subversive language, cf. Psalms II, XVII, XVIII, XXIX, LII, LXXVI, LXXXIX, XCII, CXXI, CXLIV.

[54] For economic concerns, cf. Psalms IIII, IX, X, XV, XVI, XXXVII, XLI, XLII, XLIX, LXXII; for comments on proper speech, divine voices, unruly tongues, cf. Psalms, XII, XXIX, XXXIII, XXXIX, XL, XLV, LXIV, LXVI, LXIX, LXXI, LXXVII.

[55] See above note on economic concerns in the Psalms.

[56] See above note on the language of political subversion in the Psalms. For millenarian claims in the Psalms, cf. VII, X, L, LXVIII, CII.

[57] For military imagery, cf. Psalms XVIII, XXI, CXLIV.

[58] It is thus not surprising that there exists a selection of Psalms translated by King James and authorized for publication by Charles I. For more on Royalist translations of the Psalms, see Hill, *The English Bible* 360-2. See Hannay, esp. 82-97, on how Mary Sidney, Countess of Pembroke, reworks the Psalms in her metrical translations to privilege the values and perspectives of a courtier of rank.

Fifth Monarchist movement: Vavasor Powell, Morgan Llwyd, and Christopher Feake.[59] Feake and possibly Powell were educated in university environments in which lyrics were circulated in manuscript.[60] In fact, the possibility that they would have known about this practice and the frequently anti-puritan, Royalist content of such lyrics suggests that their composition of verse was meant to counteract those poems created within poetic coteries having ideologies opposing the Fifth Monarchists.[61] Given Trapnel's self-comparison to Feake and Powell upon her imprisonment and her carefully maneuvered public preaching, it is possible that she composed her songs, on one level, to affiliate herself further with the male leaders of her group.[62]

While the poetry of Trapnel and the male Fifth Monarchist leaders shares the same political thrust and certain formal features (e.g., simple diction and rhymes, and the frequent use of ballad meter), Trapnel's lyrics differ significantly from theirs.[63] Most importantly, those male leaders write short, discrete lyrics, which tend to fall clearly into the categories of metrical translation of scripture, poetic meditation on a scriptural verse or idea, or personal religious meditations employing non-scriptural figures. Hence, they indicate their sources if they write a meditation on a biblical theme and do not claim that their own verse is divine. Their poetry constitutes a display of earthly learning whether it calls attention to its precision in translation or to its poetic prowess. In *The Bird in the Cage, Chirping*, for instance, Powell includes his metrical translation of the Lamentations of Jeremiah. He signals the straightforward relationship between that biblical text and his own by naming his paraphrase, aptly enough, "The Lamentations of Jeremiah in Meeter." He breaks his translation into chapters and verses and includes occasional marginal glosses referencing the Hebrew version. Similarly, Llwyd, who wrote at

---

[59] Llwyd worked closely with Powell. Capp specifies that "Powell and Llwyd were responsible for the whole movement in North Wales" (78). On the poetry of Powell and Llwyd, see Smith, *Literature and Revolution* 268-75.

[60] For more on the education of these Fifth Monarchists, see Capp 94, 248-9, 259; on the transmission of verse in manuscript in university environments, see Marotti, *Manuscript* 31-5.

[61] See Marotti, *Manuscript* 75-133.

[62] Capp indicates that Trapnel was associated with a number of officers and gentlemen (102, 111). Lewalski's comment about Donne's view of the Psalms is compelling in light of Trapnel's lyric preaching: " . . . Donne developed in the sermons an impressive theoretical basis for regarding the Book of Psalms as the central model for the religious lyric poet and the preacher" (*Protestant Poetics* 52).

[63] The poem by a male Fifth Monarchist most similar to Trapnel's songs is "Mr Feakes Hymne: August ye 11: 1653 Christ Church," a hymn in ballad meter transcribed in a manuscript.

least 52 lyrics in Welsh and English that are collected together in *Gweithiau*, calls one "A Hymne Upon I. COR. I. 30" (17) and another "Canticls. [sic] Some Select Verses on the Song of Songs, or the Churches Hymn after Breaking Bread" (10-11). Such poems display learning in their references to specific verses in or books of the Bible and distinguish between their own mundane responses to scripture and the divine word itself. The male Fifth Monarchist leaders also use non-scriptural tropes fairly often. Llwyd, for example, writes a set of lyrics divided according to the seasons (19-31) and includes this nationalistic bird imagery in "The Excuse":

> All English swans that are alive and Scottish
>   cuckowes sing
> and some Welsh swallowes chirpe and chime
>   to welcome pleasant spring
> The chickens now are lifted up, upon that
>   eagles wing . . . (7-9)

Similarly, Powell structures the beginning of his verse meditation "A true CHRISTIANS PILGRIMAGE, Or, AFFLICTED-STATE" around the conceit of the believer as a sun-dial:

> O Glorious *Sun* that run'st with joy thy race!
> And daily shewst the world thy goodly face,
> Shine forth upon my *Dyal* (tho but clay)
> That I may rightly know the time of Day.
> I thought it was scarce *Noon*, but now I see,
> The shadows of the *Evening* covering me. (1-6)

Even for this poem, which ultimately incorporates scriptural images as well as this more secular one, Powell provides scholarly glosses indicating the poem's allegorical dimensions.

Unlike her fellow radical sectarians' verse, Trapnel's claims to be divine rather than calling attention to the difference between it and scripture, and it pushes the notion of plain speech to its limit by almost exclusively using figurative language found in the Bible (when it uses any obviously figurative language at all).[64] Any show of mundane learning in the style of her male counterparts, of course, would disrupt the logical consistency of her role as God's handmaid. Trapnel's particular, complex style of appropriating scripture is especially evident in *A Voice for the King*

---

[64] One might argue that Trapnel's untitled folio of verse works towards being a biblical compendium much like David's Psalms themselves.

of Saints and Nations (1658). In the first segment of this work, she appropriates the tropes and themes of the Song of Songs and fuses her imitation of its repetitive, cyclical construction with the ballad meter and simple vocabulary that her psalms share with the Sternhold-Hopkins psalter; ultimately, her adaptation of Canticles justifies her own public speech and underwrites her poetic production.

Like many interpreters in a long tradition of patristic, Roman Catholic, and Protestant exegetes, she represents Canticles both as a spiritual allegory and as having a narrative structure despite its (and her own resulting text's) non-linear presentation of that narrative (Lewalski, *Protestant Poetics* 59). However, unlike contemporaries who write meditations on a few lines of Canticles or provide (very careful) metrical translations of it, Trapnel blurs these categories. She neither writes a personalized, introspective meditation on a specific verse or aspect of the Song, nor attempts to translate it as accurately as possible. Her mingling of categories is significant because most poets went to great lengths to keep them separate. Because the Song of Songs, as Hill indicates, "so manifestly is not about the love of Christ for his church" (*The English Bible* 363), it inspired many annotated metrical paraphrases that attempted to limit its meanings to unquestionably theological ones.[65]

---

[65] Hill notes, for example, that Henry Ainsworth's commentary on it "[gives] his readers seventy-seven pages of comment to eleven pages of text" (*The English Bible* 365). Sir Henry Finch's *An Exposition of the Song of Songs* has a "commentary [that] amounted to five times the length of the text" (Hill, *The English Bible* 365). Furthermore, Hill reports, "In Brightman's *Commentary* the text occupies less than ten pages out of a hundred; in Cotton's *Exposition*, twelve pages out of 233 . . . The longest commentary I have encountered is that by John Collinges, published in 1676 and 1683 but almost certainly composed in the 1640s and 1650s. This [*The Intercourse of Divine Love*] runs to 1,439 pages on Chapters I and II" (*The English Bible* 368-9). For more on Canticles, see Hill, *The English Bible* 362-70.

For verse meditations on or appropriations of a verse or aspect of the Song, cf. Herbert's "The Search" and "Dullness"; Herrick's *"To His Saviour, a Child; a Present, by a child"* (N-59); Eliza's *"The Lover"*; An Collins's *"Another Song"* [*"The Winter of my infancy"*]; and Llwyd's "Canticls. Some Select Verses of the Song of Songs, or the Churches Hymne after Breaking Bread." Ranter Abiezer Coppe's prose appropriation of the Song of Songs in *The Fiery Flying Roll* describes his personal, sensual union with Christ: "externall kisses, have been made the fiery chariots, to mount me swiftly in to the bosom of him whom my soul loves . . . where I have been, where I have been, where I have been hug'd, embrac't, and kist with the kisses of his mouth, whose loves are better than wine, and have been utterly overcome therewith, beyond expression, beyond admiration" (46). Hill observes that "Ranters [an antinomian group] naturally enjoyed the Song of Songs" (*The English Bible* 366). On Lanyer's use of the figure of Christ as bridegroom, see Woods, *Lanyer: A Renaissance Woman Poet* 141-4.

By dramatizing and expanding upon key verses from Canticles, Trapnel radicalizes the figure of the spouse.[66]   According to Trapnel's portrait of her, the spouse deliberately postures herself against patriarchal authority and becomes the creative agent behind the production of the Song of Songs. By vacillating between this bold figuration of the spouse and more traditional representations of her and by alternatively identifying herself with and distinguishing herself from the spouse, Trapnel protects herself from potentially hostile reactions to her public performance while she places her poetic efforts on the same level as the Song of Songs--at the top of the biblical hierarchy of verse.

Trapnel interprets the dramatic moments in the Song of Songs in which the watchmen beat the spouse and tear her veil (Song 5:7) and the daughters of Jerusalem question the spouse about why she thinks her beloved is the most desirable lover (Song 5:9) in order both to suggest that she is very much like the spouse and to provide acceptable grounds for a woman's public speech. Whereas the Song of Songs gives no explanation for the watchmen's attack on the spouse, Trapnel interprets this incident in terms that refer to her own situation as God's handmaiden just before the Restoration:

> The spouse comes forth with lovely song,
> And it was envyed,
> What note is this thou bringest forth,
> Was to her often said.
> What spirit is this; O it is strange,
> It differeth from other,
> They did against the song complaine:
> But she sings of her lover,
> And maketh unto him complaint,
> That they at her doe strike.
> For they did tear and rent the vayl
> Of Christ's beloved wife,
> She doth complaine unto her King;
> What injuries and smites,
> O spouse my love saith he still sing,
> Thou art the married Wife,
> Matter not though they at thee throw,
> Nor what jears thou hast had,

---

[66]   For a reading of *Voice for the King* that emphasizes its intertextual relationship to Revelation, see Richey 208-11, who interprets the text as "reveal[ing], with all the authority found in otherworldly ecstasy, the place of woman in the Gospel" and as "enabling [Trapnel] to clarify . . . the origins of feminist prophecy" (208).

I will appear unto thy sight,
And in singing make glad. (A3)

Trapnel expands one verse from the Song of Songs into several quatrains of
ballad meter.   While the spouse in Canticles merely states that "The
watchmen that went about the city found me, they smote me, they wounded
me; the keepers of the walls took away my veil from me" (Song 5:7),
Trapnel implies that the spouse's attackers "[envy]" her song: "They did
against the song complaine."   Trapnel's watchmen add verbal insult to their
physical abuse of the spouse, calling her song "strange" and "jear[ing]" at
her.   These changes make the song address Trapnel's situation: her enemies,
too, ridicule her for holding forth in song.   In *The Cry of a Stone*, for
instance, she prays:

> o then what are thy thoughts O lord,--though the Enemy begin to jeer them
> concerning those blessed songs; well says God, are my people jeered
> concerning their Excellencies, their songs, their *Hallelujahs* that are of my
> own making, that are before my Throne? the Lord cannot endure that these
> Excellencies of his Saints should be trampled upon, which are so perfect,
> so pure. (16)

In *The Cry of a Stone*, the Lord defends the songs of his "[Saint]," Trapnel;
in *Voice for the King*, the King defends the songs of his spouse.   The
dialogue Trapnel inserts into *Voice for the King* (in which the spouse
complains to her beloved about the abuses that she receives on his behalf,
and he consoles her), especially in conjunction with the analogous dialogue
she relates in *The Cry of a Stone* above, legitimates Trapnel's singing
through her implied comparison to the spouse.

   According to Trapnel, the watchmen do not just tear the spouse's
veil because they oppose her singing about her beloved but because they do
not like what the spouse says about him.   Relating how "she describes her
Lord," Trapnel provides the spouse's perspective on the male beloved's
beauty:

> O he is lovely to behold,
> His Temples they do shine,
> His looks like to Pomgrannet
> They are most choice and fine. (A3)

She then conveys the watchmen's objection to the spouse's song:

> Dost thou Christ compare, say they,
> To Pomgranet dost thou,

Liken him to such things,
We cannot it allow. (2)

The watchmen specifically oppose the spouse's use of comparisons in describing her beloved; in a sense, these male representatives of the law object to the spouse's audacity in blazoning the beloved. Speaking for the spouse, however, Trapnel makes it clear with whom the powers of representation lie. "I will describe him through out," she has the spouse retort, "Even from his head to feet" (2).[67]

Not only does the spouse's singing inspire the watchmen's hostility, but Trapnel implies that the spouse sings in knowing defiance of such objectors:

The spouses eyes are opened,
And she sets out her Christ,
And sends a challenge unto all,
And saith is any like.
Her challenge it is bold and high
Is any like to him,
Hath any such a flaming eye,
There is not such a thing;
Her challenge is bold and loud,
She doth not fear her foe,
Nor what they say, nor how they smite
But praises for him flow,
She cometh forth with challenge bold,
And saith, O there is none,
Can show me one so fair as he,
He is the onely one.
O she cometh with challenge bold,
Unto professors great,
That did so much despise these things,
And so against them speak.
O he is fair, he is fair, saith she,
To me he is most dear,
She runs about her lord to seek,
None doth like him appear. (3)

The Song of Songs includes two separate incidents in which the spouse leaves her chamber at night to wander the city streets in search of her beloved (3:1-4 and 5:2-7) and a few instances in which she boasts of him

---

[67] Interestingly, other women poets also appropriate Canticles' blazoning of Christ. Cf. Eliza's *"The Lover"* and Aemilia Lanyer's *Salve Deus Rex Judaeorum* lines 1305-20.

(e.g., 2:3 and 5:10). In Trapnel's account, however, the spouse unceasingly declares Christ's singularity in a public space where her singing places her in physical danger. These stanzas exemplify Trapnel's tendency to structure her lyrics around a refrain to which she returns repeatedly and which she usually alters with each return. In this instance, the lines referring to the spouse's "challenge" that someone find a lover better than hers serve this structuring function. In returning to the word "challenge" throughout these stanzas, Trapnel emphasizes her interpretation of the spouse's behavior; Trapnel's spouse deliberately opposes the patriarchal authority that would silence her. That Trapnel had been imprisoned--as a direct consequence of her public outspokenness--for several months prior to this performance supports the notion that she would expect an audience familiar with her history to recognize the similarity between the spouse's plight and her own.

Trapnel's self-comparison with the spouse is reinforced in the last eight lines in which she claims that the spouse "cometh with challenge bold,/ Unto professors great." Nowhere in the Song of Songs does the spouse meet objections from an audience defined through their claims to specific religious beliefs; here, especially, Trapnel writes herself into the biblical text. For it is she who has met with opposition from "professors great," and it is she who frequently asserts that her own knowledge about scriptural matters is superior to institutionally approved knowledge. For example, later in this song, she asserts:

> O glorious is the vision Lord,
> Of the latter dayes time,
> And yet this generation,
> Doth not the vision minde.
> Except it be through Rabbies voice
> Their wise and prudent men. (17)

Her anti-clerical stance, as discussed above, is essential to her justification of lay preaching.

Trapnel makes the comparison between herself and the spouse explicit when she clearly distinguishes her representation of the spouse's point of view from her assertion of her own perspective:

> Christ was bright to the spouse's view,
> And she did fear no harme,
> And my strength it is much renew'd
> For the same glorious arme,
> I have been layd within his breast,
> O how lovely is he,

> I must declare he is my rest;
> So did the spouse him see. (2)

Trapnel distinguishes between the spouse's voice and her own to make the implicit equation of her own singing and the spouse's evident. She even uses the text of the Song of Songs to describe her own relationship with Christ when she writes, "I have been layd within his breast" (Song 1:13). Hence, Trapnel holds in tension her relationship to the spouse; she identifies with her, but she is not identical to her. This distinction enables her to inscribe herself into scripture, in which she does not replace or displace the spouse, but through which she makes the significance of the spouse's narrative point to her own life. So much do Trapnel's experiences inflect her revision of Canticles that she represents the spouse's relationship to the Song of Songs such that, in a strictly theological sense, she, like Trapnel herself, is merely the passive conduit for the outpouring of the Holy Spirit. Trapnel tells her audience that "Christ doth cause her [the spouse] thus to sing" (2). Apparently, the spouse, too, is but God's handmaiden. To emphasize this interpretation, Trapnel dramatizes the lines from the Song of Songs in which the male beloved comes to the spouse's door for a nighttime visit and then disappears (5:2-6) so that this moment becomes the spouse's spiritual awakening:

> She know's that the King had been there;
> It was his very touch,
> Because the King had drawne her heart,
> She therefore loved much.
> It was the King opened her eyes,
> And caused obedience,
> And presently she sung of him
> With a deep loving sence. (2)

In Trapnel's version, the spouse knows that her beloved is the type of Christ, and she runs out into the city streets at night to search for him not primarily out of sensual desire, as the Song of Songs would suggest, but out of obedience. This moment of opening--the opening of the door in Canticles transforming into the opening of the spouse's eyes in Trapnel's reading of the poem--causes the spouse to sing. The spouse, this interpretation suggests, sings of Christ because she is extraordinarily compelled to do so.

Trapnel protects her unusual appropriation of the best of lyrics, the Song of Songs, by suggesting that the Holy Spirit is actually the creative agent behind both "great" poems:

Think not that poor one here doth speak,
Be not at it displeas'd.
Though the vessell be very meane,
Wherein this Counsell be

....
O it is not of Creatures make

....
It gives counsell to all,
It doth not lead from Scripture rule;
But doth poor sinners call.
O the King liketh well of it

....
O what am I, O what am I,
But a poor silly one,
A bruised reed thou mak'st abide,
That cannot stand alone;
But o my strength is from above,
It doth come forth from thee;
Which makes me so inflam'd with love,
And so in singing be. (21)

Trapnel includes almost every imaginable excuse to reinforce the premise
that she has not created her songs herself. She is just a "vessell . . . very
meane," "a poor silly one," "A bruised reed . . . That cannot stand alone." In
fact, she does not really speak at all: the audience must "Think not that
poor one here doth speak," for her poetry "is not of Creatures make." The
Holy Spirit *makes* her "so in singing be." Although what she speaks may
"[give] counsell to all/ It doth not lead from Scripture rule." Here she does
not presume to teach or advise her audience, and even if her words do
provide spiritual instruction, she insists that they accord perfectly with
scripture. Most importantly, "the King liketh well of" her verse; mere
creatures, therefore, ought not object to it.

Despite this series of disclaimers and qualifiers, immediately
following these stanzas Trapnel betrays an authorial interest in her poetic
creations. She directs her words to God, praying:

Lord thou giv'st much, and here dost come,
Thanks be given to thee.
O take it, I it here present,
Its thine, its not from me,
And thou sayest so I will dear Child,
Then Father, I am content,
To suffer for thy sake awhile,
And for thee to be spent. (21-22)

In thanking God for his gifts, Trapnel offers him a gift in return. "O take it," she says, "I it here present." Although the pronoun "it" is somewhat ambiguous, the greater context of this section rife with protestations that her verse comes from the Spirit suggests that "it" is that verse. Although Trapnel claims that "Its thine, its not from me," her proposition that she will make of God's gift to her a gift to him reveals a sense of ownership of her verse. If Lady Mary Carey and the shipwright's daughter have little else in common, they share this poetic tactic for circumventing the notion that all creation belongs to God. The paradox of the gift exchange that Trapnel suggests points to the conventionality of ascribing her poetic agency to God as a strategy for keeping her audience and maintaining her "prophetic" credibility; she thereby maintains the illusion that she does not overstep her prescribed womanly bounds despite her public poetic utterances. Her scripting of God's acceptance of her "gift" of his own verse--"And thou sayst so I will dear Child"--is ironic given Trapnel's series of disclaimers that God speaks through her.

A second look at Trapnel's description of the event that initiates the spouse's singing--the revelation that sends her into the night to seek her beloved--reveals a similar possibility for reading an assertion of the spouse's poetic agency against the grain of the theological premise of her passivity. Christ's role in the production of the spouse's song is analogous to the function of the beloved-as-Muse in courtly love poetry. Describing the occasion in which the spouse leaves her chamber at night to seek her beloved, Trapnel relates that the spouse "loved much" "[b]ecause the King had drawne her heart" (2). Much as the female beloved in the courtly love tradition has the capacity to steal the male lover's heart, Christ or "the King" "[draws]" out the spouse's heart. That the spouse's love for her beloved results in her singing about him--"presently she sung of him/ With a deep loving sence" (2)--likewise parallels the manner in which the courtly male lover produces poetry to express and assuage his desire. Furthermore, Trapnel's refrain during this segment--"It was the King opened her eyes" (2) --sanctions the spouse's poetic objectification of him while it simultaneously recognizes Christ as the source of her revelation in the theological sense. The "King" might have agency in "open[ing] her eyes," but she subjects him to her gaze:

> It was the King opened her eyes,
> And then she viewed him thus,
> And so described every part,
> For her soul loved much;
> She describeth his teeth and eyes
> His Temples that are rare,

His head, and mouth, and saith of him
There's nothing can compare. (3)

The spouse's revelation grants her descriptive power over the male beloved; her eyes opened, she blazons her lover.

Trapnel begins *A Voice for the King of Saints and Nations* with the assertion that "The Spirit doth come in the way,/ That the spouse did before." This elegantly simple first couplet is theologically complex. In a condensed form, Trapnel states her typological, millenarian interpretation of the Song of Songs: the words of the spouse in the Old Testament Book of Canticles prefigure the announcements and workings of the Holy Spirit in the New Testament. This first couplet appropriately frames Trapnel's poem because its parallel structure suggests a comparison between the Spirit and the spouse, implying a similarity between their respective creative agencies --a bold implication to make on behalf of the spouse. By referring first to the Spirit and then to the spouse, Trapnel creates tension around questions of priority and authority and thereby contains the potential theological paradox in the statement that the Spirit--which, in Christian belief, pre-exists Creation itself--actually follows a precedent established by the spouse. Trapnel plays this tension to her advantage throughout her revision of Canticles: her figuration of and vacillating identification with the spouse offer the possibility of reading the spouse as an example of female creative agency underwriting Trapnel's own poetic enterprise.

Chapter 4

Penelope, Prophet, or Poet? Strategic Self-Figurations in Katherine Austen's "Book M"

"ffor my part," Katherine Austen explains in her commonplace book, "Book M," "I declined all things might give a vaine encouradgement and told him I was like pennelope, always Employed" (96r).[1] Through her allusion to *The Odyssey*'s Penelope, this wealthy widow signals to a persistent suitor that his efforts are hopeless. Austen's transcription of his response indicates that the significance of her classical reference did not escape him: "I, ses he, her lovers could not abide her for it" (96r). Being Penelope, it seems, makes suitors impatient. Austen's invocation of this mythic model of the faithful wife not only served her immediate purpose of discouraging an unwanted prospective second husband; it also reveals much about her self-representation--the complicated and strategic nature of which will be the focus of this chapter.

Austen, who lived from 1628 until 1683, resided in London during the tumultuous events of the Civil War and Restoration. She was from a wealthy mercantile family and married Thomas Austen, a man of similar wealth and rank. She and Thomas shared a strong interest in increasing their socioeconomic standing. However, Thomas did not live long enough for them to satisfy their interest during his lifetime. He died in 1658, leaving their children and property under her management, which included hiring lawyers and attending hearings at Parliament to fight for possession of an estate, building houses as investment properties, and investing in the

---

[1]   In transcribing Austen's manuscript, I have attempted to preserve its characteristics while making it accessible. I have added light punctuation for the sake of clarity, expanded some abbreviated words (using brackets), broken unusual compound words in two, and placed "<>" marks around Austen's interlinear revisions. For alternative transcriptions of excerpts from "Book M," see Todd, "A Young Widow" 215-37, Houlbrooke 79, and Stevenson and Davidson 313-16.

East India Company. Thomas's will restricted her ability to marry for seven years--a detail which gave "seven" a special significance for Katherine.[2]

Austen was very concerned with status and social propriety; "Book M" suggests that she was anxious to display the proper appearances associated with having a high social rank and that her anxieties about her social status were compounded by her status as a widow. Her manuscript reveals that when she became a widow, she became acutely aware of her gender as a liability, because she discovered how it rendered her less capable of protecting her material holdings than her late husband was. While I do not claim that Austen, as a result of the changes that widowhood brought to her life, became actively conscious of the conflicts between her status (and her ambitions for ever higher rank) and her gender, I show that the inconsistencies engendered by this conflict underpin Austen's complicated, discontinuous self-representations, which she often presents in the form of lyrics.[3] In "Book M" Austen mobilizes simultaneously at least three such discontinuous figurations of herself--as Penelope or assailed widow, as powerful prophet, and as amateur poet--in order to negotiate between her gender and her rank. Ultimately, Austen's verse performs the advance in social rank so important to her and so jeopardized, in her view, by her gender.[4]

Like Penelope, Austen was left to manage property in the absence of her husband. The early modern English woman refers to her ancient Greek counterpart specifically to signify that she has no interest in remarrying, that she, too, exemplifies the faithful wife. More importantly,

---

[2] Sources for this biographical information include Austen, Todd, "A Young Widow," 207-11 and "The Remarrying Widow" 76-7. Todd specifies that her most important sources are "the Orphans Finding Book and Account Book of Money Received for Orphans (Corporation of London Record Office Mss. 93C and 94A) and the wills of Thomas and Katherine Austen in the Public Record Office, PROB 11/285/388 and PROB 11/PROB 11/375/1" ("A Young Widow of London" 214n1). Stevenson and Davidson's anthology of early modern women poets' works also includes biographical information about Austen (313-14).

[3] On the theoretical incompatibility between the notion that a man and woman can have equal rank and the ideology of gender hierarchy, see Jordan, "Renaissance Women and the Question of Class," 94. Also see Mendelson and Crawford 55-8 and 349-65 on the complicated relationship between gender and status. While Todd reads Austen's text as "offer[ing] direct insight into [her] mind," suggesting that "Book M" acts as a widow looking onto her thoughts and emotions, I propose that Austen strategically fashions portraits of herself in her manuscript ("A Young Widow" 207). Hence, I do not assume that "Book M" gives us unmediated access to Austen's internal states.

[4] On Austen's ambition, also see Todd, "A Young Widow of London" 209, 212, 215.

however, by comparing herself with Penelope, Austen reveals her acute awareness of the economics underpinning marriage. If she "was like pennelope" (96r), then her suitor must be like an unwelcome guest in Ithaca: he is analogous to those visitors who drain Penelope's resources and who hope to marry her primarily to access Odysseus' riches and power. By referring to Penelope, however, Austen does not just express suspicion of her suitor's potentially economic motivation for wooing her. Her self-figuration as Penelope exposes an inconsistency in her portrait of herself as a gentle, assailable widow, which I discuss in detail below. Austen's concern throughout her manuscript with acquiring and retaining property and with shoring up her social status suggests that her self-figuration as Penelope is an especially condensed trope through which she constructs an image of herself as a wealthy, powerful woman. If Austen is like Penelope, then she is like a queen (even if Penelope's realm is relatively small and unproductive).[5]

Why would Austen--a wealthy widow--need to imagine for herself a less assailable, more powerful social role than the one that she actually had? Why would she represent herself, in part, as weak to further her interest in power? One reason relates to the ambiguity surrounding Austen's actual social rank, which seems difficult to define precisely. Sara Mendelson, for instance, categorizes her as a gentlewoman (183 and 205n13), while Barbara Todd indicates that she and her family aspired to become members of the gentry. It is clear that "she was well-to-do by contemporary standards" (Todd, "A Young Widow" 209), but it is also clear that she was anxious to gain the highest social status that she could. One factor that potentially complicated Austen's social status was the amorphousness of "gentry" as a category. After analyzing the many complications involved in defining this social rank, Felicity Heal and Clive Holmes declare, "At the risk of tautology, we therefore must conclude that the gentry were that body of men and women whose gentility was acknowledged by others" (19).[6] Austen's anxieties about rank seem related to the "[f]lexible definitions of gentility" that Heal and Holmes discuss as "a necessary feature of the rather mobile society of early modern England" (9); to the need for others'

---

[5] For an extensive analysis of Catherine de' Medici's self-presentation as Artemisia, another ancient figure of the widow, see ffolliott.

[6] "[L]and, lordship and local acknowledgment" and wealth are among the most important partial criteria defining the gentry; however, virtue, "blood lineage and the ability to exercise martial skills" could also be considered essential attributes (Heal and Holmes 7, 9). For a more complete discussion of the complexities involved in defining the "gentry," see Heal and Holmes 6-19.

recognition as a measure of social status; and to her family's lack of qualities especially crucial for gaining recognition as gentry (e.g., having a public office, which Todd seems to use as one definitive criterion for establishing rank ["A Young Widow" 210]).

Gender could further complicate matters of rank. Constance Jordan's explanation of the problem encountered by Renaissance social theorists who suggested that men and women of the same rank were equals reveals the incompatibility between this notion and theories of gender hierarchy:

> In theory such writers proposed a social and (in some cases) political equality between men and women of the same rank. Here the relevant variable was not sex, but blood, or its mystical equivalent, which conferred upon or exacted from a person of a certain rank a correlative kind of behavior. Reasoning along these lines preserved the social hierarchy at its most public aspect, but tended to confound its domestic and private expression. The notions of "gentle" and "common" were no longer qualified by sex; the political implications of "male" and "female" were accordingly lost. ("Renaissance Women and the Question of Class" 94)

Given these observations, especially in conjunction with the uncertain status of Austen's material holdings, her pervasive anxieties about increasing her rank are less surprising.[7] However, those anxieties may seem unnecessary in light of Austen's widowhood, since widows are usually considered exceptions to the rule that early modern women were disenfranchised as a group.[8] Yet Austen's self-portrait as a widow suggests that a widow's place

---

[7] An episode that Austen relates in which a male pedestrian calls her an "old goat" illustrates her frustration when the outward signs of her wealth--her coach, for instance--do not guarantee respect: "Surely I have not deserved in my conversation among men his most abusive and Scandalous Speech. I ride in my coach while I dare to let the way be so bad for them to walke./. old goat. The rudest Speech not proceeding from a gentleman as he pretends but from a Hinde, a Soughter" (22v). Her angry response to the pedestrian's insult is to deny his gentle status, a gesture that suggests her awareness of the ideal correspondence between decorous behavior and rank. Sidonie Smith's analysis of Margaret Cavendish's relationship to her coach resonates provocatively with Austen's story. Smith explains, in reference to Cavendish: "Thus, for an 'ideal' woman cloistered within the protective walls of bashfulness but desiring an audience larger than her Lord to validate her true originality, the carriage becomes the vehicle that promises both assertive self-display and the requisite self-concealment of an inner goodness so critical to the chaste, virtuous woman" (126).

[8] See, for instance, Constance Jordan's "Women and the Question of Class" esp. 104n3 and her *Renaissance Feminism: Literary Texts and Political Models* esp. 46, 71-2. Mendelson and Crawford contradict this view: "Isolation, loneliness, poverty, and increasing

in society could be difficult to define, especially if, like Austen, she were to oppose the dominant cultural stereotype of the wealthy widow as insubordinate and licentious.[9]

Austen's choice in figuring herself as Penelope is particularly compelling because it suggests a parallel between the ways in which these women are "always Employed" (96r)--between the English widow's writing practices in composing "Book M" and the mythical Greek noblewoman's endlessly incomplete weaving, whereby she held her suitors at bay by weaving during the day and surreptitiously unraveling her work at night.[10] Because "Book M" is a commonplace book, the process by which Austen produced it is similarly non-linear. It represents a process of transcribing, writing, revising; it is a document of variable, uneven accretion, bearing marks of retreat as well as advancement. Given the regularity with which Austen took up her pen, she must have derived humorous satisfaction from her punning declaration of *Pen*elope as her classical analogue. Despite the fact that "Book M" is not an autobiography in the modern sense, I will demonstrate that through it Austen negotiates the conflicts between her status (and her ambitions for ever higher rank) and her gender by strategically figuring herself as an innocuous, vulnerable widow; as a visionary upon whom God has bestowed special revelations; and as a poet whose authority is linked to the status conferred by land and wealth.[11] Although all of these roles advance Austen's interest in social status and personal power, they do so in different, sometimes contradictory

---

dependence may have been the lot of many widows in seventeenth-century England; independence and autonomy were enjoyed by only a few" (184).

[9] Conger describes the peculiar social location of the widow: "Widows presented a particular problem in that they were neither maiden nor wife, neither yoked nor independent, neither mother nor father. Widows, therefore, did not fit anywhere in a well-ordered hierarchical society. Or maybe the problem was not that they were none of these things but rather that they were all of these things" (57). Also see Conger 24-5, 119, 121.

[10] The possibility that Austen could have known Robert Green's *Penelope's Web*, which relates stories told among Penelope and the women of her household as they unravel the winding cloth by night, reinforces the relevance of the widow's self-comparison to Penelope since that work emphasizes Penelope as a producer of texts, as well as textiles.

[11] de Grazia, Quilligan, and Stallybrass write, "even in recent critiques of Renaissance autonomy, the focus has remained the same: the subject at center and the object beyond the pale. What happens, we wish to ask, once the object is brought into view? What new configurations will emerge when subject and object are kept in relation?" (2) As we will see, Austen's self-figurations, especially that of herself as poet, depend upon her awareness of the way in which things--her material possessions, particularly land--underwrite her social identity. For especially insightful arguments on similar topics, see de Grazia's "The Ideology of Superfluous Things: *King Lear* as Period Piece" and Montrose.

and disconnected, ways. As we will see, there are significant differences among the helpless, persecuted widow who calls on God's help; the visionary whose divinely inspired dreams provide her with extraordinary knowledge of the workings of human mortality, the outcomes of legal contests, and the business of the nation; and the poet who produces verse that simultaneously performs and legitimates Austen's desire for higher status. Before analyzing Austen's self-figurations, however, it will be helpful to gain a more detailed understanding of her manuscript, "Book M."

"Book M"

"Book M" includes Austen's spiritual meditations, sermon notes, comments on her economic status and business affairs, family correspondence, and about thirty-five occasional and religious poems. Austen's commonplace book thus supports Marotti's observation that "[t]ypically, lyrics were inserted in books given over to other sorts of texts" (*Manuscript* 17). Making an example of Bod. MS Douce 280, the commonplace book of John Ramsey, Marotti also indicates that although a manuscript may contain relatively few lyrics, they "are certainly embedded in a context of an individual's intellectual, political, and familial, as well as literary interests" (*Manuscript* 21). While any writing in a commonplace book has a potentially significant relationship to the owner and can reflect her or his interests, the variable nature of those contents can complicate the question of what an individual owner transcribed or summarized and what she or he actually composed. Austen cites sources for enough of the contents of "Book M" to suggest that when she leaves a text uncited, it is likely that she wrote it herself. For instance, her sermon notes--whether copied from a printed document, memorially reconstructed from an oral performance, or composed by Austen herself according to a broad theme introduced by the sermon--usually include the name of a spiritual leader in the title, e.g. "Sermon: Doc: ffeatlyes" (17r) or "Obser[vation]:of The Last Judgement: D: Taylor:" (30r). In one instance, she precisely references a recorded text by adding, "these too Last [Sides] out of Doc Taylour of presidents of Gods way for our help" (37v). Austen cites an author for only one of the poems in "Book M": "Out of a poeme of Doc Corbets: to his ffriend when she might be a Widow:" (71v). As we will see, Austen's inclusion of this excerpt is as significant as her own verse on the theme of widowhood insofar as "Book M" provides a specialized context for interpreting the fragment. While a few of Austen's poems (especially those entitled

"Meditation") are so generic that anyone could have written them, many of them refer so specifically to autobiographical events that Austen's authorship seems clear.

The marks of revision also suggest that Austen composed much of its contents.[12] She wrote "Book M" primarily between 1664 and 1666, and she appears to have returned to it periodically, editing and amending it, until at least 1682.[13] Not only are her editorial revisions visible on several of her poems, but she also methodically struck out one long poem, to the point of illegibility, line by line.[14] The differing quality of the ink across a single page in some cases also suggests that she added to older compositions or transcriptions at a later date. In fact, she explicitly comments on her practice of reviewing her writings:

> When I view over the assurances and hopes I have had in this book of my meditations As Sometimes I am puting on wreathes of Victory, I have overcome my Enemies and my feares But such is the Unsurenes of Every ground in this World to Anchor on as I Soone come to wade in deep places againe. The Moone hath not more variations then the affaires of this life. Then the Ebes and flowes of ffortune. (Austen 112v)

Writing and reading her life are thus ongoing organizational and analytical practices for Austen: she reviews her compilation of texts and categorizes them according to the degree to which they represent success or failure, good fortune or bad.

Using such writing to organize one's life conceptually, especially to isolate the providential workings of God, was typical of seventeenth-century spiritual meditations.[15] Many of Austen's poems entitled "Meditation"

---

[12] Todd claims that Austen's poems "were carefully transcribed from other notebooks [of Austen's]" ("A Young Widow" 207).

[13] Austen indicates 1664 as the starting date for her entries in "Book M" in its prefatory pages. Most of the ensuing dates that she mentions range between 1664 and 1666. At the bottom of folio 10v, however, she includes an account of a dream that she heads "1682 Sr Edward Thurland." There are three other entries on the same page, all of which concern supernatural occurrences. Austen thus appears to have added the last dream account years after she started composing "Book M." The fact that she included it with similar texts exemplifies her efforts--visible elsewhere as well--towards organizing her book in a manner that was meaningful to her.

[14] On poems struck out in other manuscripts, see Ezell, *Social Authorship and the Advent of Print* 30, 33.

[15] Mendelson explains that "[t]he providential interpretation of life's accidents which moulded contemporary spiritual diaries offered a coherent and satisfying explanation of world-historical events. It could also transform an outwardly dull and unhappy life into

discover a divine hand in seemingly bad events; such verse makes a claim for transcendent purpose underpinning misfortune. Austen's occasional poem "On My ffall off the Tree" is an especially rich example of her dramatization of her daily experience through figuring herself at the center of a cosmic battle between forces of good and evil; providence, intervening to save her, effectively serves--figuratively speaking--as a kind of knight in shining armor (98v-9r). In the above passage in which Austen reflects on "Book M" as a whole, however, providence is strangely absent, and Austen is left with the stark, uncertain changeability of life (figured alternatively as the sea and moon). Her revisionary glance at her commonplace book exposes the constantly fluctuating emendations of her life, in which she discerns not the hidden yet ultimately straightforward trajectory delineated by providence but "the Ebes and flowes of ffortune." That Austen sees her compilation of texts in "Book M" as representing her life is essential to my argument about the different roles that she constructs for herself to negotiate the contradictions inherent in her position as a socially and economically ambitious widow.

Austen's composition of occasional poems not only represents a specialized effort at documenting, organizing, and analyzing her life, but it also overlaps with the tradition of circulating lyrics in manuscript in courtly and satellite-courtly environments--such as the universities and Inns of Court--and within the household from the Tudor period through the Restoration.[16] Although as a woman Austen could not attend a university,

---

scenes of high drama, punctuated by hairbreadth escapes from death or damnation" (186). Mendelson also indicates that "the narrative of God's mercies to the author" "helped to shape both form and content of female reminiscences" (187). On recording successful prayers, see Thomas 115 and Todd "A Young Widow" 212-13. Lewalski indicates that Anne Clifford's diary, *Life of Me*, similarly attributes many "trials, enemies, new legal claims, and providential deliverances" to Clifford's widowhood (*Writing Women* 128). Lewalski attributes Clifford's resistance to earthly patriarchy to her belief in providential design: the "firm conviction that God himself supported her claims because she was in the right enabled her to oppose the patriarchal power structure at every point while at the same time demanding that it make a place for her as a species of female paterfamilias" (*Writing Women* 133).

[16] Marotti specifies that "[m]anuscript miscellanies and poetical anthologies were kept mainly by individuals or groups of people associated with the following environments: the universities, the Inns of Court, the court, and the household or the family (by both aristocratic and middle-class individuals and their extended social circles)" (*Manuscript* 30). For more on the manuscript transmission of lyrics in these social locations and on women's participation in the circulation of lyrics, see Marotti 30-61. On women and scribal publication, see Love 54-8. On women participating in the exchange of lyrics in manuscript through coteries and for an especially helpful analysis of the unexamined and limiting assumptions that have led feminist scholars to overlook the importance of early modern women's manuscript writings, see Ezell 39-65.

her accounts in "Book M" indicate payments towards her son Thomas' education at Oxford. Moreover, a long letter to Thomas (43-4v) and her entries about her Scottish suitor reveal her awareness of university and court affairs (e.g., 97r). Conversations with her suitor, in particular, apparently made her familiar with the precariousness of a courtier's life. Although she rejects his advances, after he has died, she is more positively disposed towards him. ·Eulogizing him, she writes:

> His eminence in learning and in all the accomplishements of a gentleman for his prudence and parts might well make him arrive at high places, and to aime at promotions in England was the occasion he left ffraunce, a place where he had dwelt 18 yeares. (Austen 97r)

While Austen was neither student nor courtier, she observed such men from the periphery as they moved within their respective, overlapping public spheres. "Book M" suggests that--perhaps as a consequence of her proximity to such men--she was aware of the practices associated with circulating lyrics in manuscript in those spheres, as well as within the family.

Many scholars have recently called attention to ways in which examining lyrics produced and circulated in a manuscript environment allows us to reconceptualize lyrical production during the early modern period more broadly. Of particular importance to understanding Austen's verse is the idea that lyrics in manuscript were not conceptualized as stable, author-centered artifacts detached from specific historical and social circumstances.[17] As Marotti writes:

> In the system of manuscript transmisssion, it was normal for lyrics to elicit revisions, corrections, supplements, and answers, for they were part of an ongoing social discourse. In this environment texts were inherently malleable, escaping authorial control to enter a social world in which recipients both consciously and unconsciously altered what they received . . . In the manuscript environment the roles of author, scribe and reader overlapped . . . . (135)

---

[17]   On the significance of rethinking the early modern lyric in light of manuscript culture, see especially Ezell, Marotti, and Wall. On the notion that lyrics produced and transmitted in manuscript were not conceptualized as author-centered, textually stable, or universalizing, see Marotti, esp. 135. Also see Wall on the social construction of "the 'closed' printed work and the 'open' manuscript" (8).

Katherine Austen does not appear to have been a coterie poet like John Donne or Katherine Philips; the lyrics in "Book M" seem to have been restricted to a fairly limited sphere. Even so, her verse still reflects the practices and values of seventeenth-century manuscript culture.

As Todd observes, in "Book M" Austen composed "drafts of important letters and other personal records" ("A Young Widow" 207), which she presumably then copied and shared with her intended audiences. Jane Stevenson and Peter Davidson assert that "The book was intended to be read by her children after her death" (314). It remains unclear whether Austen circulated her poetry by copying it or allowing others to do so. However, certain of her poems appear to have had a specific audience as surely as her letters did. One can reasonably speculate, for instance, that Austen might have at least shown her sister Lady Mary Ashe the poem that she wrote when her niece Grace died. Likewise, she may have intended for her children to read her poem, "Meditation on my death." Finally, as I discuss in detail below, she circulates lines from one of her poems within the pages of "Book M" and transcribes select lines from a poem by Corbett that speak to her personal concerns as a widow, suggesting an awareness on her part of the acceptibility of editing lyrics within a manuscript context to fit one's interests.

Austen may well have imitated those "educated and fashionable gentlemen and gentlewomen" who "purchased printed poetry collections and pamphlets of individual poets' work partly to gain access to such socially restricted literary communications" (Marotti, *Manuscript* 214-5). In addition to indicating that she read some of Corbett's verse, she reveals that she read some of Donne's writings (certainly his sermons, possibly his poetry) and was familiar with legendary events concerning Donne and Sir Henry Wotton.[18] Her child loss poems (discussed in detail in Chapter Two)

---

[18] She begins a prose meditation by commenting, "The Most remarkeable points I have observed out of all the workes of Doc: Dun I doe refer to two points. Which are prosperity and Advarsity." Further down the same page, she adds, "Advarsity and prosperity: both conduce for good: And the place of riseing: and ye place of falling is most at Courts:" (91v). She includes page references after this entry: "see: pag: 13: book:C: pag-26:book [J?]:" (91v). Further research is necessary to discern whether these are other manuscripts that Austen has written or a shorthand for cataloguing the books that she owns or has read. It is intriguing that her explicit reference to Donne's writings immediately follows her prayers asking God to save her from allowing a suitor to gain her affections; perhaps Austen honed her cynicism towards courtly wooing on Donne's seduction lyrics. Austen also writes of Donne: "When D^c: Dun was in ffrance, with Sr Henery Wotten. He left his wife in Engl[and] big with child. One day the Docter was a siting a reading in a passage Roome wch had two dores. He saw his wife goe by him with a dead child in her Armes, and she lookt as paile as

and country house poem (discussed in detail below) perhaps best reveal her knowledge of the conventions associated with particular kinds of lyrics. Austen's verse meditations suggest that she frequently studied David's Psalms; she also may have become familiar with religious verse through hearing lyrics interspersed with sermons.[19]   The preacherly practice of incorporating lyrics into church services, for example, may have influenced Austen's composition of this brief poem:

> Salm. When D: Hobson preachet at Twic[kenham]:
> My think's this text speakes much to me.
> What waight I for My hopes in thee.
> Then why disquieted Then why opprest.
> While in the liveing fountaine be refreshet. (35v)

As a literate woman of means living in London, Austen had ample opportunity to encounter lyrics in different settings.

The titles and themes of many of Austen's poems reveal her awareness of the formal conventions associated with the composition of lyrics in manuscript anthologies. Marotti indicates that it was common for scribes and poets to "[attempt] to preserve the information that enabled [any given lyric] to be read in its social contexts" (*Manuscript* 15). Likewise, he writes that "[t]he manuscript environment was especially receptive to occasional poetry, especially to elegies and epitaphs about members of one's own family or social circle" (Marotti, *Manuscript* 173-4). The precise title of the poem that Austen numbers her seventh, "Upon Courtiers at ye Com[mittee] of Parlia[ment] Striving for Highbury: ye 14th ffeb: that I was there 1664," indicates, for example, her knowledge of the practice of providing contextualizing information for lyrics in manuscript, as do her country house poem, "On the Situation of Highbury"; her maternal legacy poem, "Meditation on my death"; and her child loss poems, "Dec[ember] 5: 1664 Upon Robin Austens recovery of the Smal Pox and Coronal Pop[oins?] Son John diing of them: a Youth of a very forward growth their ages the Same Popoins: 3 yeares for growth more" and "On the Death of My

---

if she had been dead. This apparition did so affright him that his hair stood up right: Sr Henry seeing him thus did not regard any Expence immediately sent poast[haste] to England. And they found that about that very time his wife was brought to bed of a dead Child very hardly Escaping her life" (11r). In addition to noting that Austen was familiar with Donne's sermons, Todd indicates that Austen refers to "Ralegh's *History of England* and Isaak Walton's *Lives*; she found inspiration in Thomas Fuller's account of the life and achievement of Hildegarde of Bingen" ("A Young Widow" 212).

   [19] For more on preachers' use of lyrics, see Wenzel.

Neece Grace Ashe 4 years." The inclusion of a title page for "Book M," and the numbering of the poems, after the first few, also point to her awareness of the formal conventions associated with verse miscellanies. Not only did Austen know the conventions associated with the transmission and preservation of verse in manuscript, but as I discuss below, her desire to rise in rank made her acutely sensitive to the social conventions corresponding to the role of the high status widow. As we will see, in fact, in the last section of this chapter, for Austen the poet, these potentially disparate sets of conventions ultimately are intertwined.

The Gentle Widow

> Men never think their wifes may be
> Neccesitate by Missery (Austen 60r)

> . . . commonly widows are so froward, so waspish, and so stubborn that thou canst not wrest them from their wills. (Swetnam 214)

A great variety of early modern English writing represented widows of high social status as seductively wealthy, sexually voracious, and absolutely uncontrollable.[20] In Shakespeare's *The Taming of the Shrew*, for example,

---

[20] While there were also many representations of low status/poor widows, they often portrayed such women as witches, rather than shrews. Willis points out that "[w]idows in some countries, including England, were represented among the accused [of witchcraft] in numbers above their proportion of the general population. . . . Most of the accused were poor, however, and had little property to pass on; English officials did not have a financial incentive to prosecute as they did in some countries" (6n6). On the stereotype of the widow, see Todd, "The Remarrying Widow," esp. 54-5 and Mendelson and Crawford 68-9. Also see Overbury's contrasting characterizations of "A Virtuous Widow" and "An Ordinary Widow" (253-4). His choice of titles alone reinforces the idea that the stereotype of the widow portrayed her negatively: he puts the "ordinary" widow in opposition to the exceptional "virtuous" one. On the connection between representations of high ranking widows' lustfulness and inappropriate (from a patriarchal perspective) second marriages in *The Duchess of Malfi* and *Hamlet*, see Jardine esp. 70-2. Jardine points out that "[i]t is the male characters who perceive free choice on the part of the female characters as an inevitable sign of irrational lust, and as the inevitable prelude to disorder and disaster" (72). For more on the actual status of Renaissance widows, see Jordan *Renaissance Feminism* esp. 46, 71-2, Keeble 252, and Mendelson and Crawford 174-84. For more on representations of widows' sexual and economic power, see Conger 87-93.

Austen is wary of accusations of impropriety. Analyzing her romantic needs, she claims that her greatest desire is not "riches" but "a person, whose soule and heart may be fit

the wealthy Widow whom Hortensio marries proves a shrew: not only will she not come when her young husband commands her presence, thereby making him lose his bet, but she also has the audacity to order him to come to her instead, embarrassing him publicly by resisting his authority in front of other men.[21] The domineering Widow's introduction into the final scene, in fact, puts Kate's "taming" into relief, while it also suggests that wealthy widows are the most shrewish of all women.   Joseph Swetnam's prose polemic *The Arraignment of Lewd, idle, froward, and unconstant Women* represents the widow as a specific, dangerous temptation to any young man who seeks wealth through marriage and provides a series of warnings against inviting an alliance with such a woman.[22]   Swetnam includes an entire section, "The Bearbaiting or the Vanity of Widows, Choose You Whether," dedicated to the evils of the widow (214-16) and provides a warning that Shakespeare's Hortensio understands too late:

> Woe be unto that unfortunate man that matcheth himself with a widow, for a widow will be the cause of a thousand woes. Yet there are many that do wish themselves no worse matched than to a rich widow. But thou dost not know what griefs thou joinest with thy gains, for if she be rich, she will look to govern, and if she be poor, then art thou plagued both with beggary and bondage . . . commonly widows are so froward, so waspish, and so stubborn that thou canst not wrest them from their wills. And if thou think to make her good by stripes, thou must beat her to death. (Swetnam 214)

In this advice to his bachelor audience, Swetnam makes explicit the connection between wealth and insubordination that Shakespeare implies: "if she be rich, she will look to govern."   Likewise, the fencing-master turned polemicist intimates that a widow cannot be tamed; in his cruel joke at the end of the passage, he makes it clear that the only "good" widow is a dead one.[23]   This stereotype of the widow as the supremely insubordinate woman has a long history.   Chaucer's Wife of Bath exemplifies the

---

for me." However, she cautions herself that it "hath a reflexion of disrepute when womens inclinations are steered all by Love."

[21] See *The Taming of the Shrew* esp. 4.2.37; 4.5.76-8; 5.2.

[22] Swetnam's pamphlet was very popular; Henderson and McManus indicate that it "ran through 10 editions by 1637 and provoked at least three defenses and a play" (16).

[23] For more on prose representations of widows, see Taylor, especially lectures 3, 4, and 7. Taylor's depictions of widows allow for the possibility that remarriage can be financially destructive to them; see Henderson and McManus 295. In *Ester Hath Hang'd Haman*, Esther Sowernam refutes the "logic" upon which Swetnam bases part of his attack on widows. For a relevant analysis of Sowernam's pamphlet, see Jordan's "Renaissance Women and the Question of Class" 100-4.

fantasized threat to patriarchy signified by a sexually active woman who makes her fortune by outliving a series of husbands and who cannot be subjugated even through her youngest (and last) husband's recourse to physical violence.[24] The misogynist cleric Janekin--Hortensio's literary precursor--becomes a long-standing model of the young man who tries to advance himself economically by marrying a wealthy, older widow but finds himself dominated by her instead.[25]

The widow's ability to remarry--which Chaucer represents as tantamount to a profession for the Wife of Bath--and to redistribute property through remarriage underpins these stereotypes of the widow as unruly and lustful. The topic of remarriage in early modern England was matter for debate, although, from a patriarchal perspective, the issue was fairly clear.[26] In *The Education of a Christian Woman*, for instance, Juan Luis Vives writes:

> It is heretical to say that second marriages should be totally rejected and condemned. That it is better to abstain than marry again is not only a counsel of Christian purity, that is, of divine wisdom, but also a recommendation of pagan, that is, human wisdom. (322)

Vives does not condemn remarriage entirely, but he weighs "wisdom" against it. Heal and Holmes observe, in fact, that "it is difficult to find a memorialist who expresses any warmth on the subject of female remarriage"(86). Representations of young men seeking financial advancement through marriage, however, such as Shakespeare's Hortensio, Swetnam's bachelor reader, and Chaucer's Janekin, indicate that from the point of view of certain men--especially young ones--the prospect of marrying a wealthy widow had its temptations.[27]

---

[24] See The Wife of Bath's Prologue and Tale esp. lines 596-632 for the intertwined representation of the Wife's age, lustfulness, and wealth in the context of her relationship to Janekin. See lines 813-22 for her domination of Janekin.

[25] The Wife's Tale, however, problematizes the patriarchal nightmare of the Prologue with a fantasy that partially reasserts male supremacy; see esp. lines 1236-56, in which the old wife rewards the rapist knight's relinquishment of husbandly mastery with her magical transformation into a beautiful, young, loyal--and most significantly--obedient wife.

[26] Conger provides a broader analysis of remarriage than this study focused on one woman's self-representations has leisure to pursue. Conger points out that "Historians of sixteenth- and seventeenth-century England and Europe generally agree that although remarriage was frequent for both sexes, it was twice as likely for widowers as for widows. Thus a significant percentage of widows did *not* remarry" (8).

[27] Marotti's contexualization of Donne's Ovidian elegies with respect to the socioeconomic desires common to young men attending the Inns of Court corresponds to

At stake in differences of opinion about second marriages was the transfer of property. According to Heal and Holmes:

> [t]he defining characteristics of the landed family lie . . . in its obsession with the continuity of the lineage through the provision of a male heir and the transmission of property in a way that provided both for the survival of the family in the long term and its success in each generation. (51)[28]

A propertied family thus faced possible internal conflicts between the immediate needs of the members of the present generation and the long-term needs of future generations. External to the family, as we have already seen, there was potential disagreement between patriarchal advocates who desired the unobstructed flow of property from the late husband to his first son and young, ambitious men who wanted the late husband's property transferred to themselves and their children. The warnings to such young men expressed through texts like *The Taming of the Shrew*, *The Arraignment*, and The Wife of Bath's Prologue and Tale shore up traditional patriarchal structures by dissuading dissenting youths from seeking their own financial advantage to the detriment of the overarching concerns of established male authority. From any of these potentially conflicting, masculinist perspectives, the widow represented a temporary repository for wealth subject to redistribution among men.[29] It is the widow's own point of view that is, so far, missing from this debate.

In stark contrast to Chaucer's, Shakespeare's, and Swetnam's portraits of young men undone by marrying rich widows are the accounts of rich widows ruined by their second husbands. Heal and Holmes, for instance, explain how:

> the transfer of wealth could become a matter of cruel jest, as when Lord St. John, having married a rich widow at the end of the 1560s, mocked her at the dinner table: "your ladyship hath only paid for your place, wherefore if any can now make a penny more of you I would he had you." (75)

Chaucer's, Shakespeare's, and Swetnam's representations of economically ambitious bachelors: "Like private-theater satiric comedies a decade later, these poems portray successful sexual adventuring among the married and unmarried women of middle-class London as young men's fantasy-triumphs over economic disadvantages, specifically as symbolic victories over a citizenry whose wealth Inns men resented" (*John Donne: Coterie Poet* 52).

[28] Also see Jardine 83.

[29] For more on the complexities of female second marriages, see Heal and Holmes 85-6 and Vives 322-26.

The notion that a widow could be financially destroyed by a second marriage was pervasive enough--and persuasive enough--to become instrumental to Jane Owen's argument in *An antidote against purgatory* in favor of rich (Catholic) widows giving money to the poor. Owen recommends that a wealthy widow reason with herself in this manner:

> *if I shall be content to enthral myself, and seventeen hundred pounds at least, to the will of a stranger, who I know not how he will use me: have I not reason to give three hundred pounds away for my own soul, for his sake, who will not suffer a cup of cold water given in his name, to be unrewarded?* (280)

The idea that a widow could lose her money as a consequence of a second marriage was thus widespread enough for Owen to use it as a justification for giving money to the poor; Owen's proposition at least allows the widow in question to retain a sense of agency in relinquishing her wealth and in strengthening her bonds with a future, celestial husband--Christ the bridegroom.[30]

This brief survey of primarily Renaissance texts exposes a significant divide in the manner in which widows were often portrayed.[31] According to masculinist representations, a widow might be a "gentle" woman in the sense of having elevated status, but she was unlikely to be "gentle" in the sense of being docile and obedient. Instead, the high status widow was likely to be among the most "froward . . . waspish . . . stubborn" of women (Swetnam 214). Yet other texts suggest that despite whatever resources for personal power a widow might have as a widow, remarriage could instantly dissipate those resources. Austen, in implicitly justifying her continued independence as a widow, inverts the stereotypical demonization of the powerful, lustful widow through figuring herself as an exaggeratedly helpless one.

---

[30] See Cavendish's play the Second Part of *Bell in Campo* for a sub-plot based on the idea that predatory young bachelors sought out rich, old widows to marry and then to abuse. See esp. Act 3, scene 12 for the bachelor's explicit interest in the widow's money and Act 4, scene 17 for the widow, Madam Passionate, giving a speech on how she loses her wealth and power when she marries Monsieur Compagnion. Todd challenges the idea that wealthy widows were pursued primarily because of their money ("The Remarrying Widow" 68).

[31] Conger's survey of the historical analyses of widows' status in colonial America suggests that scholarship falls along a similar divide: "Their analyses can be separated into two widely divergent categories: those who argue that widowhood provided women with economic independence and social power, and those who argue that widowhood spelled poverty and social dependence" (16).

Sara Heller Mendelson asserts that Austen's widowhood "plunged [her] into a sea of economic difficulties" and observes that "Austen continually bemoaned the sad state of her financial affairs since her widowhood, railing at the treachery of friends and relations who took advantage of her naive lack of business acumen" (199). While accurate in that Austen often does complain about financial matters, this characterization of Austen's representation of her economic status simplifies the significance of that representation within the broader contexts both of "Book M" itself and of contemporary depictions of widows. As we have seen, many well-known masculinist representations of widows could leave today's reader with the sense that widows were indeed unambiguously powerful women who had escaped the bonds of patriarchy.[32] Austen's self-figuring, however, in which she tries to hide the power that she does have whenever she explicitly writes about her widowed state, suggests how much the notion of a woman having *any* recourse to independence and self-empowerment was threatening to patriarchy. Austen thus downplays her personal resources, including intellectual agency and material possessions, lest they attract envious or punitive attention.[33] The disparity in her manuscript between the glimpses we receive of her actual property and her self-representation as a poor, helpless widow that I discuss below reveals that her self-figuration was strategic both as a refutation of her culture's pervasive stereotyping of widows and as a deflection of attention away from her economic and social ambitions.

---

[32] Jardine observes that "there was an area of early modern society in which apparently, although not actually, women had become frighteningly strong and independent . . . This was the area of inheritance and property, and Land Law" (78). She argues that early modern women "are technically strong (strong enough to have some 'economic leverage', and cause patriarchal anxiety), but actually they remain in thrall" (Jardine 88). For an extensive, accessible discussion of Land Law and its relationship to women, see Jardine 78-88.

[33] Mendelson and Crawford observe that "Widows at all social levels appealed to the stereotype of the poor, distressed, and weak individual. . . . Some who were neither poor nor weak still deployed the same rhetoric to urge men to help them" (175).

In "Book M," it is clear that Austen had enough wealth to make several loans. She writes a short, bitter essay on the theme "Upon Lending Mr C: Money," in which she reveals that she loaned Mr. C money on trust, so he refused to pay her back (Austen 52r). She also lists expenses, such as money spent on property maintenance; funds she lost through being cheated; and loans or financial gifts to a few cousins (99v). Todd indicates that Austen "invested in the East India Company" and that "She was concerned about the profitability of twelve new houses she was building near Covent Garden as investment properties" ("A Young Widow" 210, 211; also see 209, 229). While, as Mendelson observes, Austen's bitterness about being cheated is palpable, her various economic transactions suggest that she was not imminently at risk of becoming destitute. Austen seems to have had enough wealth to have been very concerned about losing it.

"Book M" suggests that Austen was quite self-conscious of her widowed state and its implications. For example, she was well aware that, for bachelors, she could represent an opportunity for economic advancement. She asks God, for instance, to help her avoid "giv[ing] so great a satisfaction as the reward of my selfe, and all my estate, ffor that which I am in a Capacity Civilly to requite by a lesser reward" (Austen 91r). This wealthy widow realizes that her affections can jeopardize her economic felicity. In fact, she transcribes her answer to a suitor who tries to convince her that one should not worry about financial matters when love is at stake:

> Tis Answered. If there is such a thing as Virtue to be loved for it Self Let my Amoret Entertaine me as his ffriend, and not victiate a Noble friendship with Enterist, or any other respect but pure amity. (Austen 95r)

Austen chooses to remain under God's protection alone (91) because "Men adoar [women's] company for aduantage to themselues" (96). "A Rich woman," she tells herself, "must not Marry with a p[er]son of meane ffortune" (Austen 50) because, as she later asserts:

> I thinke it is a great folly of which ones <my> self is the onely accessary by impairing the prosperity God hath given use . . .The best way is not to stay by the temptation which may insinuate in to a weekenes of consent and bring an undervalueing alteration of life. (Austen 94v)

Further justifying her own refusal to remarry despite what she represents as the necessarily troubled life of the widow, she makes this analogy: "The King courts the city and loves it because it is rich . . . As a Rich Wise woman is loved" (Austen 96).[34] She thus curtly tells her suitor that "he was mistaken" when he "protested if I was a very begger women if I wud have him he wud have me" (Austen 95). Austen recognizes her wealth as one of her most desirable traits.

Her cynicism is thus evident even in an especially romanticized narrative of a conversation with her suitor. Austen curtails his courting by first deflating his amorous rhetoric with a skeptical rejoinder and then engaging him in a pious discussion of human mortality:

---

[34] One entry in Austen's commonplace book, "In Answer to one why not to marry to Ease me of my burdens," suggests that she would not want to involve someone else in her material difficulties and asserts that she will need to dedicate herself entirely to her children in the event that they lose the estates for which they have been fighting.

When I was returning home from Mrs Al: he sed, You would not take pity if one should grow distracted for you. Their is noe fear of y^t [that], sed I. Then <as> he took me by the hand, he sed, What a hand was there to be adoar'd! I answered him, looking Upon a tuft of gras w^{ch} [which] had growing in it a yellow flower, That that spier of gras was fitter to be adoared then my hand: I allas, ses he, we are all but gras, but Shadowes. And when ever we see the gras we are to adoar the Creator in it. (Austen 96v)

Austen represents herself as a fair, chaste heroine who not only sees through the inflated rhetoric of courtly love but who also has such spiritual influence that she instantly corrects her suitor's wayward, fleshly thinking: by the end of their conversation, he replaces his misdirected adoration of Austen with proper adoration of "the Creator." Austen manages to star in her own prose romance, while she escapes the potentially licentious connotations of the genre.[35] Yet even in this dramatized scene of courtship, the widow suspects her suitor's motives.

In her self-figuration as a "gentle" widow, Austen not only expresses her awareness of the risks of a second marriage and suspicions of suitors; she also generalizes the threat to widows as potentially coming from any man. Hence, the question of a second marriage aside, Austen characterizes the widow as helpless, harmless, and persecuted. "I am in the hands of potent men," she writes, "Men skilful to distroy of subtil men, who lay traines to ruine y^e [the] widow and ffatherles" (Austen 65r). Praying to God, she writes:

> Surely My God is prepairing for me Halcione daies, for daies of trouble and Molestation I have found from men Who considers not afflicted widows. They take advantage of them, who has little help and gives frequent occasion of more disturbance. (Austen 35v)

On yet another occasion, she entreats God, praying, "O God tho my enemies seek to take advantage upon my week and destitute and helples condition A woman without Alliance of the ffamily to help me. Yet o God help me . . ." (Austen 69r). Austen the widow is "week and destitute and helples," surrounded by "[m]en skilful to distroy." It is thus surprising when Austen reveals that she is in a legal dispute over "the Red Lion" with her sister-in-law, "Sis Austen" (64v). Even after Austen reveals this detail, however, she

---

[35] For an interesting discussion of the problematics of early modern women as writers and readers of romance, see Hackett.

continues to refer to men as her economic assailants when she generalizes about her various contested properties, and she considers "Sis Austen" merely her father-in-law's pawn. Speculating about whether she can rightfully ask for God's help in this legal battle, Austen writes:

> I dare not judge it a self acqusing act. I shal have that charity to my Sister in Law. (Tho cannot have to her ffather by reason of his protestations to doe all the offices of love and ffriendship to our ffamily when his actions speake a ruine to it) ffor her, her Judgement may be falsely informed and her duty wrongly inforced. I shal construe it an Errour in Judgement. (82r)

Refusing to regard her sister-in-law as a primary agent in the legal action against her, Austen extends her self-representation as weak and helpless to "Sis Austen," whom she characterizes as unable to escape negative patriarchal influences.

Although Austen portrays herself as the potential victim of any man, she does not represent men as aggressors only. She connects her vulnerability to men at large to her lack of immediate, adult male relatives. The "subtil men" who are "skilful to distroy" specifically "lay traines to ruine y^e [the] widow and fatherles" (Austen 65r), women and children defined through their lack of a private patriarch. Part of Austen's self-figuration as a gentle widow relies on her implied wish for patriarchal protection against her male aggressors. After all, a gentle widow--one who does not conform to the stereotype of the lustful, power-hungry, shrewish widow and who respects social hierarchies out of her own ambition to be recognized as elite--would not be so critical of the patriarchy as to oppose it altogether. To demonstrate her need for male protection, Austen periodically relates dreams in which her late husband, his father, and his brother protect her from hostile men (e.g. 64r, 65), and she consoles herself with the idea that, if her husband's male relatives cannot aid her in reality, she can rely upon the assistance of the patriarch of patriarchs--God--against the men who conspire to take her estate (65r). Thus, in a verse prayer in which she emphasizes her own weakness, she entreats God the Father for his divine assistance:

> Then come and help in my extreame
> My strength is not compos'd so strong
> But subltile violence will wrong
> And in this world shall be a prey
> Unles the aid of widdowes stay

Unles thy blessings doe concur
Shall find all comforts to demur. (Austen 58)

This widow does not roam free, unfettered from patriarchal control and surveillance despite her lack of a husband; rather, she represents herself (and her property) as an object contested over by men. However, her male protectors of choice--God and her dead male relatives--are all positioned outside her mundane, material reality.

A poetic fragment that Austen copied into her manuscript centers on the notion of male protection from beyond the grave. The presence of this transcribed fragment in "Book M" is especially significant because it provides insight into how Austen participated in manuscript culture. Although she did not write this fragment, she helps to shape its possible meanings. She selects particular lines that are relevant to her own situation as a widow, and her manuscript provides a context for those lines and thus a specialized interpretation. Hence, this instance of transcription exemplifies how attending to lyrics transmitted through manuscript helps us to refine our understanding of authorship (and readership) during the period. Austen's transcription represents a collaboration between herself and another poet (whom she specifies as "Doc Corbet") and provides evidence of her playing several roles related to textual transmission. She is a reader of other poets' work; she is an editor who decides which lines to borrow for her own book; she is a scribe who copies those lines; and she is an author insofar as her own writing (the surrounding context of "Book M") participates in the manner in which the transcribed lines create meaning.[36]

She includes these lines "Out of a poeme of Doc Corbets: to his ffriend when she might be a Widow" (Austen 71v):

And as the paphian Queen by her griefs show'r (1)
Brought up her dead Loves Spirit in a fflow'r
So by those precious drops rain'd from thine Eyes
Out of my dust, O may some Vertue rise:
And like thy better Genius thee attend, (5)
Till thou in my dark period shalt end.

---

[36] For more on the complexities of manuscript authorship, see Ezell, *Social Authorship and the Advent of Print* esp. 40. Also see Ziegler 35, on the comparable way in which Esther Inglis's participation in manuscript book production and transmission expands notions of early modern authorship. On "[c]opying, transcribing, and compiling . . . [as] often crucial aspects of manuscript writing," see Burke 135-6.

In a rare engagement with a Renaissance tradition of love lyrics, Austen transcribes this fragment containing a conceit in which the poetic speaker compares himself to the slain Adonis and his wife to the mourning Venus. Austen presumably includes these lines to reflect on her own situation: her late husband, like the poetic speaker, is like Adonis, and she herself is like "the paphian Queen" (1). Her inclusion of this fragment is consistent not only with her self-figuration as an especially gentle widow, but with her tendency towards social conventionality or conservatism. While her own poems indicate in various ways her familiarity with the formal conventions associated with the manuscript transmission of lyrics and with specific poetic traditions, such as child loss poetry, spiritual meditations and prayers, country house poetry, and maternal legacy verse, Austen's lyrics tend to avoid explicit engagement with any tradition of amorous verse.[37] It is not surprising that Austen would limit her experimentations with literary forms that could associate her with the derogatory stereotype of the lustful, aggressive, uncontrollable widow. Hence, she carefully circumscribes her appropriation of the prose romance in relating her encounters with her gentleman suitor, and she transcribes, instead of composing, lines from a love lyric that has widowhood as its theme.

The implicit self-comparison to Venus in Austen's transcription allows the widow the compliment of being like the goddess of love but attempts to define the terms of that comparison very strictly. Venus, for instance, is never explicitly named as such in the fragment; instead she is the grieving "paphian Queen" (1), a high-ranking woman who properly mourns her dead husband and who recalls Austen's self-troping as Penelope, the faithful wife. In the context of Austen's accounts of her dreams suggesting her wish for her husband's spirit to protect her, the playfully

---

[37] See Marotti's *Manuscript* esp. 75-133, on the frequency of controversial sexual and political themes--with which Austen does not engage--in manuscript verse miscellanies. Also see Wynne-Davies xxiv, on the "unexpected . . . lack of love poetry" in her recent anthology of Renaissance women's verse. Jones writes that "the ideological matrix that associated open speech with open sexuality in women made love poetry an especially transgressive genre for them" (7).

Austen's poem, "On Vollantines Day this 14 ffeb: 1665/ My Jewel," represents her most explicit engagement with any tradition of amorous verse (108v-9r). Her Valentine's Day poem to herself celebrates a jewel that she found, which she takes as a providential signifier of good fortune. Calling the jewel "ffirmer to me than Lover's twines" as a Valentine's Day gift (2), Austen locates her poem against the tradition of verse written to accompany material gifts exchanged by lovers. Her poem to herself on Valentine's Day, claiming the superiority of her providential gift to that of any from a human lover, answers back to lyrics such as Donne's "*A Ieat Ring Sent*" and "*The Funerall*," Carew's "*Vpon a Ribband*," Shirley's "*To a* L.[ady] *upon a Looking-Glasse sent*," and Waller's "*On a Girdle*."

erotic subtext underpinning the figure of the dead lover as a "better Genius" who "attend[s]" his beloved diminishes in significance (5). In the context of Renaissance love poetry, it is difficult to avoid the potentially bawdy connotation of Venus' "dead Loves Spirit" (2); likewise, even a mournful "paphian Queen" seems only slightly less licentious than Venus in hot pursuit of the classical paragon of male beauty.[38] Further, when considered within the tradition of Ovidian erotic verse, the "Vertue" that "rise[s]" like a Phoenix from its own ashes in line four suggests a speedy post-coital phallic recovery. In the context of "Book M," however, which Austen fashions as textual proof and attribute of the chaste, helpless widow, one can interpret the figure of the ghostly husband's "Genius" so that it not only offers protection, but also ensures the beloved's continued chastity. Neither the beloved, nor a suitor, after all, could escape the watchfulness of such an attending spirit, and the implication that Austen wishes for such an attendant itself protects her from the stereotype of the insubordinate, lustful widow. The environment of Austen's commonplace book also highlights how this fragment domesticates the female agency behind the central transformation in the Ovidian account of Venus and Adonis. While the primary metamorphosis in Ovid's story is Venus's magical transformation of her dead male beloved into a flower memorializing her passion and sorrow,[39] here the female agent behind the teardrops (3) that engender "Vertue" out of dust (4) falls under the surveillance of that resurrected aspect of the dead male lover. The metamorphosed synecdochical figure for the male lover accompanies the female beloved to the end of her life, which turns out to be circumscribed by the male poet's sentence: the "better Genius" will attend her "Till [she] in [his] dark period shalt end" (5, 6). Austen's inclusion of this fragment thus contributes to her self-representation as a gentle widow who eschews personal agency and power to the extent that she wishes to be subjected to patriarchal control in the form of her late husband's ghostly attendance.

While Austen similarly dramatizes her vulnerability in her poem "Upon Courtiers at the Committee at Parliament Striving for Highbury," she simultaneously critiques male power. This poem is especially interesting

---

[38] For the potentially bawdy connotation of "spirit," cf. Shakespeare's Sonnet 129, and see Booth's discussion of it, 441-3. The commonplace resonance of "dying" with orgasm increases the potential for reading "spirit" as a sexual pun in this context. For more on the poetic speaker's meditation on his own death in amorous complaints, cf. Donne's *"The Apparition," "The Dampe," "The Funerall,"* and *"The Relique"* and Shakespeare's Sonnets 71-4.

[39] See Ovid 10.708-39.

because it both shows how she represents her abject weakness as a widow and reveals her awareness of traditional poetic practices. In the first six lines, for example, she participates in the widespread practice of translating biblical passages into metrical verse:[40]

> Wise Sollomen he tells me true (1)
> There is a time for all thinges due
> A Time to Spare, a time to spend
> A Time to Borrow time to lend
> A time of Trouble time of rest (5)
> A time there is to be opprest. (Austen 59v)

Austen's generalized rendering of the teachings of Ecclesiastes in the tetrameter typical of such metrical translations focuses on issues relevant to her embattled economic situation.[41] The first couplet corresponds loosely to Eccles. 3:1; the second paraphrases Eccles 3:6; and the last appears to be Austen's variation on Eccles. 3:8.[42] While Austen's careful imitation of the repetition and syntactical balance characteristic of the third chapter of Ecclesiastes makes her brief metrical paraphrase seem at first glance to be a more straightforward translation than it is, an attentive comparison of Austen's verse with the biblical text reveals that she summarizes it to fit her particular circumstances. Most significantly, Eccles. 3:6 ("A time to get, and a time to lose; a time to keep, and a time to cast away") becomes more explicitly economic in Austen's translation. The gentlewoman renders "get" and "lose," "spare" and "spend"; "keep" and "cast away" become "borrow" and "lend." Likewise, in Austen's version, time itself calls in debts--"There is a time for all thinges due" (2)--rather than simply existing as a neutral medium through which humans organize their life experiences.

Austen's verse paraphrase of Ecclesiastes appears twice in "Book M." It first appears early in the manuscript in a version that seems an initial

---

[40] For more on the popularity of metrical paraphrases of biblical texts, see Christopher Hill's *The English Bible and the Seventeenth Century Revolution* esp. 338.

[41] For more on Austen's struggles concerning the Highbury estate, see Todd, "A Young Widow" esp. 229-30. Todd explains that "A private bill had been introduced in Parliament to take Highbury away from the Austens. Katherine hired lawyers and also attended the committee meetings herself" (211). Also see my discussion of Austen's country house poem, "On the Situation of Highbury," below.

[42] Cf. the relevant verses from Ecclesiastes: (1) "To everything there is a season, and a time to every purpose under the heaven" (3:1); (2) "A time to get, and a time to lose; a time to keep, and a time to cast away" (3:6); and (3) "A time to love, and a time to hate; a time of war, and a time of peace" (3:8).

effort at an extended metrical translation of or meditation on the biblical passage. Yet Austen breaks off her attempt, stopping after the seventh line: "A time of ffolly. Time to be" (40v). She simply leaves the rest of the page blank. She circulates these verses, however, between the pages of her own manuscript: they reappear in the opening lines to her critique of the courtiers at parliament--with a significant revision. She replaces the seventh line from her first version ("A time of ffolly. Time to be") with a new one ("Such is this time now men of power"), which enables her to move beyond the limitations of metrical paraphrasing to incorporate the biblical passage into a more explicitly autobiographical lyric. Austen's new seventh line becomes a point of transition:

> Wise Sollomen he tells me true (1)
> There is a time for all thinges due
> A Time to Spare, a time to spend
> A Time to Borrow. time to lend
> A time of Trouble time of rest (5)
> A time there is to be opprest.
> Such is this time now men of power
> Doe seeke our well faire to devoure
> Confederated in a League
> By an ["oppresive" struck out] <unjust and> Dire intrege (10) (59v)

Austen makes a supremely patriarchal text--Solomon's legendary kingly wisdom is, at times, thoroughly misogynist[43]--the authority prefacing her critique of "men of power," whom she represents as banded together against her. Here Austen dramatizes her unprotected helplessness both by attaching references to her particular, personal circumstances to an ancient, sacred exposition on the universal effects of time and by using especially forceful, vivid diction. The legal contest over the Highbury estate to which the poem's title refers becomes tantamount to political conspiracy at court, where the stakes are high and the rules Machiavellian.

A section of another poem is similarly dramatic, but it focuses on Austen's recognition of widows as a particular group of women, rather than on "League[s]" of "men of power":[44]

---

[43]   See, for example, Proverbs (traditionally attributed to Solomon) esp. 11:22, 12:4, 21:9, 21:19, 22:14, 23:27, 27:15.
[44]   Todd's transcription suggests that she considers "Men never think their wifes may be" a continuation of "Upon Courtiers at the Committee of Parliament Striving for Highbury." However, Austen frequently uses a slash mark to end her poems, and such a

Men never think their wifes may be (1)
Neccesitate by Missery
Or their children be a prey
When them selves are gone away
I not resented Widdowes teares (5)
Before I was distreased with feares
This retribution doe I find
To meet with all the World Unkind. (60r)

Thus does Austen characterize the new knowledge that her widowhood brings. She implies that she knows now what "Men never think": that widows can indeed be made "Neccesitate by Missery" and that "children" can "be[come] a prey" as a direct consequence of their fathers' deaths. This passage reveals Austen's socially conventional tendency to align her views with those of the patriarchy (she apparently used to agree with the men who did not worry about widows), but it also shows how her representation of her economic embattlement as a widow challenges the dominant masculine perspective. In line five, she places her "I" in the same position of un- knowing as the "Men" who "never think" in the first. Austen did "not [resent] Widdows teares"--she did not feel anger on behalf of the injustices done to bereaved women--before she came to occupy that position in society herself. Hence, the "I" in line five serves as a transition in identification; it is the pivot point around which Austen shifts to take a position against that which "[m]en never think": that widows might actually need financial advice or assistance, that the dominant stereotype of the unambiguously powerful widow is inaccurate.

Despite Austen's revised epistemological position as a widow, despite the critical view of the patriarchy that it gives her, she retains her interest in social conservatism. Indeed, her desire to attain higher status outweighs any sense of allegiance to women as a significant cross-class social group.[45] Instead of identifying with women of all social ranks, she betrays a deep anxiety about and bitter resentment toward her gender's ability to undermine class distinctions among early modern women. She

mark precedes "Men never think." Also, Todd transcribes "not" in line five as "hot." See Todd, "A Young Widow" 231-2.

[45] The co-existence of Austen's gender-awareness with her conservatism aligns her ideologically with other early modern women writers, such as Katherine Philips and Margaret Cavendish. As Pacheco observes, "During the seventeenth century, this concurrence of political conservatism with a consciousness of gender inequality was in fact the rule rather than the exception" (11). For a compelling discussion of the relationship between absolute monarchy and the conceptualization of the absolute, private self, see Gallagher.

"hope[s]" that her body "is the worst part of [her] and that w^{ch} [which] every Servant Made and Country Wench may excel [hers], and can give the Same Satisfaction as [hers]" (95v).[46] Here, by conceptualizing her body as her "worst part," Austen suggests that her body is separate from those aspects of herself that she values more highly (e.g., her mind, virtue, status). This effort to distance her gender-marked body from the rest of herself corresponds with and points to her desire to distance herself from lower-class women as well. Austen's new awareness--coincident with her widowhood--of the importance of gender as a social category does not eradicate her elitism. Rather, it alerts her to the possibility that the weakness she associates with being an unprotected woman could undermine her social rank.

Yet she also uses that weakness as an occasion for an odd kind of boasting. "I have pased extrordinary troubles and greviances," she asserts, "as w^t [what] woman more and goe through with so litle outward dismay or did not seek a shelter by a second marriag" (Austen 76r). While she frequently represents herself as a widow so vulnerable that any man could take her material possessions, here she congratulates herself for having more "troubles and grievances" than any other woman while managing to hide signs of "outward dismay." Having resisted a second marriage as a means of gaining male protection becomes a victory in an implicit competition with other widows. Surprisingly, given Austen's efforts elsewhere to portray herself as a helpless widow assailed by powerful men, she extends this sense of social competitiveness to men, too: "Also for blesings w^t [what] woman nay or man can tel the like (<with> out Marchandize help or a Trade) as I But not to me But the great God hath done it" (76r). In her comparison of her blessings with those granted to men, she evens the playing field, implying that the blessings to which she refers signify continued material success in the absence of work--"<with> out Marchandize help or a Trade." She reverses what would be the economic advantage of men--the ability to participate unproblematically in the public sphere--into a claim both to special protection from God and economic prosperity. Catching herself making such a bold statement,

---

[46] See Mack: "While a woman's breeding and deportment were crucial in reflecting and transmitting the status of her family, underneath her clothes and manners a middle or upper class woman was often portrayed as having potentially more in common with a peasant woman or a prostitute than with the men in her own household . . . contemporaries tended to define the male character in terms of the individual's position in the class structure, while women were defined in terms of underlying occult qualities that were irrelevant to their social position" (29).

however, she contains her boast by ascribing responsibility for her successes to God. She thus negates her agency, her "I," by specifying that her blessings in this social competition are due "not to me But the great God." Despite her belated self-negation, however, we see a glimpse of the widow's social ambitions, a glimpse supporting the proposition that her self-figuration as a weak, helpless widow is strategic.

Austen's preface to "Book M" is similarly strategic in its attempt to construct the commonplace book as the sort of unassumingly personal, private work that would be appropriate for a respectable, decorous, wealthy widow to write and compile:

> Whoso ever shal look in these papers and shal take notice of these personal occurrences wil Easily discerne it concerned none but my self and was a private exercise directed to my self. The singularity of these conceptions doth not advantaige any.

While Mendelson reads this announcement as an example supporting her claim that "most [Stuart] women diarists took active steps to conceal their writing from all other eyes" (183), I would contend that Austen's prefatory statement does not fall into the same category as other women writers' use of a private shorthand to ensure the illegibility of their personal compositions or some women's attempts to destroy their writing when faced with death.[47] Austen's preface assumes a reader for "Book M"; it addresses "Whoso Ever shal look in these papers and shal take notice of these personal occurrences." It does not warn readers away or instruct them to close the book. Rather, it attempts to qualify what readers will find in "Book M" as personal and private. Austen addresses her reader in order to construct her writing as perfectly acceptable: she rhetorically circumscribes herself as a writing woman strictly within the bounds of the private sphere, which was increasingly associated with proper femininity (especially for middle and upper class women) in seventeenth-century England.[48]

---

[47] See Mendelson 183-4.

[48] On the emergence of the divide between the public and private spheres, see Hobby 3.

Mendelson generalizes the differences between early modern men's and women's diaries according to this divide: "Women's diaries are more apt to be centered around the household and its personnel. The prevailing picture of everyday life evoked in their writings is of women going about their domestic tasks, retreating to their closets to perform their devotions, entertaining and being entertained in each other's houses. Men's diaries exude more of the atmosphere of public life: occupations outside the home, social gatherings in

However, Austen did not restrict her writing to private concerns.[49] "Book M" contains brief entries, for example, concerning events of national importance, such as her meditations "Of Eng and Duch Quarrel: 1665," "On the battel at Sea: June 1666:" (73v), and "On the Sickenes" (86r). In the last third of "Book M," many of Austen's entries concern the plague's ravages on the general population. While one expects the "gentle" widow--helpless, economically vulnerable, pious--that Austen figures herself to be to devote her writing entirely to appropriately godly meditations, Austen explores topics beyond such a perfectly defined private sphere.

Katherine Austen's self-construction in "Book M" as an especially innocuous, vulnerable widow is her answer to her culture's widespread representation of the widow as a woman who had, at the best, humorous, and at the worst, horrifying power over men. Although she strategically represents herself as a proper widow who knows that frailty's name is woman, her stern independence becomes evident nonetheless. Austen's gentle widow is only one aspect of her multi-faceted, discontinuous self-figuration, through which she negotiates the incompatibilities between her socioeconomic ambitions and gender. As a woman interested in securing social and economic power for herself and her children, she mobilizes the potentially public role of the prophet to her advantage.

---

alehouses, political gossip interwoven with narratives of local affairs" (199). However, Austen's "Book M" unsettles these generalizations. Also see Todd, "A Young Widow," 213.

[49] Wilcox observes that early modern English women's "autobiographical texts are full of evidence of the blurring of these distinctions [between the public and private spheres]," and notes that "In their lives and their texts, these women intertwined matters of domestic and national importance" (59). For more on the insufficiency of "public" and "private" as descriptive categories for late seventeenth- and early eighteenth-century texts, see Ezell, *Social Authorship and the Advent of Print* esp. 38-44.

The Ambivalent Visionary

> If men doe listen to Wispers of fear, and have not reason, and observation
> Enough to confute trifles . . . Every old woman shal be a prophetes. (Austen
> 25r)

> Was not one of my Dreames the presaigment of blesing to the Nation As
> the Dream of a poor Stranger did confirme Gedion to goe on with the more
> confidence to his Victory? (Austen 15r)

In 1664, when Austen began composing "Book M," the monarchy had been restored, and there were increased restrictions against the more radical religious sects--Quakers, Seekers, Fifth Monarchists, Baptists, Ranters, etc. --which had proliferated during the revolutionary period.[50]   As many scholars have noted, the 1640s and 1650s saw an unprecedented number of women involve themselves publicly in the various debates concerning the intertwined religious and political issues of the day.   Women petitioned Parliament; they helped found new religious sects; and they acted as missionaries, as Mack indicates, "in New England, the Atlantic colonies, the Caribbean, even to Catholics and Moslems on the island of Malta and in Turkey" (1).[51]   Prophetic activity, in particular, flourished during this period.   According to Hill, the role of the prophet was "almost a new profession" for men and women alike (*The World Turned Upside Down* 73). Hobby notes, in fact, that "Well over half the texts published by women between 1649 and 1688 were prophecies" (26), and Mack points out that "Women as prophets enjoyed virtually the only taste of public authority they would ever know" (5).

As the discussion of Anna Trapnel's prophetic writings and performances in Chapter 3 indicates, being a prophet in seventeenth-century England did not simply involve predicting the future. As Hobby explains, many of the women who wrote prophecies between 1649 and 1688 "present[ed] themselves as divinely inspired counterparts of the Old Testament prophets, whose role was to report and interpret God's messages to His people . . . Women prophets were possessed by the Lord, burdened

---

[50]   See Hill, *The Century of Revolution* 211.

[51]   There are numerous studies on women's participation in the religious and political events of this period.   A brief survey of those studies includes Mack; Hobby, esp. 26-75; Ezell, *Writing Women's Literary History* esp. 132-60; Purkiss; Laurence; Wiseman; Hinds; Cross; Dailey; Irwin, esp. Chapter Five; Ethyn Morgan Williams; Burrage; Greaves; Ludlow; Berg and Berry; Cohen; Blecki; Carroll; Rickman; Irene L. Edward; and Stone 337-40.

with the duty to speak" (26). Such women prophets were not simply seers who could tell the future; they were divine messengers. The nature of a prophet's messages could be complex and could derive from multiple traditions, as Keith Thomas explains:

> The real boost to ancient prophecy . . . came with the Civil War, when Galfridian prophecies joined astrological prognostication and religious revelation to place an unprecedented amount of prophetic advice before the lay public. Although the three genres were distinct, their separate identity was not always preserved . . . The literature of the Civil War period suggests a disposition to welcome any kind of prophetic utterance, regardless of the foundation upon which it purported to rest. (409)

Austen's ambivalent engagement with prophecy in "Book M" suggests her familiarity not only with the role of female prophets from radical religious groups during the civil wars but also with the generic mixing of prophetic traditions that Thomas describes.

While her self-fashioning as a prophet in "Book M" contrasts with her self-portrait as an especially weak widow, both roles represent strategies for negotiating the incompatibilities between her gender and her socioeconomic desires. Thus she simultaneously dissociates herself from a specific figure of exaggerated female power (the wealthy widow) and experiments with underwriting her social and economic ambitions with divine power. Both roles allow her to hide her personal agency, and therefore, to distract attention away from her financial and intellectual resources and her aspirations for social and economic advancement. Prophecy, like poetry, becomes a specialized means through which Austen organizes and ascribes meaning to her life in "Book M."[52] While the widow's participation in manuscript culture potentially associates her with elite social groups, her claims to prophetic insights align her with rebellious lower and lower middle class urbanites during the revolutionary period.[53]

---

[52] Todd observes that "To help herself through these crises [related to protecting her estates] she also relied on the consolation of analyzing her dreams and recording examples of predictive visions and other cases of prophetic foreknowledge that she discovered in reading or conversation" ("A Young Widow" 211).

[53] Marotti argues that "one of the obvious reasons for the persistence of the manuscript system of literary transmission through the seventeenth-century was that it stood opposed to the more democratizing force of print culture and allowed those who participated in it to feel that they were part of a social as well as an intellectual elite" (*Manuscript* 34). Ezell, in *Social Authorship and the Advent of Print*, challenges the characterization of print as democratizing and manuscript authorship as aristocratic; see esp. 40-4 and 101-2. However, the greater context of "Book M" suggests that Austen was interested in

Hence, her occasional verse that touches upon prophetic matters and requests divine revelations represents an odd hybridization: Austen flirts with a discourse which, in the wake of the revolutionary period, is marked as low class, but she inscribes that discourse into a potentially conservative, elitist form. Austen's self-figuration as a prophet is especially fissured and inconsistent due to her ambivalence both towards exposing her social and economic ambitions and towards the association of prophetic activity with disreputable persons: the urban rabble and outspoken women.

Austen's account of her "Dreame on 2^d of Jan: 1668" not only points to her concerns about how her gender impacts her economic status, but also suggests that she is able to assert a sense of interpretive authority through her claim to prophetic abilities.[54] She dreams of leaving her mother when she goes to a wedding where she sees her late husband talking to another man in a room with a long table. To her mind, her later, actual experience at Parliament confirms the visionary quality of her dream. The room in which she conducts her business concerning her estate is the one that she saw in her dream, and the man whom she saw with her husband looks just like a person who was present at Parliament, "Sr John Birkenhead."[55] Retrospectively, she concludes that "This busines was a Weeding: for it was a Contract, a Confederacy to take away our Estate. And I shal noe more be of that opinion generally observed in Dreames that a Weeding foretels a burning and a burning a Weeding. But that it is danger

---

representing herself as elite. Burke also challenges the assumption that manuscript culture was elitist; see 141.

Quoting from John Lilburne's *Come out of her my people* (Amsterdam, 1639; 19) in his discussion of the widespread interest in prophecy during the revolutionary years, Hill argues that "[t]here is overwhelming contemporary evidence that the strength of the sectaries lay with what Lilburne called 'the base and obscure fellow of the world'" (*The World Turned Upside Down* 80). Also see Capp 82, 85, 93.

[54] Austen's critique of the legal system reveals both her assumption that she cannot protect herself in this situation and her sense of economic vulnerability: "If there is such a power can take away that w^{ch} [which] the Lawes of the Land dus affirme to us I know noe other remedy, then to prepaire my self to work for my liveing, for I must expect all that I have may be gone: And I bles God I shal be able to doe it" (72v).

For other examples of Austen's prophetic interpretations of her dreams, see 38, 54, and 70v.

For information about Margaret Clifford's prophetic dreams, see Lewalski, *Writing Women in Jacobean England* 136.

[55] Austen is very similar to prophets like Anna Trapnel insofar as her personal visions turn out to include figures from the public sphere.

of Conspiracy against one -- as This was to us" (Austen 60v-1).[56] Austen's vacillation between plural and singular pronouns in this passage provides a starting point for unraveling her overlapping concerns about her gender, her financial situation, and her prophetic authority.   First, Austen conceptualizes her contested estate as the property of herself and her late husband, who appears seated at the negotiating table in her dream. She specifies that there is "a Confederacy to take away our Estate." She switches to the first person singular, however, in asserting that her accurate prediction in the case of this dream gives her the authority to contest the popular notion that dreaming about a wedding "foretels a burning" in order to claim instead that such a dream signifies "danger of Conspiracy against one." It is in this moment of claiming a right to interpretation that Austen acknowledges that on the most immediate, material level, she--not her dead husband (except insofar as his heirs stand in for him)--is the one in a position to lose the estate. Yet when she moves away from the significance of the dream--"it is danger of Conspiracy against one"--and back to her account of what transpired at Parliament, she again uses a plural pronoun: "as This was to us." Austen's prophetic dream thus allows her to assert interpretive, organizational authority over her experiences, even if she does not conceptualize herself as an economic agent absolutely independent of her late husband.[57]   Ultimately, Austen interprets her difficulties with Parliament as signifying at the national level. And it is in this moment of making her personal grievance against Parliament tantamount to a general, public concern and of suggesting that Parliament's behavior will doom the nation to a recurrence of the upheaval of the previous decades that Austen sounds most like the radical female prophets of the Civil War period. In an essay entitled "On, report at Parliament" Austen writes:

---

[56]   Todd reads "burning" as "burying" ("A Young Widow" 233).   Either interpretation is possible, and each leads to slightly different resonances of meaning. Unfortunately, Austen's writing is unclear in this case.

[57]   Austen's self-representation with respect to her husband is complicated, as is evident in the above discussion of her self-figuration as a "gentle" widow who wishes for his ghostly surveillance. She does not simply assume, however, that he still represents her legally and economically, as if he were alive. In a passage directed to her children, she writes, "think when you receive my blesing that you receive that of yo[ur] Dear ffathers also. (I representing him al)" (Austen 42).

Austen's linking together of her waking material vulnerability and her dream about the wedding, incidentally, provocatively implicates the institution of marriage in women's economic disenfranchisement.

ffor this Complaint of oppression, God hath punishet the Land fformerly, in the great Callamities w^ch [which] fell upon the times, And Surely if they pursue, and commit the same Crimes, of Unjustice, and Injuries to poore men. And Especially to acte violence on Widdowes and orphanes, how will their cries an greviances perce the Eares of Heaven, who will hear and Judge their cause, against an Unjust Nation. (67v)

In a fleeting instant of solidarity with the lower classes ("Surely if they pursue, and commit the same Crimes, of Unjustice, and Injuries to poore men"), Austen threatens that Parliament's unjust handling of her economic affaires will bring down the wrath of God on England--again.

Austen is not only similar to the prophets of the revolutionary period in castigating the nation, but she also shares with the female prophets of those decades the tendency to compare herself to biblical figures.[58] Across her manuscript, she compares herself several times to David, a particular favorite among female prophets, as well as to Abraham, Isaac, Ester, Judith, Deborah, Job, Hezekiah, Peter, and Paul (21r, 56r, 75r, 85v, 155r).[59] Although one might contend that she compares herself to such figures only to emphasize her membership in the community of the faithful, elsewhere she clearly connects her similarity to biblical figures to her own prophetic claims. Of Hezekiah, for example, she writes:

Nor was Hezekiahs death foretold to him by a plainer demonstration then I had: ffor w^t [what] could be more certaine to perswaide my self of the reality, then the agreement there was of My Husbands age and mine to be the same at the periode of the time Limited to live: So was the Counterintimation the same as to Hezekiah. Nay I received it by a wonderful providence ascertained to me in the words the prophet David Spoake: corresponding to those of y^e [the] pro[phet] Esaj: which were sent to hezekiah. (Austen 75r-v)

That Austen's self-comparisons to all biblical figures had weight for her is evident in her concern about suggesting too strong a comparison between herself and Christ:

---

[58] See Mack 105 and Hobby 26.

[59] For instance, she writes: "Remember David And all His afflic: Remember thy Servant and all her afflictions to" (56r); "And as Isack lay at the Alter so did my life lye a sacrifice at the Will of my God:" (75r); ". . . the lively and infalliable assurances of the Almighties succours and assistances of his favour and tendar regard over them who flye to him for refuge May Convince of the truth of such Religion Which I have found. As well as Abram and Isack: As well as David: and St Peter and St Paul. As well as Ester and Judeth and Deborah" (85v).

> I shal conclud my Meditations with my Sauiours resignation (when the Sin
> of all mankind depresed him) And tho I dare not make a parralel between
> momentary earthly troubles And my Sauiours for worlds of sinneres Yet I
> am incited from him our Captaine. And in my soule shal say his words of
> releasement, w^ch [which] refreshes me. (112r)

Her concern about the potential arrogance implied in comparing herself to
Christ seems evident in her omission of the words of her "Sauiours
resigation" and her qualification that she only thinks this way because
Christ has "incited" her to do so.

Austen was not only ambivalent about comparing herself to Christ;
she also had doubts about the validity of any claims to special revelations in
contemporary times. The association of prophetic activity with the lower
classes during the revolutionary period made asserting oneself as a prophet
of questionable, but tempting, value to Austen.[60]   Mack explains the
tensions between issues of social rank and gender among the prophets:

> The prophets of the Civil War period, many of them laborers, farmers, or
> artisans, understood their condemnation of an engorged clergy and
> aristocracy as both spiritual and social protest. And since women were
> commonly identified with the poor and deprived, both in Christian tradition
> and in popular and legal language, one would expect that those radical
> movements that championed the poor and deprived would also champion
> the increased authority of women. Yet we will see that those sects that
> were most radical in challenging traditional social and economic
> relationships were least likely to be attentive to the needs and rights of
> oppressed people who were female. Conversely, those women who were
> most conscious of their authority as females, Quaker and non-Quaker, were
> also those middle and upper class women who had the least affinity with
> the plight of the laboring classes. (4)

---

[60]   In his discussion of the popularity of prophecy, Hill indicates that "for
seventeenth-century English radicals the religion of the heart [the indwelling spirit or light]
was the answer to the pretensions of the academic divinity of ruling-class universities" (*The
World Turned Upside Down* 76). For a woman who could not attend a university but whose
son did, the appeal of claims to uninstitutionalized spiritual knowledge could have created a
powerful tension.
    Lady Eleanor Davies may come to mind as a possible model of the high status
female prophet from whom Austen could have borrowed. However, Davies' notoriety (she
was imprisoned and sent to Bedlam) and her utter disregard for social propriety (she tarred
the hangings behind the bishop's seat at Lichfield) might have instead made Austen even
more ambivalent towards pursuing a prophetic role had she known about Davies (Spencer
51-3).

While laying claim to uninstitutionalized knowledge and divine power may have been attractive options for Austen, her aspiration to rise in rank must have made any seeming similarity to low-ranking prophets an uncomfortable proposition for her.

As an aspirant to the gentry and a Royalist, Austen had some significantly different views from the radical sectarian prophets of the previous decades. As a landowner and a parent with a son at Oxford, she was invested in a national church and thus in a mandatory church tithe.[61] It is therefore not surprising that she disapprovingly refers to "the beginning of the troubles [in] 1643 When Ministers was put out of their liveings" (10r). This observation from her account of "Doc: Hammonds Dreame:" indicates that she would be opposed to the beliefs of women prophets like Anna Trapnel, who argued vehemently against the tithe. Austen's record of Hammond's dream dramatizes the nonconformist threat to the established ministry and projects a fantasy of Anglican vindication after the Restoration. Austen relates how Hammond and a small group of followers were mysteriously separated from a "multitude" and assailed by "a most tempestuous Storme." Amidst rain, violent wind, and "Bals of ffire," the doctor heard a voice say "Be stil, and ye shal receive no harme." Hammond then apparently prayed until the end of the storm, when "he heard began that Cathedral Antheme 'Come Lord Jesus. Come away.'" Austen concludes her account of the divine's prophetic dream--the storm signifying, apparently, the threat to the established church represented by the events of the revolutionary period--by writing "The correspondent evvent of all which he found verrified in the preservation of himself and ffriends in the doeing of their duty" (10). Austen presumably records Hammond's dream as evidence of valid prophetic activity on the side of the established church. By providing this account of an established church leader's accurate vision, Austen opens a space, distinct from that occupied by radical sectarians, for her own claims to extraordinary inspiration.

A survey of a few of the titles Austen includes at the beginning of her book reveals her pervasive interest in dreams: "Doc Duns Apparit of

---

[61] See Hill, *The World Turned Upside Down*: "The attack on tithes, common to all the radicals, undermined the whole concept of a state church, since if parishoners could not be legally compelled to pay tithes there would be no 'livings' for the clergy to occupy, no impropriated tithes for the gentry to collect in the forty per cent of livings which were lay fees. Disestablishment of the church would deprive the gentry of another property right--the right of presentation to a living, a right for which they or their ancestors had paid hard cash and which gave them useful opportunities of providing for a younger son or poor relation" (79).

Wife," "Divers other Dreames & of Germaine prince {D. Hol?}," "Observat
of My Dreames."   "Book M" suggests that she was simultaneously
fascinated and disturbed by the possibility that such visions could have
prophetic significance. The juxtaposition of two titles in "Book M's" table
of contents--"How ill to desier to know our ffortune" and "Some Dreames
not to be slighted: of S: of Serpent"-- points to the widow's competing
interests in the conservative didactic moralism that would reject the
possibility of extraordinary interventions through dreams and in the
opposite stance, espoused by many nonconformists, that understood divine
visions, including dreams, as important, fairly frequent interruptions of the
supernatural into the realm of the mundane.   Through these two titles,
Austen both acknowledges that it is inappropriate to guess what divine
providence has in store and intimates that this restriction does not always
apply, that it is sometimes crucial to read the significance of one's dreams.
In an essay entitled "Of the ffeare of God," Austen records the spectrum of
arguments against concerning oneself with the significance of dreams. She
writes, "Dreams are without rule, and without reason. They proceed very
much from the temper of the body and trouble of the minde.   Tho
Sometimes from some Daemon good or bad" (25r). (Even here, however,
she displays belief in the idea that dreams could result from supernatural
influences.) In the same essay, she writes that "The fancy may be vexed in
to a representation of it Now if the Events of our Dreams doe answer in one
instance, we becom credulous in twenty, and so we discourse our Selves
into folly and weak observation, and give the Devil power over us in those
circumstances we can least resist him" (26r). Here, Austen suggests that
reading prophetic significance into one's dreams can be dangerous to one's
soul. Whether she composed such assertions or simply recorded them from
other sources, they indicate her awareness of claims against reading
meaning into one's dreams. Her acknowledgement of potentially satanic
forces influencing dreams is especially striking given her many efforts to
interpret her own dreams.

Austen remains ambivalent towards prophetic activity--particularly
towards the potentially prophetic significance of dreams--throughout much
of her manuscript. This mixed feeling is evident in how she occasionally
converts her boldest claims of having spiritual or extraordinary gifts into the
conventional attributes of spiritual autobiography. For example, in her
essay "Observation on my Dream of Monition," she writes:

> Certainly I may have an expectation, a dependance of something
> extrordinary, to be fal me at the period of that time When I find stories

from Monitions and Notices given to some persons, yeares before it come to pas. Yet I have hardly heard of anything with so much plainnes and certainty, as w^t [what] I have received. And yet in this certainty I have found a contradiction that I shal not dye but live and declare the works of Lord. As if that was the meaning, After the being excercised with divers trials and afflictions that I should continue to declare the workes and manifestations of his goodnes . . . Thou hast showed thy wonders to me as well as to David: as well as to Kings. (Austen 21)

Austen first suggests that she, like those extraordinarily gifted people in the stories she reads, will receive special gifts. She asserts that the gift she has already received, to her knowledge, has greater "plainnes and certainty" than any other. After making such bold claims, however, she implies that her divine gift is the promise of eternal life resulting from Christ's sacrificial death and resurrection ("I shal not dye but live . . ."). Her fascination with special revelations gives way to a standard confession of Christian faith. The ambivalent visionary lapses into a commonplace spiritual meditation.

Austen's occasional poem, "Upon My Dreame the 20th Oct 1664 When I Dreamet I Saw 4 Moones in a Clear Sky: Meditation," similarly highlights the tentative role of prophetic claims with respect to Austen's writing:

Will ffoure Moones more my ffate declare?
Waight I in hope? or in Dispaire?
Dus life or Death my date Unfold?
I know not Lord thou are my hold.
Which state is fittest Lord for thee (5)
To that most willingly agree
If through the pavement of y^e [the] grave
Heavens providence more beauty have
My God I doe Submit and know
More glory unto me will Show (10)
Then this fraile life can contribute
When pleasures to our hearts most Suite
The mean time Lord prepare my heart
ffor what thy ["purposes" struck out] <goodnes shal> impart
ffor what thy purposes intend (15)
In Embassaige of life, or end.
Addorne my Soule and beautify
That chiefest part, I may comply
O fit me Lord, to dye or live
To doe my Duty while I breath. (20)
Then weelcome life or death Each one

> If thou Entitle me thy one
> If thou convert this litle Sand
> To Stand the Shoke of thy Command. (63v-4r)

Austen integrates her interest in the possibility that her dreams have prophetic significance with her concern for writing an appropriate kind of verse--verse befitting the commonplace book of a woman of rank. Thus, she turns her questioning of her dream's meaning into a conventional articulation of her submission to God's will. I include the poem in its entirety to demonstrate, first, the degree to which Austen compensates through generalized, unobjectionable entreaties to God for the opening lines in which she explicitly wonders about the meaning of her dream, and second, the coherence of the poem despite this shift from prophetic interrogation to humble prayer. Austen converts her potentially controversial effort to read meaning into her dream, to determine whether it foretells further life or imminent death for her, into a prayer accepting whichever alternative God dictates. Therefore, although the poem strays from the topic of prophetic dream interpretation so provocatively suggested by its title, it is still tightly constructed around the problem of an uncertain future, whether Austen will live or die. (Austen's playful repetition and reversal of the phrase "life and death," in particular, contribute to this thematic coherence; see esp. lines 3, 16, 19, and 21.)

Austen's conflicted opinions about the validity of prophetic activity are especially evident in her collection of arguments that could be made either against the prophetic claims of particular radical groups or against the possibility of contemporary prophecy altogether.[62] For example, Austen records arguments opposing Quaker and Ranter beliefs that an individual's direct access to God--the presence of the indwelling spirit in a man or woman--supersedes any external assessment (including the scriptures) of that direct, supernatural contact. Austen writes that "w^t [what] a man pretends he hath herd we can enquier if it agree to Gods word" (14): she asserts that divine inspiration can be tested against the higher authority of

---

[62] While Austen seems to target specific radical sectarian beliefs with her criticisms of claims to latter-day revelations, she does not satirize puritans in the manner in which the lyrics in some Royalist collections do. See Marotti, *Manuscript* esp. 118-124. Similarly, Austen does--like the radical sectarians--express anti-Catholic feeling, yet she does so in much milder terms than they. She is arguably less concerned with refuting "papist" beliefs than she is with proving radical Protestant beliefs wrong. For instance, she concludes a paragraph relating a Protestant view of the Catholic belief in praying to saints for intercession by simply asserting, "But to pray to any saint theirs noe president in Scripture from the first of Gen: to the last of Revelations" (Austen 19).

the scriptures.[63] Austen also seems to target the Quakers when she includes these observations about the classical fortunetellers, the Sybils: "The ffathers observe of the Sybels, and other oracles That they were possesd with such shakings and transports as bereaved them of their reason. But Divine inspirations, and oracles preserve the harmony of the Soule" (12v).[64] Real prophets do not shake; by implication, Quakers cannot be legitimate visionaries. Furthermore, Austen writes that "God is not prodigal of these special favours but for some great designes are they indulged" (12v). Prophetic abilities do not manifest themselves frequently. Given Austen's social elitism, this statement could signify that members of the lower classes could not possibly be the main recipients of such divine favors. After all, it is "but for some great designes" that God grants them. Against the ecstatic behavior of nonconformist groups, Austen posits the fundamental value of rationality in measuring God's extraordinary communications. "When God dus give signes," Austen writes, "he gives also illustrations of the understanding, that they may be discerned to be his signs and not esteemed natural accidents." Likewise, the widow argues that "One rule in discerning and Judging a miracle or of a Revelation is to consider whether it be done in confirmation of a Necessary Truth. Otherwise it may be suspected a delusion" (Austen 15).[65] Austen even recounts the oft-cited, bottom-line argument against any special contact with the divine after the days of the apostles.[66] She writes:

> Had God continued to us persons of unfalliable gifts and of extraordinary spirits, as hertofore th[e?] prophets and Apostles were of, it had been a means to take us off from studing and searching the scriptures Now God hath left us to hear what his son speaketh, and we are to know the mind of God out of his word which he hath spoken. (Austen 16)

The age of prophecy, according to this argument, passed long ago. Although Austen does not explicitly or specifically target any of the radical

---

[63] On the controversy about the relationship between the Holy Spirit and scripture, see Nuttall 20-33.

[64] On neosibylline prophecies, see Thomas 393. Hill points out that "Fifth Monarchists in the 1650s cited ['the prophecies of Merlin, Mother Shipton and many others'] as well as the Sibylline prophecies, Nostradamus, Parcelsus and astrologers" (*The World Turned Upside Down*, 72). Austen's questioning of the validity of sibylline prophecies could also, therefore, register her disbelief in Fifth Monarchist claims to prophetic knowledge.

[65] On appeals to reason in trying the spirit, see Nuttall esp. 43.

[66] On the question of whether the same spirit that acted upon the apostles was similarly acting upon seventeenth-century English men and women, see Nuttall esp. 28-9.

groups who made prophetic claims in the previous decades, an awareness of their role in the upheaval of that period could have prompted her either to contradict the validity of their specific prophetic activities or to record someone else's assertions to the same effect.

Austen's letter to her son Thomas at Oxford reveals her awareness of the manner in which nonconformist beliefs could become socially disruptive, challenging the conventions of civility dear to the elite classes. Austen warns her son away from his apparent flirtation with the socially iconoclastic resistance to paying "hat honor":[67]

> This Custome in my weeke opinion may be diclined as the introduction to rudenes, to lofty and conceited carriadg, and w^{ch} [which] renders yo[ur] self in yo[ur] own Esteeme far better then yo[ur] Correspondent. Tom: w^t [what] ere the ffashione is I wud have yo[ur] demeanour otherwayes. And tho you may goe Scot-free Hat ffree be not so rude in yo[ur] Carriadg but if a Beggar puts off his hat give the like. And now I see the rise and orriginal of Person Wilsons Surly Nod from his prestine preheminence. (44r)

Austen worries that her son, acting in the public sphere of the university, might indulge in a "ffashione" that could be "the introduction to rudenes." Given the widow's concerns about rising in status, it is not surprising that she disapproves any "ffashione" that makes a spectacle of disrupting social conventions. Tellingly, Austen connects what she sees as "rude" behavior with puritan excess: she "see[s] the rise and orriginal of Person Wilsons Surly Nod from his prestine preheminence." Austen's mocking alliteration

---

[67] Hill remarks, "Even what seems to us the innocent eccentricity of refusing to remove the hat in the presence of social superiors, or to use the second person plural to them, confirmed conservative contemporaries in their suspicions. The former was a long-standing gesture of popular social protest, practised not only by Marian martyrs but also by the seditious Hacket, Coppinger and Arthington in 1591, by John Lilburne on many famous occasions, by Winstanley and Everard in the presence of Fairfax in 1649" (*The World Turned Upside Down* 198). Capp relates an incident in which Fifth Monarchist leader "Feake and his supporters kept on their hats as a protest as psalms were sung at Christ Church in 1654" (144). Also see Bauman, for an explanation of how the Quakers' rejection of "politeness phenomena," including paying hat honor, "challenged the very fabric of social relations and social interaction" (43) and see Hill, *The Century of Revolution* 144 and Hazard 202-3. Todd interprets Austen's letter as referring to "A college tradition [which] allowed students of his standing not to remove their hats in respect of others." However, Todd's transcription leaves out the line referring to "Person Wilsons Surly Nod," which suggests that Austen has nonconformists in mind. The widow may have conflated two different sets of customs concerning the etiquette of wearing hats. Todd also reads "diclined" as "described" ("A Young Widow of London" 220, 221). For more on hat etiquette at the universities, see Stone 172.

in referring to the parson's "prestine preheminence" reveals her scorn for what she considers his puritanical, holier-than-thou attitude--an attitude that, to her mind, replaces a social hierarchy with an exclusively religious one and does so to her disadvantage.[68]

Not only does Austen's social elitism thus inflect her attitude towards prophetic activity, but so does her more specific awareness of her gender as a potential threat to her rank. Mack observes that "*all* enemies of the propertied classes and of the religious establishment, both male and female, were portrayed symbolically as women . . . while actual female visionaries were portrayed as tramps, in both the sexual and economic sense" (57). As the first epigraph to this section suggests, Austen appears to have been familiar with the derogatory association of prophetic activity with women: "If men doe listen to Wispers of fear, and have not reason, and observation Enough to confute trifles . . . Every old woman shal be a prophetes" (Austen 25r). Given Austen's angry essay in reaction to being called an "old goat" by an anonymous male pedestrian (see note 7 above), it is clear that she is sensitive to the implication that she qualifies as such an "old woman," an epithet she considers the worst of insults. ". . . I should be unwilling to call a woman of foure score old," Austen writes, explaining the negative connotation of the expression as she sees it, "Ancient is honourable: old is despicable. Old belongs to Old Shooes. Old clothes. Not to my self" (22v). Given Austen's unequivocal understanding of "old woman" as disparaging, her comment about how superstitiousness leads foolish men to think "every old woman . . . a prophetes" reveals her bitter sense of the potential ridicule associated with being a woman prophet.[69]

The representation of radical sectarians in the newsbook *Mercurius Fumigosus* from the week of 16-23 August 1654 exemplifies the written treatment of such groups that a literate Londoner like Austen might have encountered. *Mercurius Fumigosus* describes two "*shee-Ranters*" who try to seduce two men in a bar: the women are thrown out of the alehouse because they are too noisy in their disrobing and dancing. The article emphasizes the extremity of the women's scandalous behavior by explaining that:

> the *women* would not hide but the next day went *stark naked* about the
> *streets*; being demanded if they had Husbands? they replyed, *Their*

---

[68] See Bauman, 55-6, for more on typical reactions to religious groups who rejected forms of courtesy.

[69] Austen's fear of being thought an old woman corresponds with her culture's tendency to stereotype old women negatively, about which, see Mendelson and Crawford 69.

husbands were within them, which was God. Oh that Women (the shape of
Angels) should prove worse then Devills. (159-60)

The "*shee-Ranter[s']*" greatest offense is their contention that "*Their
husbands were within them, which was God.*" This hostile representation of
the belief in the indwelling spirit--an anti-hierarchical belief that could
logically lead to claims of individual prophetic revelation--exemplifies the
manner in which radical sectarian membership by women was coded as
doubly shameful. Their "heretical" (antinomian) beliefs, unveiled for shock
value only at the end of the narrative, are prefigured in their unruly,
licentious behavior. As a woman strongly invested in social hierarchy and
anxious to augment her rank, Austen would certainly have avoided any
possible identification with such women. Had she read any of the
newsbook articles describing Fifth Monarchist Anna Trapnel's prophetic
activities, she might have seen even more reason to reject women prophets
as a group. The newsbook *Severall Proceedings of State Affairs*, for
instance, reporting for the week of 12-19 January 1653 [54] includes
Trapnel's prayer asking God to help gentlewomen renounce their material
vanities. The newsbook reports Trapnel's plea:

> [t]hat the Lord would cause the people of this Nation, to leave their sins
> and profaneness, As Gentlewomens black Spots and Patches, Powderings
> of Hair, Gold and Silver-Lace, and other wickedness; and that she did
> believe God hath some of his Elect even among such, and prayed to God
> for their Conversion. (165)

Austen, so driven to gain gentle status herself, seems unlikely to have
appreciated the shipwright's daughter's disdainful speculation that "God
hath some of his Elect even among such."

Given the tensions between the gentry and the urban lower classes
during the revolutionary decades and the demonizing association of women
represented as whores with such low ranking groups, it is no wonder that
Austen distinguishes herself from the radical prophets of the 1640s and 50s.
As I indicate above, Austen shares with the female prophets who precede
her the tendency to compare herself to biblical figures; however, she also
mixes her biblical self-comparisons with her material desires. In drawing a
parallel between her own life and a biblical episode that few radical
sectarians would draw, for example, Austen compares the estate at
Highbury that she hopes to own with the Land of Canaan. She hopes that
God will not delay in assisting her in her legal battles, "if it seemes good in

this sight of God to lend us that pleasant and fruitful Canaan to posses to his Glory" (Austen 68r).   Later, in reference to the same property, she speculates that God has made her take "six yeares in Learning how to receive and entertaine the blesing to Enter into y^e [the] land of Canan a rich Soile flowing with Milk and honey. Silver and Gold" (76v). Austen wants her own personal promised land; unlike radical sectarians, she does not seriously await the imminent arrival of Jesus and the establishment of his kingdom on earth.

Perhaps Austen's most striking difference from the radical women prophets of the 1640s and 1650s is her use of non-biblical historical figures in evaluating and asserting her authority.[70] For example, she asserts:

> When a vehement calamity lies long I can plead, out of Gods precidents, That this wil not last. David was not ten yeares in banishment but he enjoyed the Kingdome forty. Queen Eliz: was 5 yeares in affliction then it did appear God had mercy for her. (Austen 37-8)

Radical sectarians--Fifth Monarchist Anna Trapnel, for example--would not compare themselves to an actual European king or queen because no earthly monarch could possibly compete in importance or majesty with King Jesus.[71] Austen, however, boldly asserts her similarity to figures at the top of the social and political hierarchy, whether those figures are exclusively biblical or not. For example, she relates how "Henery a Germaine prince" read writing on "an old wall" that ultimately signified his political advancement to "Emperour of Germany." Austen uses this anecdote not only to support her belief that extraordinary signs similarly construct her life into a divinely-inflected narrative, but also to further her hopes that those signs have a similarly positive meaning. She thus explains how she

---

[70] Her particular interest in legends concerning Elizabeth I is not unique or unusual. Wynne-Davies notes that "the most recurrent political topic utilized by women poets of the time is the life and reign of one of their own number: Elizabeth I. Perhaps her popularity as subject matter rested on the fact that, in issues of government and national policy, Elizabeth offered the unique combination of absolute power and female gender" (xxiv). Also see Wynne-Davies xxv.

[71] As Capp indicates, "Anna Trapnel prophesied that God would make the saints earls and potentates" (145); however, the position of monarch was inevitably held in reserve for Jesus. Capp describes the proposed Fifth Monarchist political structure: "Until Christ arrived, the government was to be by the small minority who formed the elect, organized into a church-parliament based on the Jewish sanhedrin . . . The tyranny of the godly over the unregenerate was one logical result of Calvinist election, and there was certainly nothing democratic in the Fifth Monarchists' programme" (138).

found a jewel, which she feels must have extraordinary meaning, in an old wall:

> I had noe fore admonishment to look for the Jewel I found. Yet I found it
> out of an Old Wall, tho by meer accident. What [?]rtarily import to me I
> cannot surely determine. Yet sure I think it nearely concernes me. I wish I
> may as piously attend a circumspection of my daies as this happy person in
> the Story.

If Austen can indeed "as piously attend a cicumspection of [her] daies as this happy person in the Story," then she, like "Henery [the] Germaine prince," would become a monarch (12r). That this is her implication is especially likely given that her next anecdote relates how a "Common Souldier" becomes a "Romaine Emperour" in fulfillment of a sign that he receives. Elsewhere the widow also muses, "I here St. Bernard til a great Queen she was as <more> honourable in her widow condition, as by being a Queene" (40). In this instance, Austen consoles herself with the thought that an ancient figure of authority, St. Bernard, values the social position of the widow as much as--or even more than, as Austen's emendation suggests --a queen.

    While Austen may desire aristocratic status, she also seems to wish that kings would listen to her. Her brief essay on the twelfth-century mystic Hildegard of Bingen suggests that Austen finds in this medieval woman, who was respected by powerful male leaders of her own day and of Austen's as well, a worthy model to emulate:[72]

---

[72]   Thomas indicates that the Catholicism of "the medieval saints, Hildegard, Bridget, and Vincent," was not an obstacle because their "apocalyptic predictions relating to the reform of the Church and the fall of Rome were easily acceptable in a Protestant environment" (393).   *The Nunns Prophesie: OR The True, Wonderful, and Remarkable PROPHESIE of St. Heldegard, First NUNN and then ABESS: CONCERNING The Rise and Downfall of those Fire-Brands of EUROPE, the whole Order of JESUITS* (1680) is representative of Protestant appropriations of Hildegard as an early anti-papal figure, even if it may have been published too late to have influenced Austen directly (although, given that the latest date recorded in "Book M" is 1682, it could have influenced her). In the preface to the pamphlet, its editor characterizes Hildegard thus: *"Tho' the Religious Writer of this Remarkable Prophesie, had the unhappiness to be Born in the very heat of Superstition, and to be bred up among all the Errors and Traditions of the Church of* Rome, *yet no sooner was she arriv'd at Years of Discretion, but her discerning Eyes easily look'd through all those gaudy-Innovations, and by a Prospective of Divine Inspiration, she both beheld, admir'd, and practic'd Christianity in its Innocent, Naked, and Primitive Shape, as Christ himself had left it before it had been corrupted in* Italy. *It was this that caus'd her (tho' she had been one her self) bitterly to inveigh against the Debauchery of* Nunneries, *the Lasciviousness of* Priests, *the Hypocrosie of* Monks, *and indeed against the Clandestine Impieties of the* Pope

Of Hildegardis

God first humbles and afflicts whom he intends to illuminate with more than ordinary grace. And tho she had afflictions God gave her wings, and raised her mounted Soule in Revelations. And St. Bernard, and the pope allow those Revelations to be authentick. She prophesied of the Mendicant ffriers and divers signs of covetiousnes And of the coming of those vermine into the World who wud rob secular princes of their prerogatives and many things concerning the abuse of the papal church. She was of the popes conclave and emperours counsel to whom they had recourse in Difficulties. Yea y^e [the] great Torches of the Church lighted themselves at her Candle, and patriarchs, and Bishops sent knots as pased their fingers for her to vntie.

Hildegardis was for certaine a gracious virgen, and God might performe some great wonders by her hand. (34r)

According to Austen, Hildegard used her prophetic gifts with the approval and admiration of patriarchal authorities (from "St. Bernard and the pope" to "emperours"), who sent her "knots" "to vntie" that they could not undo. This aspect of Austen's representation of Hildegard is consistent with that in *The Nunns Prophesie* (1680), which reports that the mystic's piety made her:

> *most deservedly respected by all the Learned and Religious Men of her Age, who generally look'd on her as one to whom God for the purity of her Life, had intrusted with the Spirit of* Prophesie. (1)

Unlike some of the radical women prophets of the 1640s and 1650s, Hildegard did not seek the sudden, violent overthrow of established (earthly) patriarchal authority. In fact, according to Austen, Hildegard predicted "the coming of those vermine into the World who wud rob secular princes of their prerogatives": Austen's Hildegard is all the more admirable for having had the foresight to be a Royalist. This medieval mystic was apparently the kind of prophet that Austen would like to have been--or perhaps, that Austen thought she was. *The Nunns Prophesie* reports that:

> *this veneration they had for [Hildegard] during her Life (as is usual) was rather increased by her death, for then they carefully collected all her Manuscripts, and finding this* Prophesie *among them, Written by her*

---

himself; so that we may more properly term her a Roman-Protestant *than a* Roman-Catholique . . ." (1).

*own hand, they all look't on it as a real thing, and expected the fulfilling
of it* . . . (1-3).

It is tempting to speculate that Austen, too, may have known about this
aspect of the post-Reformation legends concerning Hildegard and that she
may have hoped for an analogously posthumous discovery of "Book M" and
its prophecies.[73] Austen's description of the source of Hildegard's authority
applies just as well to herself. Much of "Book M" records her prayers and
meditations concerning her afflictions. That she begins her essay on
Hildegard with the statement that "God first humbles and afflicts those
whom he intends to illuminate with more than ordinary grace" suggests that
she, like Hildegard, will be given "wings" and that God will "[raise] her
mounted Soule in Revelations." Her claims to prophetic dreams and
accurate predictions, in fact, suggest that she has already been granted such
special "Revelations." Hildegard, as a historical model of the female
prophet, is the perfect alternative to Austen's more immediate prophesying
sisters, the radical sectarians of the revolutionary period: Hildegard is no
"*shee-Ranter*," and neither, Austen would presumably hope, is she.

That Austen periodically displays less ambivalence about her own
prophetic claims is evident in the occasional poem she numbers her twenty-
first. While "Has Conduct Carried me through Seaven great yeares" retains
the commonplace features--such as the acceptance of affliction and desire
for contrition (e.g., lines 14 and 17-18 below)--of some of Austen's
generalized verse spiritual meditations, it integrates Austen's prophetic
concerns more thoroughly with those thematic conventions:

> Has Conduct Carried me through seaven great yeares
> Great in perplexities, and great in feares
> Great Griefes with Job: could hardly be Exprest
> Neither by Sighings or by teares redrest
> Six folded trials and a seaventh as great (5)
> By a perticular and genneral waight
> Hard knot Negotiates by oppresion knit
> A Dread consuming Sickenes came, And Yet
> Mercy out Shined all those dark Eyed Clouds
> Design'd to me, in Seaven yeares ruged folds (10)
> The Wise Egiptianes deemed six compleate
> The Divine Scriptures dus the same repeate

---

[73] Mendelson and Crawford relate an interesting anecdote, in which Sarah Henry
reads the religious reflections of a recently deceased female friend, that supports the view that
Austen might have anticipated a posthumous readership for "Book M" (228).

Six hardest trials, and to give renowne
There comes a Seaventh. This is afflictions Crowne
My Gracious Lord Wilt Thou admit to me (15)
Thy Dearest <speciall [inserted below the line]> favours Soe much glory
  See
O that Upon thy Alter I may lay
A Contrite heart and perfectly obay
That Every day and minute be Confind
Thy bright Memorials to bear in minde (20)
And to the future generations tell
How high, how Excellent, Thy glories swell. (102v-103)

In "Upon My Dreame the 20th Oct 1664 When I Dreamet I Saw 4 Moones in a Clear Sky: Meditation," the ninth poem that Austen numbers in "Book M," she incorporates her brief initial prophetic interrogation into a very conventional, unexceptionable spiritual meditation. In this much later poem, however, she maintains her interest in prophetic interpretation throughout. The first fourteen lines not only meditate on the numerological significance of the seven years Austen interprets as her allotted period of suffering before she gains some great reward (which corresponds to the stipulation in her husband's will that she not remarry for seven years), but they also justify that meditation through biblical and legendary references. Hence, Austen cites Job as the scriptural model of endurance (3-4); she borrows from the ancient authority of "The Wise Egiptianes" who, like her, see six as a symbol of "compleate[ness]" (11); and she confirms the sacred significance of six and seven by alluding to the six days of creation and the seventh day of rest in Genesis (12-14). Rather than diminishing the implications of her numerological meditation by retreating into a purely conventional prayer after line fourteen, Austen incorporates an explicit plea for extraordinary gifts into her address to God. In line sixteen, Austen changes her request for God's "Dearest favours" into a request for "<speciall> favours." Austen's revision, in fact, alters the rest of the prayer such that it suggests that her ability to "lay/ A Contrite heart" upon God's "Alter" and "perfectly obay" depends upon God's granting her those "<speciall> favours" (17-18). Austen thus combines prophetic discourse with the conventions of meditative verse. The last two couplets similarly merge these discourses. Lines nineteen and twenty continue the series of conditional results of God's bestowal of "<speciall> favours" upon the poetic speaker; this divine gift will enable the poet "every day and minute" to "be Confined/ Thy bright Memorials to bear in minde." The gift of "<speciall> favours" here appears to assist the speaker's meditative self-discipline, but it does not seem to give her access to anything particularly extraordinary. The image of constant "Confine[ment]," in fact, suggests that the poet will simply engage in the most private--and therefore the most appropriate for a seventeenth-century woman--of religious exercises. The final couplet, however, calls the privacy of that "Confine[ment]" into question. The "<speciall[y]> favour[ed]" poet will "the future generations tell/ How high, how Excellent, Thy glories swell" (21-2). The implication connecting these last two couplets as a logical sequence of thought is the act not only of writing, but of textual transmission, of "publishing" in the sense of making public. The fruits of contemplation in an isolated, private space will transform into a public declaration across generations.

The final lines (12-19) of Austen's nineteenth numbered poem include a similar linkage of Austen's plea for an extraordinary gift from God with her promise to make a public declaration of the deity's greatness in return:

> Declare me what to doe, Something reveale
> Since grace and glory all high things wilt give
> Teach me with circumspection how to live
> ffrom Special favours begs Enlardged desier (15)
> My Soule in all its motions may move higher
> That Heaven and Earth to all I may display
> The Love of Jesu, and his Soveraigne Stay
> And by an outward, and an inward Story
> Render my praises to that immense glory. (101v)

The poet requests that God "reveale" "Something" (12) to her and suggests that "Special favours" cause one to be that much more zealous in one's faith, to have "Enlardged desier" (15). The speaker claims that she makes this request for a special dispensation so "That Heaven and earth to all [she] may display/ The Love of Jesu" (16-17). While on one level, the speaker suggests an exchange with God--if God "reveale[s]" "Something," the speaker will publicize God's greatness in doing so--on an another level, she justifies through this implied exchange a woman's public speech. Given the speaker's proposed terms of exchange, if God were to grant a special revelation, it would have to be because he does indeed want the recipient of his gift to "display" "to all" "The Love of Jesu"; God's granting of "Special favours" would be tantamount to a license to speak publicly. In the final couplet of this poem, Austen again distinguishes between private spiritual exercises and public declarations of faith to make clear her willingness to serve God publicly. If he will only "Declare [her] what to doe, Something reveale," she will "by an outward, and an inward Story/ Render [her] praises to that immense glory" (18-19). While Austen's distinction between "an outward, and an inward Story" could signify her intention to show her devotion to God through her outward behavior as well as her inner thoughts, the greater context of "Book M," in which the widow betrays an interest in making her writing public, suggests that this distinction could also indicate her willingness to enter the public sphere on God's behalf.[74]

Austen the ambivalent visionary, negotiating between the private and public spheres, proclaiming in a personal, never-published manuscript her willingness to praise God through both "an inward" and "an outward . . . Story," thus struggles to develop an acceptable model for a decorous woman poet of rank--a model which will not undermine her proper femininity through too obvious a desire to intervene in the public sphere, but which will, nonetheless, legitimate and perform her status for some unknown audience.

The Landed Poet

> Am I the person am to reap the first fruites of that long expectation, and enter into those pleasant feeldes of a faire inheritance. And that it should be appointed for my Children. Tis a blesing I know not how to receave. Yet let me and mine ever remember that we receive our prosperity, and enter into a Lardge revenue through the Jawes of death, and by the heapes of Mortality . . . let the name bear the same rememberance. Highbury. To bury those that are mounted never so high in this world. (Austen 103v)

In "On the Situation of Highbury," the twenty-third numbered poem in "Book M," Austen appropriates select topoi from the tradition of country house poetry to ascribe value to the estate and to negotiate her position in relation to it. In doing so, she creates a socially acceptable, if paradoxical, voice for a wealthy widow eager to increase her social rank. As we will see, Austen's country house poem warrants especially close attention because it represents a significant, unapologetic departure from her usual religious verse (which constituted the least objectionable poetry a seventeenth-century woman could write) and because the poetic voice

---

[74] Wilcox notes that "The obligation to use the gifts of God and display the works of providence compromises the notion that women's devotional lives can be inviolably private" (57).

Austen constructs in it speaks from an innovative position--neither patron/proprietor nor guest--within the tradition of the genre.[75]

The most striking characteristic of "On the Situation of Highbury" is Austen's tentative relationship to estate about which she writes. As Malcolm Kelsall observes, "the English country house tradition is originated by, and belongs to, outsiders" (40).[76] Such "outsiders" can be social equals to the hosts for whom they write their epideictic verse (as in the case of Carew's "To Saxham" and Fane's "A Peppercorn or Small Rent Sent to My Lord Campden for the Loan of His House at Kensington, 9 February, 1651"), or they may have unequal status, either lower or higher, with respect to their hosts (as in the case of Jonson's "To Penshvrst," Lanyer's "The Description of Cooke-ham," or King James's "Verses Made by the King, when He was Entertained at Burly in Rutland-shire, by my Lord Marquess of Buckingham. August 1621"). Austen, however, is not simply an "outsider," a visitor to Highbury; "On the Situation of Highbury" praises an estate that she hopes to secure as her own. She appears to have composed her poem in September 1665, when Highbury came out of lease to another holder and entered into Austen's possession. Yet waiting for the estate to come out of lease had been only one obstacle to her ownership of the estate. There had been a separate movement in Parliament earlier that year that would, if successful, have made the estate unavailable to her.[77] Hence, while Austen seems to have been positioned to receive the estate in September, she still relates to it as a somewhat uncertain prospect. Thus, strictly speaking, there is neither a host, nor a guest in Austen's country house poem until the very end. Hesitant in her ownership of Highbury, the ambitious widow marshals the traditional topoi of the country house genre so that her desire for elite status and her assertion of an authoritative voice--

---

[75] Fowler's *The Country House Poem: A Cabinet of Seventeenth-Century Estate Poems and Related Items*, an extremely helpful anthology of over 70 poems within or relevant to the country house tradition, demonstrates the popularity of the genre. Although Austen's poem is not in Fowler's collection, he does include poems by other women writers, such as Aemilia Lanyer, Margaret Cavendish, and Anne Finch. Fowler observes that "[f]rom 1560-1700, virtually every poet attempted at least one poem of country life," whether an estate poem or related kind (e.g., verse on the happy life) (*Country House Poem* 14). Fowler associates such poetry, in general, with the "affirm[ation of] traditional values," which suggests that Austen's composition of a country house poem was perfectly consistent with her tendency towards social and political conservatism (*Country House Poem* 14). On the conservative nature of country-house poetry, also see Dubrow 126-30.

[76] For more on outsiders in relation to country-house poetry, see Dubrow 129.

[77] On Austen's problems in gaining Highbury and for some illustrative excerpts from "Book M," see Todd, "A Young Widow" 229-37.

both complicated by her awareness of her gender as a potential liability in advancing her socioeconomic desires given her widowed state--become intertwined and mutually reinforcing. Austen the poet reinforces the value of the estate soon to augment her status by inscribing it within the country house tradition alongside other celebrated, monumentalized sites; the worthiness of the estate, which will soon reflect on Austen as owner, legitimates the authority and propriety of her verse.[78]

Austen's "On the Situation of Highbury" clearly indicates her familiarity with the tradition of country house poetry. Her verse praises the estate's fertility and abundance; locates pleasure and joy in relation both to that self-producing abundance and to the masterful prospect of the land available from what is presumably the site of the house; and remarks the paradisal absence of hard labor at Highbury.[79] Austen, however, also excludes topoi usually associated with the genre. Most significantly, she does not praise the hospitality of the owner of the estate and his or her family; she does not portray the harmony between the members of the resident family and their servants and tenants; and she does not provide glimpses of the family's history, its cross-generational existence at the estate.[80] Likewise, although Austen's representation of the fruitfulness of

---

[78] Wayne's observations about seventeenth-century changes in notions of self in relation to possessions suggests how owning Highbury could help Austen to further her aspirations to gentility: "whereas the terms 'property' (or 'propriety') had formerly signfied a relationship, by the seventeenth century the relational concept was subordinated to the more reified notion of a thing.

In precapitalist English society property was understood as a *right*, that is, a right to revenue (in service, produce, or money) based on title to land. With the ascendancy of a market economy and its accompanying ideology, the distinction between the right and the thing became blurred: property became the thing itself" (23). On the importance of understanding subjects in relation to their objects, see de Grazia, Quilligan, and Stallybrass.

[79] On fertility and plenitude in the genre, see Fowler, *Country House Poem* 3 and Dubrow 126. See Goldberg 226 and Kelsall 33, on those commonplaces in Jonson's "To Penshvrst." On the prospects, see Fowler 51n54. On estates as paradisal, see Fowler 3-4 and Dubrow 126. See Harp esp. 81-3 on biblical precedents for associating nature's abundance with prelapsarian humanity. Also see Williams 31-2 for an argument relating Edenic figurations of estates to the erasure of labor.

[80] See Cain 35 for the traditional scholarly association of "generosity, hospitality and . . . 'natural' harmony" with "To Penshvrst," and see Fowler, *Country House Poem* 8-11 on hospitality in general. Rathmell proposes that Jonson's awareness of Lord Lisle's financial difficulties may have influenced the poet's depiction of "[t]he distinguishing characteristics of the Penshurst household" as "the warmth of its hospitality, the generosity and humanity of its owners, and its importance as the focus of the local community" (260). See Fowler, *Country House Poem* 7-8 and Lewalski, *Writing Women* 236 on family history in the genre. In addition to leaving open the position of Highbury's proprietor and therefore not including

the land participates in the expected conventions of the genre, she does not convey the typically emblematic, derivative relationship of the estate's Edenic qualities with respect to the resident aristocratic or gentle family.[81] As we will see, Austen selectively appropriates topoi from the country house tradition to negotiate her hesitant, but ambitious, relationship to Highbury. She praises the place through the use of conventions rendering it legible as a site deserving of poetic monumentalization, while she leaves its lord unnamed, the role of proprietor unspecified, and therefore open to the possibility that the poet herself will fill that position. I include the poem in its entirety because it is not widely available:

> So fairely mounted in a fertile Soile
> Affordes the dweller plesure, without Toile
> Th'adjacent prospects gives so sweet <rare> a Sight
> That Nature did resolve to frame delight
> On this faire Hill, and with a bountious load (5)
> Produce rich Burthens, makeing the aboad
> As full of joy, as where fat vallies Smile
> And greater far, here Sicknes doth exhile
> Tis an unhappy fate to paint that place
> By my unpollishet Lines, with so bad grace (10)
> Amidst its beauty, if a streame did rise
> To clear my mudy braine and misty Eyes
> And find a Hellicon t'Enlarge my muse
> Then I noe better place then this wud choose
> In such a Laver and on this bright Hill (15)
> I wish parnassus to adorne my quill. (Austen 104r)

---

commonplace observations concerning the proprietor's family history, Austen excludes the typical opposition of old, modest, organic houses with new, ostentations, prodigy ones (about which see Fowler, *Country House Poem* 2, 18, and Kelsall 32), and she does not participate in the allegorical contrasting of houses of holiness with houses of sin (see Fowler *Country House Poem* 5 and McClung 78). That Austen does not reveal much about the house itself, however, is typical of the genre: Fowler asserts that "'Country house poems,' so called, are not about houses: a better label is 'estate poems'" (*Country House Poem* 1). For more on generic commonplaces, see Fowler, *Country House Poem* esp. 16-17; Kelsall 49; and Lewalski, *Writing Woman* 236.

   [81]   Fowler asserts that "[m]ost estate poems are epideictic, urging the subject's praises. Any feature of an estate may emblematize the owner; but often the poem culminates in explicit eulogy of the family's virtues" (*Country House Poem* 7; also see 21). Arguing that "To Penshvrst" is concerned with a new, emergent definition of the "home," Wayne writes that "Penshurst is represented as a place where everything that is natural and good is in abundance; this abundance is administered by a family, which is, in turn, represented as everything that is humanly natural and good" (39).

Austen's poem divides into two main sections exactly at its midpoint (after line 8). The first half adjusts the commonplace representation of an estate's fruitfulness to link Highbury's abstracted qualities of abundance, pleasure, and beauty to each other, while it leaves undeveloped the suggestion of the typically vital connection between such idealized qualities and an especially virtuous owner. The second half develops a complicated relationship of mutual valuing between the poet / owner and the land.

For the most part, Austen depicts Highbury's paradisal attributes as a self-feeding, uninterrupted circle; although she mentions an anonymous "dweller" who benefits from the estate's delightful productivity, that unspecified owner is not explicitly responsible for the estate's ideal functioning. Austen does not name a particular person who provides a center of virtue around which the estate's abstracted Edenic qualities fall into a coherent, meaningful association with each other, as in Jonson's "To Penshvrst," for example; instead, if any aspect of the estate serves as the foundation of its value, it is sheer productivity itself. For instance, the alliteration in the first line, "So fairely mounted in a fertile soile," emphasizes the connection between Highbury's beauty and productivity; the fertility of the site contributes to its aesthetic value. Productivity also underwrites the property's emotional value: Highbury has "a bountious load" that "Produce[s] rich Burthens, makeing the aboad/ As full of Joy, as where fat vallies Smile" (5-7). Austen explicitly makes Highbury's agricultural fruitfulness responsible for the abundance of joy one finds there. In fact, "Joy" becomes an almost material product of the estate in this line; "the aboad" is "full of joy" as if the emotion itself could be accumulated in a cellar. Her alliteration linking the constellation of words "bountious," "Burthens," and "aboad" also highlights the place's productivity. What may seem a failed simile in these lines--"as where fat vallies smile"--instead perfectly fits Austen's repeated emphasis on the estate's abundance. This comparison asserts that the productivity of the land at Highbury is very much like that of productive land, "fat vallies." Her comparison is tautological except insofar as it compares the specific, Highbury, to the general, "vallies." In this simile, the "Joy" that fills the "aboad" finds its outdoor counterpart in the "fat vallies" that "smile." The "Joy" that seems material enough to expand and fill the "aboad" metamorphoses through this comparison into an expression of the now personified land's pleasure. Whereas Ben Jonson's belly presumably grows as a consequence of Penshurst's detailed material copia (if the poet gets his wish), which is represented as an aspect of Lord Lisle's hospitality, Austen's valley is "fat" and "smil[ing]" with pleasurable satiety. Her tautological comparison is all the more interesting because it simultaneously intimates consumption and production: the land seems both gorged with its own plenty and pregnant, poised to be fruitful and multiply.

Among Highbury's positive attributes is the fact that it "Affords the dweller plesure, without Toile" (2). This follows in the tradition of "To Penshvrst," in which Jonson concludes his praises of the estate and its owner by asserting that the lords of "proud, ambitious heaps" "haue built, but thy lord dwells" (*The Forrest* 2.101, 102). The distinction between "building" and "dwelling" in Jonson's poem has multiple resonances. For instance, it recalls the opening lines of "To Penshvrst," in which Jonson initiates his monumentalization of the Sidneys' country house by exclaiming its superiority to those houses "built to enuious show/ Of touch or marble" (*The Forrest* 2.1-2). The poet praises the fact that Penshurst cannot:

> boast a row
> Of polish'd pillars, or a roofe of gold:
>   Thou has no lantherne, whereof tales are told;
> Or stayre, or courts; but stand'st an ancient pile,
>   And these grudg'd at, art reuerenc'd the while.
>
> (*The Forrest* 2.2-6)

By detailing the ostentatious features of prodigy houses in contrast to Penshurst's organic development across many years, Jonson highlights the association of the former with a glaring, excessive expenditure of human labor--a display of work undermining any Edenic figuration of them. Jonson intimates that such buildings arouse not the prelapsarian emotions of joy and delight but the envy and resentment typical of the world after the fall. "[B]uilt to enuious show," such extravagant buildings attract hostility from onlookers; they are "grudg'd at," possibly by those who perform the back-breaking labor necessary to erect them so quickly.[82] An owner who "builds" thus does not found his or her house upon the right principles and human relationships. An owner who "dwells," by contrast, legitimately

---

[82]   Many scholars have addressed Jonson's representation of labor in "To Penshvrst"; for a range of relevant arguments, see Williams, 30-3; Wayne 75-6; Kelsall 34-5; Cain 37-40; and Harp 74. Robert Herrick's "*A Panegerick to Sir* Lewis Pemberton" (H-377.59-64), in which Pemberton "never grudged at" sharing food equally with all his guests, reverses the direction of potential resentment. Jonson and Herrick, however, both use this expression to emphasize that in a proper country house, there are no abuses of privilege or power to arouse bad feeling. Also cf. Jonson's "To Sir Robert Wroth," where "dwelling" suggests the mental peace one achieves by avoiding envy through shunning the capricious, competitive activities typical of a courtier's life (*The Forrest* 3.61-94).

constitutes the virtuous center of an ancient, harmonious estate. His or her possession of the estate is as natural as the organic, gradual construction of the country house across successive generations of his or her family. Furthermore, the presence of such a rightful "dweller" guarantees the maintenance of proper relations across the social hierarchy of the estate. Far from "grudg[ing] at" Penshurst's plenty, for instance, the locals "bring a capon . . . a rurall cake, / Some nuts, some apples . . . The better cheeses . . . [and] their ripe daughters" to their master's house to "expresse their loue" (*The Forrest* 2.51-4, 57). "Dwelling" at a country house like Penshurst summons the conservative fantasy of a socioeconomic microcosm where proprietor, guests, servants, and tenants all know their places, perform their respective duties willingly, and evince no desire to hold any other place in the estate's hierarchy.

Because "to dwell," in the wake of "To Penshvrst," implies so much about the proper ownership and management of an estate, it is telling that Austen refers to Highbury's nameless occupant as its "dweller." That she understands the conventional significance of the term is evident in her claim that the estate "Affords the dweller plesure, without Toile," for she specifically associates the absence of "Toile" or extreme labor with the owner's pleasure. Her precise choice of "Toile" suggests her awareness of the fact that estate poems can acknowledge the presence of labor (as Alastair Fowler points out, even the proprietor supposedly works by overseeing the estate) but that they must banish excessive labor lest it threaten the figuration of the estate as Edenic.[83] Like Penshurst, Highbury is a place where there is abundance without "Toile"; hence, there can be no resentment--or strife, an additional resonance of "Toile"--to disturb its paradisal order or its "dweller['s] plesure." Austen's claim that Highbury "Affords the dweller plesure, without Toile" is not only interesting because it reinforces the proposition that she was very familiar with the conventions of the genre but also because it points to her tentative relationship to the estate. As I indicate above, Highbury's "dweller" is unnamed; Austen does not clearly identify herself (or anyone else) with this role. When Austen

---

[83]   Fowler 17. Robert Herrick's estate poem, "*A Panegerick to Sir* Lewis Pemberton" (H-377) and his poems on the happy life are especially instructive in delineating notions of labor in these (usually) socially and politically conservative genres. On the owner's virtue as a kind of labor, see "*A Panegerick to Sir* Lewis Pemberton" (H-377.112-14); on the proprietor overseeing the estate's maintenance, see "*The Country life, to the honoured Master* Endimion Porter, *Groome of the Bed-Chamber to His Majesty*" (H-622.19-45); for a frank description of low-ranking laborers' efforts as the source of the estate's plenty, see "*The Hock-cart,* or *Harvest home: To the Right Honourable,* Mildmay, *Earle of Westmorland*" (H-250.1-4, 47-55).

refers to Highbury's occupant or owner as its "dweller," she invokes associations (natural, virtuous, ancient ownership) that together establish a proper place at the estate for that person to occupy, but she leaves that place empty. That her reference in line 2 to the issue of labor so common to the genre is highly condensed relates to this vacancy. Concerns about labor reflect upon the proprietor's management of the estate and his or her interactions with its lower-ranking occupants. Because Austen's poem is structured around the possibility that she will fill the position of proprietor herself, she avoids topoi that depend upon a more thorough representation of the owner's relationship to the estate. If Austen cannot yet fill the vacancy at Highbury, neither will anyone else.

The significance of a known, secure relationship between the owner of the estate and the servants and tenants becomes evident in the constrast between "On the Situation of Highbury" and Mildmay Fane's "My Hock-Cart or Reaping Day." Although Fane's poem is not, strictly speaking, a country house poem, it provides a useful example of a proprietor / poet's composition about his own possessions.[84] Fane unabashedly details the work necessary to bring *his* harvest home:

> Yet there will more go to't:
> > Words will not do't;
> But hands employed must be,
> And sickles used with rakes and furmety;
> And binders, too, be got
> With the black jack and flagon pot,
> That whilst with working each do sweat
> Those may allay and temper heat.
>
> And for to add to these
> > The bacon pease,
> The scythe and pitching fork
> Must all in season, too, be set a work. (17-28)

While Jonson arguably treats issues of labor and social hierarchy with critical awareness, he nonetheless represents them carefully in the interest of securing the patronage that would guarantee him a comfortable position

---

[84] About Fane, Fowler remarks that he has been "[u]ndervalued as a poet, perhaps because of his sincere but repetitive piety, perhaps because his large oeuvre of nondramatic verse has mostly remained in manuscript" (*Country House Poem* 213). Thus, Fane's works have been impeded by the same obstacle (remaining in manuscript) that has reduced the attention given to the works of many early modern women writers.

within that hierarchy. In contrast, Fane's speaker is not critical in the least of the hierarchical relations underpinning the assumed acceptability of the idea that the laborers at his estate will happily exchange their sweat for such edible rewards as "furmenty," "the black jack and flagon pot," and "The bacon pease." As both proprietor and poet, as a landowner secure in his elevated position in the social hierarchy, Fane represents the workers that he oversees with unusual frankness. Austen, however, does not experience this kind of security. Presumably, Austen would hope to become a center of power at Highbury analogous to that represented by Fane in "My Hock Cart or Reaping Day"; she, too, would like to be the point from which other, lesser social positions would measure their respective places and from which the land and house would derive their virtues. Yet because of her embattled recent history with respect to the estate, she does not easily express a fantasy of hierarchical but harmonious labor in service to her interests.

Although Austen's unspecified "dweller," does not oversee the details of estate management, she does gain pleasure from accessing the prospect overlooking the estate and its environs:

> Th' adjacent prospects gives so sweet <rare> a sight
> That Nature did resolve to frame delight
> On this faire Hill . . . . ("On the Situation of Highbury" 3-5)

While this view is not as majestic as that, for example, which Lanyer represents as the privileged view of Margaret Clifford, Countess of Cumberland in "The Description of Cooke-ham" [which includes "A Prospect fit to please the eyes of Kings" (72)], it still suggests a masterful objectification of the landscape that would convey a sense of ownership of the place. Austen not only aestheticizes the view from Highbury, calling it "sweet" and linking the act of seeing with pleasure through the end rhyme "sight / delight," but she renders that "prospect" an artwork. That "sight" is so "sweet" or "rare" (Austen's interlinear revision) that "Nature did resolve to frame" it.

Austen's manner of bringing together Nature and Art recalls Thomas Carew's "*To my friend* G.N. *from* Wrest," in which the poet represents the best "worke of Art" as the product of a partnership between Nature and Art in which the two are so closely associated as to be conflated. In claiming the aesthetic superiority of Wrest's ornamental waters over the classical statues of other estates, Carew writes:

Yet we decline not, all the worke of Art,
But, where more bounteous Nature beares a part
And guides her Hand-maid, if she but dispence
Fit matter, she with care and diligence
Employes her skill . . . . (69-73)

While one can interpret these lines so that they clearly distinguish between
Nature, who provides "Fit matter," and Art, her "Hand-maid," who "with
care and diligence / Employs her skill," the use of feminine pronouns to
refer to both entities throughout the passage tends to confuse them,
suggesting a difficulty in determining where Nature ends and Art begins. In
a similar but more complete conflation of the two, Austen's Nature is an
artist who stands back from her work and decides that all it needs is the
proper frame. Hence, a view that was already "sweet" or "rare" translates
into "delight" when regarded from the right point of view, when limited and
positioned according to a perspective offered only from a certain physical
location, when seen through the right eyes in the right place. From the
vantage point of the country house, nature becomes visually contained;
Austen's choice of the term "to frame" in conjunction with her revision of
"so sweet a sight" to "so rare a sight" suggests that the landscape is
simultaneously a natural domain and a valuable painting, a commodifiable
art object reinforcing the status and prestige of its unnamed possessor.[85]

The first personal possessive pronoun in "On the Situation of
Highbury" appears in its last eight lines, which constitute a distinct section
of the poem.   After her very condensed, abstracted description of
Highbury's beauty, pleasures, and abundance--or perhaps more accurately,
its beautiful, pleasurable abundance--Austen begins to construct her poetic
voice in relation to the place. Her hesitancy about her position with respect
to Highbury corresponds to the fusion of traits that one would usually
ascribe either to amateur or to laureate poetic identities.[86] The first couplet
in the second section of the poem exemplifies this fusion. Recalling the
aestheticized, framed landscape subject to the masterful, delighted gaze of

---

[85] Fowler indicates that picture galleries were frequently associated with country
houses and points out the connection between prestige and art collecting (especially with
respect to garden statuary) (*Country House Poem* 6-7). Poems referring explicitly to
paintings include Richard Lovelace's "AMYNTOR'S GROVE, *His* CHLORIS, ARIGO, *and*
GRATIANA. An Elogie" (29-32); Sir Richard Fanshawe's "The Escuriall" (67-96); and
Thomas Randolph's "On the Inestimable Content He Enjoys in the Muses: To Those of His
Friends that Dehort Him from Poetry" (143-50). For more on country-house galleries, see
Hazard 162-3.

[86] I borrow these terms from Helgerson.

Highbury's owner in lines 3-5, Austen laments in lines 9-10 that "Tis an unhappy fate to paint that place/ By my unpollishet Lines."[87] "Paint" reinforces the image of the landscape as a framed painting but marks the differences between Nature and the poetic speaker as creative agents, between the land as it really is and as Austen represents it in her poem. Austen's first direct self-reference--"my unpollishet Lines"--is an assertion of ownership, yet what she possesses is verse, not land. This creates the kind of distance from owning an estate found in Lanyer's and Jonson's poems: laureate poets write poems for proprietors of country houses; such owners typically supply patronage, not lyrics.[88] While Jonson may gain a vicarious sense of mastery over Sidney's estate through his blazoning of its commodifiable material pleasures, and while he establishes a special place for the poet in Penshurst's and the nation's hierarchy through his creation of "To Penshvrst," his propriety is only over his poetic construction of Penshurst.[89] Lanyer locates herself even further from any actual

---

[87] Here Austen again echoes Jonson. Her reference to her "unpollished Lines" recalls Jonson's portrait of Penshurst as the kind of country house that is not so ostentatious as to "boast a row / Of polish'd pillars" (*The Forrest* 2.2-3) and suggests a parallel between Austen's modest poem and Jonson's idealized Penshurst.

[88] Writing a country house poem, in itself, can suggest a claim to laureate poetic authority. Helgerson specifies "serious public poems of history and topography" as "poems that corresponded in the career of a laureate to the active public service of the amateur" (30). For the poet claiming ownership of verse, rather than an estate, also see Thomas Randolf's "On the Inestimable Content He Enjoys in the Muses: To Those of His Friends that Dehort Him from Poetry" (169-82) and Sir Thomas Salusbury's proem to "Kensington Grove" (3-4).

[89] Many scholars have analyzed the centrality of "To Penshvrst" in Jonson's construction of the poet's role in relation to his community. Cain asserts, for instance, that "[w]hen Jonson introduces himself into the scene, he is claiming recognition for the poet's place in society: the poet is a man of worth and dignity, who ought to be accorded the respect of others and welcomed to the communal celebrations. Jonson does not detail the poet's function within the banquet-scene, or within the network of relationships at Penshurst. Instead, we are to accept the poem itself as emblematic of what the poet contributes to his community" (40). Similarly, Goldberg argues that the poem provides "the very image of an endlessly fertile and yielding estate. What it gives to be devoured become the words on the page which give back to the estate as much as it yields. The poem repeats again and again this poetic economy, exchanging word and food, a paradigm of sustenance and the concrete valorization of the poet's play" (226). Also see Schoenfeldt, who asserts that "[i]nto the poem's fabric of praise . . . Jonson insinuates the possibility that Lisle needs him as much has he needs Lisle . . . Jonson's 'faire acceptance' of Lisle's hospitality dignifies the feast, the estate, and the noble hosts by making them, and what they stand for, legible" (74). Likewise, Wayne asserts that "[t]he only freedom from a rigidly hierarchical social structure attainable for him depended on the willing subjection of his power as a writer to the legitimation of the existing hierarchy. Yet in serving that function in exchange for the recognition and consecration of his genius, the writer became an embodiment of a new ideology, one that

proprietorship over the estate she praises and objectifies. Her valedictory poem gives her poetic power not over Cooke-ham itself but over her memory of it.[90] Lanyer's increased distance from owning Cooke-ham, however, does not prevent her from using her poetic description of it to claim laureate status for herself: "This last farewell to Cooke-ham here I give: / When I am dead, thy name in this may live" (205-6).[91]

Like these unpropertied poets, Austen mediates her desire for a place at Highbury through the powers of objectification and mastery involved in poetic description. She, like Lanyer and Jonson, claims propriety at least over "[her] . . . Lines." However, she characterizes her verse in a manner appropriate to the amateur poet who wants to advertise his or her gentle status: her lines are "unpollishet."[92] Similarly, Austen belittles her poetry by ascribing to it a "bad grace," which contrasts sharply with Lanyer's multifold attribution of "grace" to the Countess of Cumberland, and by association, to her poem. Cooke-ham is where the poet "first obtain'd/ Grace from that grace where perfect grace remained" (1-2). Lanyer's poetic speaker explains that "The gentle winds did take delight to be / Among those woods that were so graced by [the countess]" (39-40). Furthermore, Lanyer can unabashedly characterize her poetry as a "work of grace" because she ascribes its origins to the graceful countess's "desires" (12). Lanyer thus makes the countess the source of grace both for the estate and her verse. The "bad grace" of Austen's verse, meanwhile, which is "Amidst the beauty" of the estate (10, 11), intermingles dangerously with Highbury, threatening to pollute it. This is surprising because in the

---

asserted the possibility of individual transcendence" (18). For more on Jonson's positioning of the poet with respect to the social hierarchy and the nation, see Cain 39-40; Goldberg 223-6; Schoenfeldt 69, 73; Wayne 77.

[90]   Lanyer's distance from owning Cooke-ham is arguably increased because "it belonged . . . to the crown, not to the Countess" (Lewalski 237). For more on "The Description of Cooke-ham," see Woods, *Lanyer: A Renaissance Woman Poet* 28-32, 115-25.

[91]   Also cf. Thomas Stanley's "Sylvia's Park" (31-40).

[92]   Helgerson asserts that the poet's representation of his--or her (Helgerson's account suggests that all available poetic roles assumed a male poet)--attitude towards his (or her) verse is fundamental to that poet's effort to establish either an amateur or laureate identity. He writes, for instance, that "Like Pope and Dryden, Spenser, Jonson, and Milton felt it necessary to keep reminding the world of their greatness. But even as we recall the sometimes annoying obstrusiveness of these assurances, we should remember too that they are often an integral part of the laureate's finest poetry" (Helgerson 11). Helgerson associates the amateur, however, with strategic "self-disparagement" (31).

country house genre, proprietors do not typically devalue their property.[93] While the countess infuses Cooke-ham with her grace, Austen, in her complex position as poet and future proprietor of Highbury, is purified by the land. Austen writes:

> if a streame did rise
> To clear my mudy braine and misty eyes
> And find a Hellicon t'Enlarge my Muse
> Then I noe better place then this wud choose.
> ("On the Situation of Highbury" 11-14)

The poetic speaker fantasizes that her body and a feature of the estate, "a streame," are intertwined in order simultaneously to elevate Highbury's worthiness and to provide an origin for her poetic authority. Austen's animated stream is her variation on the *sponte sua* motif, in which nature makes itself serviceable to elite human beings. While Austen's "streame ris[ing]" is her only representation of the inanimate gaining agency, she does much with this image. Although at first it might seem to undercut her amateurish discounting of her "unpollishet lines" by making a subtle, conditional claim to Orpheus's power to move objects or Amphion's ability to build walls through song, she gives the "streame" agency beyond mere movement, and she correspondingly diminishes her own agency as poet. She calls upon the "streame" "To clear [her] mudy braine and misty eyes": this water source will purify her occluded "braine" and "eyes," her impaired faculties of thought and sight.

---

[93] The seventh stanza of Marvell's "Upon Appleton House" renders somewhat ambiguous the manner in which an estate conforms itself to a proprietor's "greatness":

> Yet thus the laden house does sweat,
> And scarce endures the Master great:
> But where he comes the swelling hall
> Stirs, and the square grows spherical,
> More by his magnitude distressed,
> Then he is by its straitness pressed:
> And too officiously it slights
> That in itself which him delights.

Marvell highlights the convention of deriving an estate's ideal qualities from the proprietor by conveying the magical, seemingly impossible physical metamorphosis of the house to accommodate its "Master great"; however, his representation of this transformation seems a potentially dubious compliment.

Austen's impaired poetic vision is entangled with her tentative mastery of the estate. Fortunately, the land and her poetry can reciprocally clarify one another's intrinsic worthiness. She portrays the land itself in the form of the animated "ris[ing]" "streame" intermingling with her body, clearing her "mudy braine" and "misty eyes." By purifying the poetic speaker's mind and vision, the stream will enable her to "find a Hellicon t'Enlarge [her] Muse." The confusion of place and speaker is so thorough here, however, that the location of that Hellicon is unclear; it appears to be both inside and outside of her. On one level the stream enters the poetic speaker and flushes her out so that the "mud" and "mist"--those polluted interior water sources--become an internal Hippocrene spring. In this sense, the place, her source of inspiration, underwrites her authority as poet. However, the Hellicon that emerges in line thirteen could also arguably be the re-viewed site of Highbury itself. With her mind and sight cleared, the poetic speaker looks at a physical site already valuable for its abundance and sees it for the elevated source of poetry that it is. It is significant that the speaker asserts her agency for the first time after this fantasy of transformation through the mingling of her body with the stream, a metonymical figure for Highbury and for Hellicon. After this transformation, she can conclude, "Then I noe better place then this wud choose" (14).[94] Austen's complicated imagery of purification in the preceding lines has simultaneously served to provide a legitimate (classical) source for her poetic authority and to elevate the value of the land so that it becomes a place deserving of poetic celebration. Inspired by a place-- Highbury--she becomes a poet; with the authority of a poet, she deems her Highbury her Hellicon.[95] Furthermore, the intermingling of the poetic speaker's body with the estate (as represented by the stream) firmly embeds her identity in the property itself. While this arguably represents the elevation of Austen's social rank (the property itself is figured as part of her), it also points to a contradiction that underpins her assertion of poetic authority.[96] The complicated poetic process through which Austen brings the estate and her verse into a mutually valuing relation to each other ultimately requires the objectification and fragmentation of the representation of her own body.

Even as Austen appears to succumb to the unavoidable influence of the masculinist tradition in which male poetic subjectivity constructs itself

---

[94] On the significance of a country house's location, see Hazard 152-3.

[95] Aglionby's "On Bolsover Castle" is explicit about the poet's ability to make a site worthy of poetry by inscribing it into verse (11-14).

[96] See note 79 for studies on the relationship between property and identity.

upon the objectified, fragmented, silenced body of a female beloved, however, she revises that tradition.[97]   While she fragments the representation of her body to the extent that she blazons her own brain and eyes, her manner of doing so mocks Petrarchan convention in the style of Shakespeare's Sonnet 130.   As in the case of Shakespeare's mistress, Austen's eyes are "nothing like the sun": in her anti-blazon of herself, her eyes are "misty" and her brain "mudy."[98]   Austen also arguably revises poetic convention in the last lines of "On the Situation of Highbury" in her deflection of the imagery of insemination (in her portrait of the animated stream rising) away from the figuration of her own body. Although Austen implies that the stream enters her body to purify her occluded poetic vision, the result of this suggestive penetration is the "Enlarg[ment]" of her "Muse." Austen redirects what could become a figure for impregnation so that it suggests poetic inspiration; in doing so, she appropriates the traditional representation (usually by male poets) of poems as offspring. At Highbury, there are no "ripe daughters" and no "fruitful" lady of the house, as there are at Penshurst (54, 90); instead, there is a widow whose Muse inspires poems--as proven by "On the Situation of Highbury" itself.[99] Austen can thus conclude by locating herself, as a poet, at the estate: "on this bright Hill/ I wish parnassus to adorne my quill" (15-16).

---

[97]   See Vickers, esp. 266, 274-79, for the idea that Renaissance male poetic subjectivity is constructed through the fragmentation and objectification of a female beloved.

[98]   Shakespeare, Sonnet 130, line 1.

[99]   Austen resists an explicit connection between the estate's fertility and human fertility. This contrasts sharply with the depictions of women in Jonson's poem. Wayne indicates that in "To Penshvrst" Barbara Gamage is not so much co-proprietor with her husband but an especially valuable piece of his property. Wayne observes that "[t]he reference to 'ripe daughters' is also metonymically related to the lady of the house, Barbara Gamage, who is identified with fertility throughout the poem" (68) and that Jonson "must have known how valuable a commodity she was at the time of her marriage" (71). Also see Wayne 68-75. For a compelling discussion of the different representations of female labor in Jonson's and Lanyer's poems, see Crane 219-22.

Chapter 5

Conclusion: The Harp in Hand

In "Upon ye Sight of my abortive Birth the 31th: of December 1657," Mary Carey writes,

> Lett not my hart, (as doth my wombe) miscarrie;
> but precious meanes received, lett it tarie;
>
> Till it be form'd; of Gosple shape, & sute;
> my meanes, my mercyes, & be pleasant frute: (73-76)

Wrestling with the cruel cultural implications of her spontaneous abortion, Carey's poetic speaker identifies her spiritual state with her "little Embrio; voyd of life, and feature" (2). Figuring her "hart" as both womb and embryo, she asks God to let her go full term, to "tarie/ Till it be form'd," and she specifies that the form it should take is "of Gosple shape." Carey thus suggests that the Bible, a particular text, will provide the shaping pattern or mold for the developing infant "hart" that stands in for the miscarrying mother's spiritual state; if God fulfills the speaker's plea, she will both bear and become "pleasant frute" in the image of the New Testament.

In the context of this study of the instrumentality of seventeeth-century English women's lyrics in the reconceptualization or alteration of those women's social positions, Carey's implication that the "Gosple" acts as a mold, as a means for imprinting the proper features on an otherwise shapeless "poore despissed creature" is especially provocative (1). While looking to the Bible for proper models of behavior was commonplace during Carey's era, her employment of this notion here has a special resonance with her use of the lyric as a medium through which to challenge both the literary and social conventions shaping her experience of child loss. While the women poets whose works I examine had different social positions, experiences, beliefs, and opinions, writing lyrics was, for all of them, part of their active social lives.

In *Literature and Revolution in England 1640-1660*, Nigel Smith asks, "Why *did* people write poetry in early modern England?" Proposing an answer to this question, he writes:

> Partly because it was in various ways an extension of being--for some being a gentleman of course, but also of being civilised or being a Christian. You *are* your genres, in so far as genre is a refraction of identity and a means through literary structure of exploring potentials and acknowledging limitations in relation to the world. Hence the large degree of generic inventiveness and eclecticism among women authors between 1640 and 1700: they were discovering for themselves the voices of authorship. (5)

The works of the women poets that I investigate in this book are consistent with Smith's observations. However, they also move beyond his description: they wrote their poetry not only as "an extension of being" but also to revise their being. Laying hands on the harp--to return to Anna Trapnel's vivid image of poetic resistance--proved an effective means for women such as herself, Mary Carey, and Katherine Austen to reshape constrictive, gender-based social roles, while also making distinct contributions to English literary history. Each of them identified with and was identified by at least one primary social role that was fundamentally determined by her female gender. Carey was a mother with a long, unfortunate history of seeing her infants and children die. She also identified strongly with her role as a Christian believer, but this role was firmly intertwined with her identity as a mother. And it is that latter social role that bears most upon her creative efforts: her many elegies for her children. However, as we have seen, the direction of influence here is not simply a one-way, essentializing one. Carey's poetic production affected her social identity as a mother, just as that role influenced her elegies. While others might discuss motherhood as if it were a matter of unmediated biology, my concern has been to show the significant connections between certain literary efforts (i.e., child loss poetry) of early modern mothers and the cultural construction of early modern motherhood. Seventeenth-century English men and women believed that mothers had very particular properties: for example, their imaginations could influence the physical shape of their unborn babies, and their own bodies could be easily penetrated (especially through their sense of vision) by their surroundings.[1]

---

[1] On early modern cultural assumptions about pregnant women, see, for instance, Cressy *Birth, Marriage, and Death* 46 and *Travesties and Transgressions* 25, Mack 35, Mendelson and Crawford 151, and Schwarz 299-300.

While some mothers responded to the cultural pressure to blame themselves for their children's deaths and to make a display of fettering their imaginative, intellectual abilities by writing the plainest possible poetry, by adhering strictly to the stark conventions of child loss verse, others--Carey especially, but also Austen, for instance--revised the expectations for maternal child loss poetry by subtly displaying their poetic prowess and questioning the accusations implicitly directed towards them. For some mother-poets, writing lyrics enabled them to reconceptualize the parameters of motherhood at a moment of crisis in which that social role was under negative scrutiny.

Anna Trapnel--the poet at the very heart of this study--explicitly represents her poetic production as an act of resistance. In her case, taking the harp in hand moves beyond a figurative or conceptual reshaping of her social role towards a material alteration of it. Upon one's initial encounter with Trapnel's writings that contain poetry, one most easily identifies her with the part of the holy handmaid, or female prophet. Although this is certainly only one among the many social roles that she plays, it is, in part, her intelligibility as a female prophet, in conjunction with the strategic interventions of her verse into the social and literary realms, that enables her to pursue the more controversial part of female preacher. Acting as a female prophet, as in the case of the early modern mother, was a specifically gendered social role with certain attendant expectations and constraints. As many scholars have amply explained and documented, the female prophet was understood to be assigned a particular function by divine forces beyond her control, and her ability to serve that function was dependent upon specific early modern ideas about femininity. Because the dominant, masculinist early modern viewpoint saw women as fundamentally irrational creatures who were more vulnerable to supernatural influences, whether divine or demonic, than men, early modern people were likely to have believed a female prophet more credible than a male one. By Trapnel's day, the role of the female prophet was so well established--the evacuation of personal agency and identity, the death-like trances, etc.--that a culturally legible script was available for taking the part of God's handmaid.[2] That Trapnel's followers recognized her as prophet set

---

[2] On Trapnel's divine inspiration, see Berg and Berry 48-50, Burrage, Cohen 422-27, Hobby 31-6, Mack 92-8, and Wiseman 186-90. On Trapnel as a weak vessel, see Mack 32-4. On female biology and the prophet's body, see Mack 24-34, Hobby 26, Purkiss, and Wiseman 192. On the prophet's trance, see Dailey esp. 453 and Mack 34. On the widespread popularity of the role of the prophet, see Hill, *The World Turned Upside Down* 73.

the stage for her poetic performances by determining, for instance, some of the assumptions behind those performances (e.g., she could not compose psalms spontaneously herself but was merely a conduit for the Holy Spirit's poetic outpourings).[3] However, her lyrics--in their intricate interplay with her prose speeches and sermons--played an instrumental part not only in lending credibility to her most immediately legible role as a prophet but, more importantly, in enabling her to act subtly as a preacher--a position of authority that most early modern English Christians believed to be utterly forbidden to women by the Pauline injunctions against female speech in I Corinthians 14: 33-35 and I Timothy 2:11-12. Trapnel's sermon-psalms enabled her to construct a conceptual space for the female preacher and to appear in a preacherly role, at least for a time, in public.

Harp in hand, Katherine Austen resisted and revised the social conventions related primarily to the role of a wealthy widow. The inconsistencies engendered by the conflicts among Austen's status as widow, her ambitions for ever higher rank, and her gender underpin her complicated, discontinuous self-representations, which she often presents in the form of lyrics. Like an early modern mother or a female prophet, a wealthy widow was understood to be a very specific sort of woman. In particular, early modern English culture stereotyped wealthy widows as insubordinate, uncontrollable, and sexually voracious.[4] Aware of these negative stereotypes and eager to surmount them and to be recognized as a woman of rank, Austen used her poetry in multiple ways to fashion her own version of wealthy widowhood. Not only does she address the cultural expectations of widows explicitly in some of her poems (e.g., "Upon Courtiers at the Committee at Parliament Striving for Highbury" and "Men never think their wifes may be"), where she presents her own competing ideas about widowhood, but she also experiments with different means to represent herself as a wealthy widow who inverts the negative stereotype (i.e., as one who is submissive to patriarchy, polite, chaste, etc.). Thus, although she flirts with a prophetic role akin to Trapnel's--a role which appears to evacuate human agency but which also associates the prophet with divine power--she constructs her prophetic poems and other writings strategically to ensure that she cannot be interpreted as a radical, rabble-rousing prophet like Trapnel. In fact, this ambivalent visionary reaches far into the past to find an appropriate model of the female prophet for herself:

---

[3] See, for example, *The Cry of a Stone* 13 and Burrage 532.

[4] On stereotypes of widows, see, for instance, Todd, "The Remarrying Widow," esp 54-55, and Mendelson and Crawford 68-9.

Hildegard of Bingen. The most striking case of influence between Austen's social roles and her poetry, however, relates to her country-house poem, "On the Situation of Highbury," in which she allows the association between an estate whose possession she hopes to secure and her poem about that estate to reinforce mutually her roles as wealthy, landed widow and as authoritative, socially proper poet.

Collectively, the women poets discussed in this study help to expand the notion of what might count as social verse. Their texts might seem at first to be entirely private. A mother's poem written to mark her child's death can seem like a perfectly domestic, self-enclosed expression of personal grief. Trapnel strategically represents her moments of poetic production as beyond the pale of her consciousness. Austen's "Book M," prefaced with claims about its personal, private nature, seems the epitome of an asocial document. However, social concerns are central to these works, and the composition of lyrics is essential to the negotiation of those concerns. The mother-poets, lyrical preacher, and ambitious widow lived in a world in which poetry had a range of social functions and was only beginning to be associated with seemingly universal, timeless emotions or truths that were separated from particular social occasions or historical moments.[5] Poetry could be exchanged, for example, to shore up bonds among courtiers, between courtiers and patrons, among university students, and among family members. Poetry circulated in manuscript was assumed to be flexible, subject to revisions and retorts--much like jokes and occasional poetry that are circulated on the Internet among communities of e-mail correspondents today. Given the typically occasional nature of Renaissance lyric poetry and the emphasis on collaboration in manuscript culture, it is easy to see the importance of understanding Renaissance lyrics as social verse.[6]

While scholars such as Margaret Ezell, Arthur Marotti, and Wendy Wall have emphasized the social nature of the lyric during this period by calling attention to the circulation of lyrics in manuscript miscellanies, to coteries of poets in friendly competition with each other, and to lyrics as a form of socioeconomic currency in the patronage system, I focus on how the sociality of the lyric relates to women's writing when that writing seems especially insular and does not fit neatly into patterns of interaction

---

[5] Marotti, *Manuscript* 137.

[6] For more on social verse, see Marotti, "'Love Is Not Love': Elizabethan Sonnet Sequences and the Social Order"; *John Donne, Coterie Poet*; and *Manuscript*; Wall esp. 1-22; Ezell, *Writing Women's Literary History* esp. 37-8, 56-7, and *Social Authorship and the Advent of Print* esp. 21-44.

predominantly followed by men. Some of the women poets that I discuss participated in poetic practices like those pursued mostly by men at the courts, Inns of Court, and universities. Aemelia Lanyer appears to have used her poetry to seek patronage from powerful court ladies; Katherine Philips circulated her verse to friends in a coterie bound together by similar attitudes and values; even Austen seems likely to have circulated her poems to friends and family.[7] However, the poets most central to this study--Carey, Trapnel, and Austen--are interesting not only for any overlap their works might have with modes of lyric sociality pursued typically by their male contemporaries but also for how they use their lyrics to reshape their social roles. When they take the harp in hand, they make valuable poetic innovations through their experimentations with convention, but their poetic production has meaning in addition to any aesthetic contributions: it helps the poets to rewrite constrictive social roles based upon their female gender.

The fact that none of the main poets in this study transmitted their texts solely through print is a crucial aspect of what makes it possible to witness how they used their lyrics to reshape their social roles. Carey and Austen both circulated their verse in manuscript: Carey's poetry was transcribed into an elegant, leather-bound fair copy with gilded pages, and although it is unclear whether Austen circulated her verse frequently or far, it is evident that "Book M" reveals her interest in other poets such as Donne and Corbett and that she shared the assumption that manuscript verse was available for circulation and revision. While Trapnel's works do not appear to have been circulated in manuscript in the typical sense, they were not simply printed either. The status of Trapnel's texts is complicated by the claims of the prophetic ones--which are the only ones that include verse--to have been performed orally, transcribed by hand at the scene of Trapnel's possession by the Holy Spirit, and then finally printed. Because there were multiple layers involved in the process of transmitting Trapnel's works, there were several different audiences for those layers: the spectators who witnessed her performances in person; the Fifth Monarchists who, much like a poetic coterie bonded through similar social and political values, oversaw the transcription and probably the printing of the prophet's words; and the much wider readership of the printed copies of her works. This especially complex transmission process requires further investigation. Despite ways in which Trapnel's texts call attention to the instability of their

---

[7] On Lanyer's participation in the patronage system, see Lewalski, *Writing Women in Jacobean England* 219-26 and Woods, *Lanyer: A Renaissance Woman Poet* 43-54 and 101-8. On women in coteries, including Philips, see Ezell, *Writing Women's Literary History* 48-57 and *Social Authorship and the Advent of Print* esp. 25-8, 52-4.

production and transmission (such as when a Fifth Monarchist amanuensis comments upon the difficult circumstances in which he strives to hear and to copy the holy handmaid's divine words), her believers might well have assumed her message to be utterly stable (because divine powers supposedly underwrote it), whereas her opponents might have interpreted the many layers in the process of textual transmission as all the more reason to be suspicious of the legitimacy of her message.[8]

Analyzing these women's works, which do not fit the print scenario that many twentieth-century scholars assumed to indicate the value of a literary work (i.e., that such works are valuable only when produced for mass consumption in a capitalist market), contributes to the ongoing effort to recover women writers' works and to discover how those works revise our understanding of literary history.[9] Investigating child loss poetry calls attention to the significance of this wide spread genre and its specific conventions, while it reveals that gender does not inflect such verse in a simple, straightforward manner. Although poems written by male and female poets writing on behalf of other people's children can be virtually indistinguishable from one another, mother-poets' verse is strikingly distinct. The early modern cultural construction not just of gender but more specifically of motherhood in relation to literary production is what is most at stake here. And when Carey, in particular, responds to those stakes, she creates poems in the maternal plain style that manage to display her impressive poetic skill, despite that poetic style's tendency to minimize the visibility of a mother's intellectual creativity. Trapnel's lyric preaching expands our knowledge of the range of ways in which early modern women could lay claim to preacherly authority. Her radical revision of Canticles to justify a woman's right to speak in public is noteworthy both for its social and political significance and for the poetic innovation Trapnel shows in taking a biblical text that had such a strong influence on Renaissance poetry and making it her own. Analyzing Austen's "Book M" calls attention to several previously unknown, compelling poems by a woman writer, and it shows how those poems are central to an ambitious widow's complex responses to her society's imposition of its restrictions on her. Her transcription of Corbett's fragment emphasizes how lyrics during this period were treated as malleable and how, like Trapnel, Austen appropriates a text from a mainstream tradition to serve her own purposes. Furthermore, in

---

[8]   See, for example, *The Cry of a Stone* 19, 58.

[9]   On twentieth-century feminists' assumptions about literary value, see Ezell, *Writing Women's Literary History* 4, 32 and *Social Authorship and the Advent of Print* 17.

transcribing part of Corbett's poem and situating it in relation to the rest of "Book M" to fashion herself as an especially chaste, proper widow, she puts herself into a poetic collaboration with Corbett. Finally, her country-house poem, "On the Situation of Highbury," contributes an innovation to the genre through the exclusion of a feature typically central to it: the celebration of the patron/landowner as the origin of the bounty and goodness of the estate.

Smith claims that "the lyric in the 1650s . . . became the possession of women" (*Literature and Revolution* 257).   This statement is very suggestive in relation to the works treated in this study, many of which (e.g., the poetry of Carey, Trapnel, and Austen) were composed in the middle of the seventeenth-century and all of which show women taking various lyric traditions in hand for their own purposes.   Smith asserts further, after discussing the impressive verse of Philips and Cavendish, "[t]hat women, freed temporarily from traditional roles by civil disruption [caused by the wars], should seize such an initiative, has been neglected for too long, and we still need to understand more about this kind of poetry before our view of the literary canon is properly renewed" (*Literature and Revolution* 259). While this analysis focusing on three specific cases of poetry in relation to different kinds of socially ascribed women's roles cannot result in a large-scale, overarching claim about the status of English women's mid-seventeenth-century poetic production, it does respond to Smith's concerns by showing that, for these poets at least, it is very likely that the civil disruption he describes helped to create the proper conditions for their appropriations of lyric tradition and their use of poetry to reconceptualize or alter their social roles. Hopefully, this study has also called attention to women poets--especially Carey, Trapnel, and Austen--who have yet to gain the attention they deserve and whose works may offer further insights that will lead us to still more revisions of this period and a fuller understanding of its literary products.   Discoveries of additional texts by early modern women writers may well revise our understanding of the significance of women's elegies.   Meanwhile, the works of Trapnel and Austen require more analysis from a variety of perspectives.   It was beyond the scope and purposes of this book, for instance, to treat thoroughly Trapnel's untitled folio of psalms, which is almost one thousand pages long.   Likewise, there is much more to be learned from Austen's "Book M," not only by literary scholars interested in poetry but also by social historians interested in glimpsing into the complex affairs of a savvy, self-aware, ambitious widow.[10] Finally, the works of poets like Carey, Trapnel, and Austen show the continuing need to investigate the relations among textual production, transmission, and reception in early modern England. I have tried to show what happens when, harp in hand, diverse seventeenth-century women poets take hold of various lyric traditions and make them relevant to their social lives; in doing so, I hope that I have also called attention to how relevant such women writers and their poetic resistance can be to the lives of later generations.

---

[10] Todd, in particular, has already performed compelling historical investigations of "Book M."

Bibliography

Aglionby. "On Bolsover Castle." Fowler, *Country House Poem* 167-72.

An Account of Mary Adams, the Ranters Monster. London, 1652.

Austen, Katherine. "Book M." British Library, Add. MS 4454, 1664.

Battersby, Christine. "Stages on Kant's Way: Aesthetics, Morality, and the Gendered Sublime." Brand and Korsmeyer 88-114.

Beilin, Elaine V. *Redeeming Eve: Women Writers of the English Renaissance*. Princeton: Princeton UP, 1987.

Berg, Christine, and Philippa Berry. "'Spiritual Whoredom': An Essay on Female Prophets in the Seventeenth Century." *1642: Literature and Power in the Seventeenth Century*. Ed. Francis Barker, et al. Essex: U of Essex P, 1980. 37-54.

Bergmann, Emilie L. "Language and 'Mother's Milk': Maternal Roles and the Nurturing Body in Early Modern Spanish Texts." Miller and Yavneh 105-20.

Bicks, Caroline. "Midwiving Virility in Early Modern England." Miller and Yavneh 49-64.

Blecki, Catherine La Courreye. "Alice Hayes and Mary Penington: Personal Identity Within the Tradition of Quaker Spiritual Autobiography." *Quaker History* 65.1 (1976): 19-31.

Booth, Stephen. Commentary. *Shakespeare's Sonnets* 135-538.

Bradstreet, Anne. *The Complete Works of Anne Bradstreet*. Ed. Joseph R. McElrath, Jr. and Allan P. Robb. Boston: Twayne Publishers, 1981.

Brand, Peggy Zeglin, and Carolyn Korsmeyer, eds. *Feminism and Tradition in Aesthetics*. University Park: The Pennsylvania State UP, 1995.

---. "Introduction: Aesthetics and Its Traditions." Brand and Korsmeyer 1-22.

Burke, Mary E., Jane Donawerth, Linda L. Dove, and Karen Nelson, eds. *Women, Writing, and the Reproduction of Culture in Tudor and Stuart Britain*. Syracuse, N.Y.: Syracuse UP, 2000.

---. Introduction. Burke, Donawerth, Dove, and Nelson. xvii-xxx.

Burke, Victoria. "Women and Early Seventeenth-Century Manuscript Culture: Four Miscellanies." *The Seventeenth Century* 12:2 (1997): 135-50.

Burrage, Champlin. "Anna Trapnel's Prophecies." *English Historical Review* 26.103 (1911): 526-35.

Cain, William E. "The Place of the Poet in Jonson's 'To Penshurst' and 'To My Muse'." *Criticism: A Quarterly for Literature and the Arts* XXI.1 (1979): 34-48.

Capp, B.S. *The Fifth Monarchy Men: A Study in Seventeenth-Century English Millenarianism*. London: Faber and Faber, 1972.

Carew, Thomas. *The Poems of Thomas Carew with His Masque Coelum Britannicum*. Ed. Rhodes Dunlap. New York: Oxford UP, 1949.

Carey, Mary. "Upon ye Sight of my abortive Birth ye 31th: of December 1657." Greer, et al. 158-62.

---. "Wretten by me at the death of my 4th sonne and 5th Child Perigrene Payler." Greer, et al. 157-8.

---. "Wretten by me att the same tyme; on the death of my 4th, & only Child, Robert   Payler;---." Greer, et al. 156-7.

Carroll, Kenneth L. "Martha Simmonds, a Quaker Enigma." *The Journal of the Friends' Historical Society* 53.1 (1972): 31-52.

Cavendish, Margaret. *A True Relation of my Birth, Breeding and Life. Her Own Life: Autobiographical Writings by Seventeenth-Century English Women*. Ed. Elspeth Graham, Hilary Hinds, Elaine Hobby, and Helen Wilcox. New York: Routledge, 1989. 89-100.

---. The Second Part of *Bell in Campo*. *The Convent of Pleasure and Other Plays*. Ed. Anne Shaver. Baltimore: The Johns Hopkins UP, 1999. 141-69.

Cerasano, S.P., and Marion Wynne-Davies, eds. *Gloriana's Face: Women, Public and Private, in the English Renaissance*. Detroit: Wayne State UP, 1992.

Chaucer, Geoffrey. The Wife of Bath's Prologue and Tale. *The Riverside Chaucer*. Ed. Larry D. Benson. 3rd ed. Boston: Houghton Mifflin Company, 1987. 105-22.

Clifford, Arthur, ed. *Tixall Poetry*. Edinburgh: James Ballantyne and Co., 1813.

Cohen, Alfred. "Prophecy and Madness: Women Visionaries during the Puritan Revolution." *Journal of Psychohistory* 11 (1984): 411-30.

Collins, An. *Divine Songs and Meditacions*. Ed. Sidney Gottlieb. Binghamton, NY: Medieval & Renaissance Texts & Studies, 1996.

Conger, Vivian Leigh Bruce. "'Being Weak of Body but Firm of Mind and Memory': Widowhood in Colonial America, 1630-1750." Diss. Cornell U, 1994.

Cope, Esther S. "Eleanor Davies and the Prophetic Office." Burke, Donawerth, Dove, and Nelson 207-219.

Coppe, Abiezer. *Abiezer Coppe: Selected Writings*. Ed. Andrew Hopton. London: Aporia Press, 1987.

Crane, Mary Thomas. "'Players in Your Huswifery, and Huswives in Your Beds': Conflicting Identities of Early Modern English Women." Miller and Yavneh 212-223.

Cressy, David. *Birth, Marriage, and Death: Ritual, Religion, and the Life-Cycle in Tudor and Stuart England*. New York: Oxford UP, 1997.

---. *Travesties and Transgressions in Tudor and Stuart England: Tales of Discord and Dissension*. New York: Oxford UP, 2000.

Cross, Claire. "'He-Goats Before the Flocks': A Note on the Part Played by Women in the Founding of Some Civil War Churches." *Studies in Church History 8: Popular Belief and Practice*. Ed. G.J. Cuming and Derek Baker. New York: Cambridge UP, 1972. 195-202.

Crum, Margaret, ed. *First-Line Index of English Poetry: 1500-1800 in Manuscripts of the Bodleian Library Oxford.* 2 vols. Oxford: Clarendon P, 1969.

Dailey, Barbara Ritter. "The Visitation of Sarah Wight: Holy Carnival and the Revolution of the Saints in Civil War London." *Church History* 55 (1986): 438-55.

de Grazia, Margreta. "The Ideology of Superfluous Things: *King Lear* as Period Piece." de Grazia, Quilligan, and Stallybrass 17-42.

de Grazia, Margreta, Maureen Quilligan, and Peter Stallybrass, eds. *Subject and Object in Renaissance Culture.* New York: Cambridge UP, 1996.

---. Introduction. de Grazia, Quilligan, and Stallybrass 1-13.

Deming, Robert H. *Ceremony and Art: Robert Herrick's Poetry.* The Hague: Mouton & Co. N.V., Publishers, 1974.

de Vere, Anne Cecil. "Four Epitaphs." Wynne-Davies 16-17.

DiSalvo, Jacqueline. "Fear of Flying: Milton on the Boundaries Between Witchcraft and Inspiration." *English Literary Renaissance* 18.1 (1988): 114-37.

A Discoverie of Six Women Preachers, in Middlesex, Kent, Cambridgshire, and Salisbury, with a Relation of Their Names, Manners, Life, and Doctrine, Pleasant to be Read, but Horrid to be Judged Of, 1641.

Dobell, Bertram. Catalogue 99. Dec. 1901. 29-30.

---. "A Unique Book." *Notes and Queries* 2.9 (1914): 221-2.

Dolan, Frances E. "Marian Devotion and Maternal Authority in Seventeenth-Century England." Miller and Yavneh 282-92.

Donne, John. *The Poems of John Donne.* Ed. Herbert J.C. Grierson. 2 vols. New York: Oxford UP, 1966.

Dubrow, Heather. *A Happier Eden: The Politics of Marriage in the Stuart Epithalamium.* Ithaca, N.Y.: Cornell UP, 1990.

Edwards, Irene L. "The Women Friends of London: The Two-Weeks and Box Meetings." *The Journal of the Friends' Historical Society* 47.1 (1955): 3-21.

Edwards, Thomas. *Gangraena, or a Catalogue and Discovery of Many of the Errours, Heresies, Blasphemies and Pernicious Practices of the Sectaries of This Time, Vented and Acted in England in These Four Last Years.* London, 1645.

Egerton, Elizabeth. "On my Boy Henry." Greer, et al. 117-18.

Ehrstine, Glenn. "Motherhood and Protestant Polemics: Stillbirth in Hans von Rüte's *Abgötterei* (1531)." Miller and Yavneh 121-34.

'Eliza.' *Eliza's Babes: OR THE Virgins-Offering.* London: Printed by M.S. for Laurence Blaiklock, 1652.

Ezell, Margaret J.M. *Social Authorship and the Advent of Print.* Baltimore: The Johns Hopkins UP, 1999.

---. *Writing Women's Literary History.* Baltimore: The Johns Hopkins UP, 1993.

Fane, Mildmay. "My Hock-Cart or Reaping Day." Fowler, *Country House Poem* 224-6.

---. "A Peppercorn or Small Rent Sent to My Lord Campden for the Loan of His House at Kensington, 9 February, 1651." Fowler, *Country House Poem* 235-45.

Fanshawe, Richard. *The Poems and Translations of Sir Richard Fanshawe.* Ed. Peter Davidson. Vol. 1. New York: Oxford UP, 1997.

Feake, Christopher. "Mr Feakes Hymne: ~ August ye 11: 1653 • Christ Church: • ." TT E710 (13). Film 4655. Reel 109.

Felski, Rita. "Why Feminism Doesn't Need an Aesthetic (and Why It Can't Ignore Aesthetics)." Brand and Korsmeyer 431-45.

ffolliott, Sheila. "Catherine de' Medici as Artemisia: Figuring the Powerful Widow." *Rewriting the Renaissance: The Discourse of Sexual Difference in Early Modern Europe.* Ed. Margaret W. Ferguson, Maureen Quilligan, and Nancy J. Vickers. Chicago: U of Chicago P, 1987. 227-41.

Fowler, Alastair. "The 'Better Marks' of Jonson's *To Penshurst.*" *The Review of English Studies* XXIV.95 (1973): 266-82.

---, ed. *The Country House Poem: A Cabinet of Seventeenth-Century Estate Poems and Related Items.* Edinburgh: Edinburgh UP, 1994.

---. "Introduction." Fowler, *Country House Poem* 1-29.

Fox, Margaret Fell. *Women's Speaking Justified, Proved and Allowed of by the SCRIPTURES.* London, 1667.

Goldberg, Jonathan. *James I and the Politics of Literature: Jonson, Shakespeare, Donne, and Their Contemporaries.* Baltimore: The Johns Hopkins UP, 1983.

Greaves, Richard L. "Foundation Builders: The Role of Women in Early English Nonconformity." Greaves, ed. 75-92.

---, ed. *Triumph over Silence: Women in Protestant History.* Westport, Conn.: Greenwood Press, 1985.

Greer, Germaine. Introduction. Greer, et al. 1-31.

---, et al., eds. *Kissing the Rod: An Anthology of Seventeenth-Century Women's Verse.* New York: The Noonday Press, 1989.

Guillory, John. *Cultural Capital: The Problem of Literary Canon Formation.* Chicago: The U of Chicago P, 1993.

---. *Poetic Authority: Spenser, Milton, and Literary History.* New York: Columbia UP, 1983.

Hannay, Margaret P. "'When Riches Growes': Class Perspective in Pembroke's *Psalms.*" Burke, Donawerth, Dove, and Nelson. 77-97.

Harp, Richard. "Jonson's 'To Penshurst': The Country House as Church." *John Donne Journal* 7.1 (1988): 73-89.

Harvey, Elizabeth D. *Ventriloquized Voices: Feminist Theory and English Renaissance Texts.* New York: Routledge 1992.

Hayes, Nancy. "Negativizing Nurture and Demonizing Domesticity: The Witch Construct in Early Modern Germany." Miller and Yavneh 179-200.

Hazard, Mary E. *Elizabethan Silent Language.* Lincoln: U of Nebraska P, 2000.

Heal, Felicity, and Clive Holmes. *The Gentry in England and Wales, 1500-1700*. Stanford: Stanford UP, 1994.

Helgerson, Richard. *Self-Crowned Laureates: Spenser, Jonson, Milton and the Literary System*. Berkeley: U of California P, 1983.

Henderson, Katherine Usher, and Barbara F. McManus. "The Debate about Women." Henderson and McManus 3-46.

---, eds. *Half Humankind: Contexts and Texts of the Controversy about Women in England, 1540-1640*. Chicago: U of Illinois P, 1985.

---. "The Literary Contexts." Henderson and McManus 99-130.

---. "The Social Contexts." Henderson and McManus 47-98.

Herbert, George. *A Priest to the Temple or The Countrey Parson His Character, and Role of Holy Life. The Works of George Herbert*. Ed. F.E. Hutchinson. New York: Oxford UP, 1945. 223-90.

---. *George Herbert*. Ed. Louis L. Martz. New York: Oxford UP, 1994.

Herrick, Robert. *The Complete Poetry of Robert Herrick*. Ed. J. Max Patrick. New York: W.W. Norton & Company, Inc., 1968.

Hill, Christopher. *The Century of Revolution*. New York: Norton, 1980.

---. *The English Bible and the Seventeenth-Century Revolution*. New York: The Penguin Press, 1993.

---. *Milton and the English Revolution*. New York: The Viking Press, 1977.

---. *The World Turned Upside Down: Radical Ideas during the English Revolution*. New York: The Viking Press, 1972.

Hinds, Hilary. "'Who May Binde Where God Hath Loosed?': Responses to Sectarian Women's Writing in the Second Half of the Seventeenth Century." Cerasano and Wynne-Davies 205-27.

Hobby, Elaine. *Virtue of Necessity: English Women's Writing: 1649-88*. Ann Arbor: U of Michigan P, 1989.

The Holy Bible. King James Version. New York: Ballantine Books, 1991.

Homer. *The Odyssey*. Trans. W.H.D. Rouse. New York: Mentor, 1937.

Irwin, Joyce L. *Womanhood in Radical Protestantism: 1525-1675*. New York: The Edwin Mellen Press, 1979.

Jardine, Lisa. *Still Harping on Daughters: Women and Drama in the Age of Shakespeare*. New York: Columbia UP, 1989.

Jed, Stephanie H. *Chaste Thinking: The Rape of Lucretia and the Birth of Humanism*. Bloomington: Indiana UP, 1989.

Johnson, Barbara. *A World of Difference*. Baltimore: Johns Hopkins, 1987.

Johnson, Lynne Staley. "The Trope of the Scribe and the Question of Literary Authority in the Works of Julian of Norwich and Margery Kempe." *Speculum* 66.4 (1991): 820-38.

Jones, Ann Rosalind. *The Currency of Eros: Women's Love Lyric in Europe, 1540-1620*. Bloomington: Indiana UP, 1990.

Jonson, Ben. *Ben Jonson*. Ed. C.H. Herford, Percy and Evelyn Simpson. Vol. 8. New York: Oxford UP, 1947.

Jordan, Constance. *Renaissance Feminism: Literary Texts and Political Models.* Ithaca: Cornell UP, 1990.

---. "Renaissance Women and the Question of Class." *Sexuality & Gender in Early Modern Europe: Institutions, Texts, Images.* Ed. James Grantham Turner. New York: Cambridge UP, 1995. 90-106.

Julian of Norwich. *Showings.* Trans. Edmund Colledge and James Walsh. New York: Paulist Press, 1978.

Keeble, N.H., ed. *The Cultural Identity of Seventeenth-Century Woman: A Reader.* New York: Routledge, 1994.

Kelsall, Malcolm. *The Great Good Place: The Country House and English Literature.* New York: Columbia UP, 1993.

Kempe, Margery. *The Book of Margery Kempe.* Ed. Sanford Brown Meech. Oxford: Oxford UP, 1940.

Krontiris, Tina. *Oppositional Voices: Women as Writers and Translators of Literature in the English Renaissance.* New York: Routledge, 1992.

Lanyer, Aemilia. *The Poems of Aemilia Lanyer: Salve Deus Rex Judaeorum.* Ed. Susanne Woods. New York: Oxford UP, 1993.

Laslett, Peter. *Family Life and Illicit Love in Earlier Generations: Essays in Historical Sociology.* New York: Cambridge UP, 1980.

Laurence, Anne. "A Priesthood of She-Believers: Women and Congregations in Mid-Seventeenth-Century England." *Women in the Church.* Ed. W.J. Sheils and Diana Wood. Cambridge, Mass.: Basil Blackwell, 1990. 345-63.

Lewalski, Barbara Kiefer. *Protestant Poetics and the Seventeenth-Century Religious Lyric.* Princeton: Princeton UP, 1979.

---. *Writing Women in Jacobean England.* Cambridge, Mass.: Harvard UP, 1993.

Lilley, Kate. "True State Within: Women's Elegy 1640-1740." *Women, Writing, History 1640-1740.* Ed. Isobel Grundy and Susan Wiseman. Athens: U of Georgia P, 1992. 72-92.

Llwyd, Morgan. *Gweithiau.* London: J.M. Dent & Co, 1899.

Love, Harold. *Scribal Publication in Seventeenth-Century England.* Oxford: Clarendon Press, 1993.

Lovelace, Richard. *The Poems of Richard Lovelace.* Ed. C.H. Wilkinson. New York: Oxford UP, 1963.

Ludlow, Dorothy P. "Shaking Patriarchy's Foundations: Sectarian Women in England, 1641-1700." Greaves, ed. 93-123.

Luecke, Marilyn. "The Reproduction of Culture and the Culture of Reproduction in Elizabeth Clinton's *The Countesse of Lincolnes Nurserie.*" Burke, Donawerth, Dove, and Nelson 238-52.

Mack, Phyllis. *Visionary Women: Ecstatic Prophecy in Seventeenth-Century England.* Berkeley: U of California P, 1992.

Margaret, Queen of Navarre. "A Godlie MEDITATION of the in*ward loue of the*

Soule towards Christ our LORD." *The Monvment of Matrones: The Second Lampe of Virginitie*. Ed. Thomas Bentley. Trans. Tudor, Elizabeth. London: Denham, Henrie, 1582. 1-35.

Marotti, Arthur. *John Donne, Coterie Poet*. Madison: U of Wisconsin P, 1986.

---. "'Love Is Not Love': Elizabethan Sonnet Sequences and the Social Order." *English Literary History* 49 (1982): 396-428.

---. *Manuscript, Print, and the English Renaissance Lyric*. Ithaca: Cornell UP, 1995.

Marvell, Andrew. *Andrew Marvell*. Ed. Frank Kermode and Keith Walker. Oxford UP, 1990.

Masten, Jeff. "'Shall I turne blabb?': Circulation, Gender, and Subjectivity in Mary Wroth's Sonnets." *Reading Mary Wroth: Representing Alternatives in Early Modern England*. Ed. Naomi J. Miller and Gary Waller. Knoxville: U of Tennessee P, 1991. 67-87.

McClung, William A., Jr. "Jonson's 'To Penshurst.'" *The Explicator* 33.9 (1975): 78.

McGrath, Lynette. "'Let Us Have Our Libertie Againe': Aemilia Lanier's 17th-Century Feminist Voice." *Women's Studies* 20 (1992): 331-48.

Mendelson, Sara Heller. "Stuart Women's Diaries and Occasional Memoirs." *Women in English Society 1500-1800*. Ed. Mary Prior. New York: Methuen, 1985. 181-210.

Mendelson, Sara and Patricia Crawford. *Women in Early Modern England 1550-1720*. Oxford: Clarendon Press, 1998.

Mercurius Fumigosus. 16-23 Aug. 1654. Raymond 159-60.

Mercurius Politicus. 13-20 April 1654. Raymond 166.

Mermin, Dorothy. *Godiva's Ride: Women of Letters in England, 1830-1880*. Bloomington: Indiana UP, 1993.

Miller, Naomi J. "Mothering Others: Caregiving as Spectrum and Spectacle in the Early Modern Period." Miller and Yavneh 1-25.

Miller, Naomi J. and Naomi Yavneh. *Maternal Measures: Figuring Caregiving in the Early Modern Period*. Burlington, VT: Ashgate, 2000.

Milton, John. *Complete Shorter Poems*. Ed. John Carey. New York: Longman, 1989.

---. *Paradise Lost*. Ed. Alastair Fowler. New York: Longman, 1989.

Moi, Toril. *Sexual/Textual Politics: Feminist Literary Theory*. New York: Routledge, 1994.

Montrose, Louis A. "Spenser's Domestic Domain: Poetry, Property, and the Early Modern Subject." de Grazia, Quilligan, and Stallybrass 83-130.

The Nunns Prophesie: OR the True, Wonderful, and Remarkable PROPHESIE of St. Heldegard, First NUNN, and then ABESS: CONCERNING The Rise and Downfall of those Fire-Brands of EUROPE, the whole Order of JESUITS. London, 1680.

Nuttall, Geoffrey. *The Holy Spirit in Puritan Faith and Experience*. Oxford: Basil Blackwell, 1947.

Overbury, Thomas. *A Wife*. Keeble 253-4.

Ovid. *Metamorphoses*. Trans. Rolfe Humphries. Bloomington: Indiana UP, 1955.

Owen, Jane. *An antidote against purgatory*. 1634. *Renaissance Woman: Constructions of Femininity in England*. Ed. Kate Aughterson. New York: Routledge, 1995. 279-80.

Payler, George. "Written by my dear Husband at ye Death of our 4th (at that time) only Child, Robert Payler." Greer, et al. 157.

Philips, Katherine. *The Collected Works of Katherine Philips: The Matchless Orinda*. Ed. Patrick Thomas. Vol. 1. Essex: Stump Cross Books, 1990.

Phillippy, Patricia. "London's Mourning Garment: Maternity, Mourning and Royal Succession." Miller and Yavneh 319-32.

A pitiless Mother. Henderson and McManus 361-67.

Powell, Vavasor. *The Bird in the Cage, Chirping*. London, 1661.

Purkiss, Diane. "Producing the Voice, Consuming the Body: Women Prophets of the Seventeenth-Century." *Women, Writing, History 1640-1740*. Ed. Isobel Grundy and Susan Wiseman. Athens: U of Georgia P, 1992. 139-58.

Randolph, Thomas. "On the Inestimable Content He Enjoys in the Muses: To Those of His Friends that Dehort Him from Poetry." Fowler, *Country House Poem* 138-44.

Rathmell, J.C.A. "Jonson, Lord Lisle, and Penshurst." *English Literary Renaissance* 1.3 (1971): 250-60.

Raymond, Joad, ed. *Making the News: An Anthology of the Newsbooks of Revolutionary England 1641-1660*. New York: St. Martin's Press, 1993.

Richey, Esther Gilman. *The Politics of Revolution in the English Renaissance*. Columbia, Missouri: U of Missouri P, 1998.

Rickman, Lydia L. "Esther Biddle and Her Mission to Louis XIV." *Quaker History* 47 (1955): 38-45.

Rogers, John. *Ohel or Beth-shemesh. A Tabernacle for the Sun: OR IRENIUCM EVANGELICUM. A Idea of Church-Discipline, In the THEORICK and PRACTICK Parts*. London: Printed by Joseph Caryl, 1653.

Rogers, P.G. *The Fifth Monarchy Men*. New York: Oxford UP, 1966.

Rose, Judith. "Mirrors of Language, Mirrors of Self: The Conceptualization of Artistic Identity in Gaspara Stampa and Sofonisba Anguissola." Miller and Yavneh 29-48.

Salusbury, Thomas. "Kensington Grove." Fowler, *Country House Poem* 153-5.

Scattergood, Antony. Verse Miscellany. British Library, Add. MS 44963, 1630s.

Schleiner, Louise. *Tudor and Stuart Women Writers*. Bloomington, Ind.: Indiana UP, 1994.

Schnell, Lisa. "'So Great a Difference Is There in Degree': Aemilia Lanyer and the Aims of Feminist Criticism." *Modern Language Quarterly* 57.1 (1996): 23-35.

Schoenfeldt, Michael C. "'The Mysteries of Manners, Armes, and Arts': 'Inviting a Friend to Supper' and 'To Penshurst.'" *'The Muses Common-Weale':* *Poetry and Politics in the Seventeenth Century.* Ed. Claude J. Summers and Ted-Larry Pebworth. Columbia: U of Missouri P, 1988. 62-79.

Schwarz, Kathryn. "Mother Love: Clichés and Amazons in Early Modern England." Miller and Yavneh 293-305.

Scodel, Joshua. *The English Poetic Epitaph: Commemoration and Conflict from Jonson to Wordsworth.* Ithaca: Cornell UP, 1991.

Severall Proceedings of State Affairs. 12-19 Jan. 1653[4]. Raymond 163-6.

Shakespeare, William. *The Complete Works of Shakespeare.* Ed. David Bevington. Fourth ed. New York: HarperCollins Publishers, Inc., 1992.

---. *Hamlet.* Bevington 1060-1116.

---. *Macbeth.* Bevington 1219-1255.

---. *Shakespeare's Sonnets.* Ed. Stephen Booth. New Haven: Yale UP, 1977.

---. *The Taming of the Shrew.* Bevington 108-46.

Shirley, James. *The Poems of James Shirley.* Ed. Ray Livingstone Armstrong. Morningside Heights, N.Y.: King's Crown Press, 1941.

Showalter, Elaine. "Toward a Feminist Poetics." *The New Feminist Criticism: Essays on Women, Literature, and Theory.* Ed. Elaine Showalter. New York: Pantheon Books, 1985. 125-43.

Smith, Nigel. *Literature and Revolution in England 1640-1660.* New Haven: Yale UP 1994.

---. *Perfection Proclaimed: Language and Literature in English Radical Religion 1640-1660.* Oxford: Claredon Press, 1989.

Snook, Edith. "'His Open Side Our Book': Meditation and Education in Elizabeth Grymeston's *Miscelanea Meditations Memoratives.*" Miller and Yavneh 163-75.

Sowernam, Esther. *Esther hath hanged Haman.* Henderson and McManus 217-43.

Spencer, Theodore. "The History of an Unfortunate Lady." *Harvard Studies and Notes in Philology and Literature.* 20 (1938): 43-59.

Spenser, Edmund. *Spenser: Poetical Works.* Eds. J.C. Smith and E. De Selincourt. New York: Oxford UP, 1989.

Stanley, Thomas. *The Poems and Translations of Thomas Stanley.* Ed. Galbraith Miller Crump. New York: Oxford UP, 1962.

Staub, Susan C. "Early Modern Medea: Representations of Child Murder in the Street Literature of Seventeenth-Century England." Miller and Yavneh 333-47.

Steinberger, Deborah. "The Difficult Birth of the Good Mother: Donneau de Vise's *L'Embarras de Godard, ou l'Accouchée.*" Miller and Yavneh 201-11.

Sternhold, Thomas, John Hopkins and others. *The Whole Book of Psalms: Collected into English meeter.* London: Printed by Roger Daniel, 1653.

Stevenson, Jane and Peter Davidson, eds. *Early Modern Women Poets: An Anthology.* New York: Oxford UP, 2001.

Stone, Lawrence. *The Family, Sex and Marriage In England 1500-1800.* New

York: Harper & Row, 1977.

Stuart, James. *The Psalms of King David.* London. Film 470. Reel 1370.

---. "Verses Made by the King, when He was Entertained at Burly in Rutland-
          shire, by my Lord Marquess of Buckingham. August 1621." Fowler,
          Country House Poem 98-100.

Swetnam, Joseph. *The Arraignment of Lewd, idle, froward, and unconstant
          women.* Henderson and McManus 189-216.

Taylor, John. *A Juniper Lecture.* Henderson and McManus 290-304.

Thimelby, Gertrude Aston. "The Death of Her Only Child." Clifford 85-6.

---. "An EPITAPH on a Sweet Little Boy of Sir William Persall." Clifford 105-
          106.

---. "No Love Like That of the Soule." Clifford 95.

---. "To H-- T--." Clifford 89-90.

---. "To the Lady Elizabeth Thimelby, on New-Yeares Day, 1655, Looking Dayly
          for Her Sonne From Travaile." Clifford 104-5.

---. "To Mr E-- T--, Who Holds Selfe-Love in All Our Actions." Clifford 90-92.

---. "To Sir William and My Lady Persall, uppon the Death of Their Little Franke."
          Clifford 99-100.

---. "Upon the Lady Persalls Parting with Her Daughter Without Teares." Clifford
          97.

Thomas, Keith. *Religion and the Decline of Magic.* New York: Scribner's, 1971.

Todd, Barbara J. "'I Do No Injury by not Loving': Katherine Austen, A Young
          Widow of London." *Women & History: Voices of Early Modern England.*
          Ed. Valerie Firth. Toronto: Coach House Press, 1995. 207-37.

---. "The Remarrying Widow: A Stereotype Reconsidered." *Women in English
          Society, 1500-1800.* Ed. Mary Prior. New York: Methuen, 1985. 54-92.

Trapnel, Anna. *Anna Trapnel's Report and Plea.* London, 1654.

---. *The Cry of a Stone.* London, 1654.

---. *A Legacy for Saints.* London, 1654.

---. *Strange and Wonderful Visions from White-hall.* London, 1654.

---. [untitled volume of verse in Bodleian Library]. Bod. S. 42. I Th. London,
          1658.

---. *A Voice for the King of Saints and Nations.* London, 1658.

Trubowitz, Rachel. "'But Blood Whitened': Nursing Mothers and Others in Early
          Modern Britain." Miller and Yavneh 82-101.

Vickers, Nancy. "Diana Described: Scattered Woman and Scattered Rhyme."
          Critical Inquiry 8.2 (Winter 1981): 265-79.

Vives, Juan Luis. *The Education of a Christian Woman: A Sixteenth-Century
          Manual.* Ed. and trans. Charles Fantazzi. Chicago: The U of Chicago P,
          2000.

Vosevich, Kathi. "The Education of a Prince(ss): Tutoring the Tudors." Burke,
          Donawerth, Dove, and Nelson 61-76.

Wall, Wendy. *The Imprint of Gender: Authorship and Publication in the English
          Renaissance.* Ithaca: Cornell UP, 1993.

Waller, Edmund. *Poems 1645*. Yorkshire, England: The Scolar Press Limited, 1971.

Waugh, Joanne B. "Analytic Aesthetics and Feminist Aesthetics: Neither/Nor?" Brand and Korsmeyer 399-415.

Wayne, Don E. *Penshurst: The Semiotics of Place and the Poetics of History*. Madison, Wisconsin: The U of Wisconsin P, 1984.

Wenzel, Siegfried. *Preachers, Poets, and the Early English Lyric*. Princeton: Princeton UP, 1986.

Wilcox, Helen. "Private Writing and Public Function: Autobiographical Texts by Renaissance Englishwomen." Cerasano and Wynne-Davies 47-62.

Williams, Ethyn Morgan. "Women Preachers in the Civil War." *Journal of Modern History* 1.4 (1929): 561-9.

Williams, Raymond. *The Country and the City*. New York: Oxford UP, 1973.

Willis, Deborah. *Malevolent Nurture: Witch-Hunting and Maternal Power in Early Modern England*. Ithaca: Cornell UP, 1995.

Wiseman, Sue. "Unsilent Instruments and the Devil's Cushions: Authority in Seventeenth-Century Women's Prophetic Discourse." *New Feminist Discourses: Critical Essays on Theories and Texts*. Ed. Isobel Armstrong. New York: Routledge, 1992. 176-96.

The Wonderful Discovery of the Witchcrafts of Margaret and Philippa Flower. Henderson and McManus 369-79.

Woodhouse, A.S.P, ed. *Puritanism and Liberty: Being the Army Debates (1647-49) from the Clarke Manuscripts*. Rutland, Vermont: Charles E. Tuttle Co., Inc., 1992.

Woods, Susanne. "Aemilia Lanyer and Ben Jonson: Patronage, Authority, and Gender." *Ben Jonson Journal* 1 (1994): 15-30.

---. Introduction. Lanyer xv-xlii.

---. *Lanyer: A Renaissance Woman Poet*. New York: Oxford UP, 1999.

Wynne-Davies, Marion, ed. *Women Poets of the Renaissance*. New York: Routledge, 1999.

Yavneh, Naomi. "To Bare or Not Too Bare: Sofonisba Anguissola's Nursing Madonna and the Womanly Art of Breastfeeding." Miller and Yavneh 65-81.

Ziegler, Georgianna. "'More Than Feminine Boldness': The Gift Books of Esther Inglis." Burke, Donawerth, Dove, and Nelson 19-37.

Index